THE BEST OF
THE GROWING EDGE

NEW MOON

PUBLISHING

New Moon Publishing, Inc., Corvallis, Oregon, USA

NEW MOON

PUBLISHING

New Moon Publishing, Inc.,
215 SW Second Street #201
Post Office Box 1027
Corvallis, Oregon 97339
503-757-0176, FAX 503-757-0028
Internet Address: talexan@CSOS.ORST.EDU

Copyright © 1994, New Moon Publishing, Inc.
First printing, March, 1994
Printed in the United States of America
ISBN: 0-944557-01-5

Compiled by Tom Alexander and Don Parker
Edited by Don Parker
Layout and Design by Diana Slater Mickaelson
Illustrations and graphics by Diana Slater Mickaelson,
Anna Asquith, Carrie Walch, Michael Spillane,
Don Parker and Sono Shinkawa
Cover Design and Illustration by Sono Shinkawa

Printed on 50% Recycled, Acid-free Paper

Table of Contents

Chapter 8
Specialized Techniques

Chapter Guide

About the Authors

George Van Patten is the author of *Organic Garden Vegetables, Gardening Indoors* and *Gardening: The Rockwool Book.*

Lawrence L. Brooke is the owner and founder of General Hydroponics in Corte Madera, California.

Don Parker is the editor of *The Growing EDGE.*

Fritz-Gerald Schröder is an agricultural engineer at the Institute of Vegetable Production at Großbeeren, Germany.

James B. DeKorne is the author of *Hydroponic Hothouse* and an independent researcher based in New Mexico.

Russell J. Antkowiak is the President and chief tinkerer at AquaCulture, Inc. in Tempe, Arizona.

Chuck Erikson is the owner of Suncor Systems in Portland, Oregon.

Dr. Cal C. Herrmann is with The Bionetics Corporation, NASA Ames Research Center, Moffett Field, California.

Kathleen Yeomans is the author of *The Able Gardener* and a freelance writer in Santa Barbara, California.

Justina Marie Kelliher is a Master Gardener in Benton County, Oregon, and has worked as a professional pest management consultant.

John McEno is an independent researcher and feelance writer specializing in pest control strategies.

Erik Ackerson is the associate editor of *The Growing EDGE.*

Thomas H. Lavallee is a freelance writer, furniture builder and amateur gardener in Salmon, Idaho.

Jay Green is a freelance writer, gardener and computer hacker.

Steven Carruthers is the publisher of *Practical Hydroponics*, the author of several books and the former manager of South Pacific Hydroponics in Sydney, Australia.

Tom Alexander is the publisher of *The Growing EDGE.*

Joelle Steele is a writer and consultant to the horticultural services industry.

Martin P. Waterman is a writer, horticultural researcher and gardener based in Petitcodiac, New Brunswick, Canada.

Michael Spillane is a freelance writer, illustrator and landscape designer based in Montreal, Canada.

Paul Przybylowicz is a professional mycological consultant and the author of several books on mushroom cultivation.

Walt Wilson is the Director of Research and chief executive officer of the Wilder Company, Inc. of Pulaski, Pennsylvania.

Stephen Jones is the president of Canadian Hydroponic Information Cooperative, Inc. and a greenhouse operator since 1978.

Roger H. Thayer is the owner of Eco Enterprises in Seattle, Washington.

Paul Olsen is a floriculturist and researcher in Madison, Wisconsin.

Michael Christian is the owner of American Hydroponics in Arcata, California.

Tom Bressan is a writer, lecturer, irrigation system designer and part owner of The Urban Farm Store in San Francisco, California.

Introduction

So what is *The Growing EDGE*? Nearly five years after the first issue rolled off the press, that remains an awkward question. The short answer usually involves phrases such as "new and innovative" or "high-tech." But the short answer is perhaps too short, leaving the impression that the magazine is nothing more than a collection of gadgets and tricks for gardeners with a fascination for such things. To be sure, there is enough information on new equipment and techniques to keep the most avid "techno-gardener" busy for years in the pages of the magazine and in this collection of past articles. It was the lack of this information in the popular gardening press that was the driving force behind the creation of *The Growing EDGE*. But there is much more going on here.

During the past five years, *The Growing EDGE* has attempted to chronicle the evolving relationship between the planet's human population and the plants that sustain it, a process that has accelerated in the past decade. In that sense, *The Growing EDGE* is more than just another gardening magazine; it represents a different way of looking at the process of cultivating plants — for food, for pleasure, or for profit. It is a view that seeks to reconcile the demand for plants and plant products with the environmental and cultural realities of the 21st century. It is more an attempt to integrate human systems with natural processes than to imitate them.

What you hold in your hands is the result of that effort. In a way, the idea for a collection such as this originated with the readers of *The Growing EDGE*. From the beginning, demand for back issues has been strong. Even now, it is not unusual to get an order for a new subscription along with a complete set of back issues. This book was designed to make it easier and more economical for the growing number of new readers to bring themselves "up to speed." (Back issue sets are still available at this writing.) It was also an opportunity to condense and organize the volumes of information contained in early issues of the magazine in a way that is easier to use, understand and store. Finally, the book format allows The Best of The Growing EDGE to introduce new readers to the technology and the magazine. Books can be marketed in places and in ways that magazines can not.

Long-time readers of *The Growing EDGE* are certain to find some of their old favorites in these pages; they may also find a few missing. This is not intended to be a comprehensive collection, something that would have taken several volumes. Articles were selected based on several criteria including the quality of the information and the overall presentation. Above all else, however, selections were made based on their ability to contribute to the book as a whole. In some cases that meant including repetitious or even contradictory information, although every effort was made to keep that to a minimum. As in any complex field, not all of our authors agree on everything. Rather than act as judge and jury, we elected to include some conflicting views and allow our readers to sort things out for themselves. In some cases, articles have been updated with new information to bring them up to date. In others, brief excerpts of longer pieces were included to illustrate specific points.

Although not designed as a how-to book, The Best of the Growing EDGE should provide new growers with the information needed to get started in high-tech gardening, indoors, outdoors or in the greenhouse. An attempt was made to include basic information on every major topic — soilless gardening, nutrients, pest controls, environmental controls, plant varieties, propagation, production methods and other techniques. Novice or professional, we believe thinking readers (we don't have any other kind) should find much here that is useful, enlightening, even provocative. — *Don Parker*

Chapter 1
Soilless Gardening

Hydroponics for the Rest of Us

by George Van Patten

To many people, hydroponic gardening conjures up images of whitecoated researchers poking and prodding their genetically manipulated plants, or of future space travelers harvesting zero-gravity salad greens from sealed growth chambers. In reality, hydroponic technology is not necessarily as daunting as those images suggest. More growers are beginning to recognize the advantages of hydroponic gardening indoors and out.

Indoors, hydroponics allows for the maximum use of space with a minimum of the mess and bother associated with dirt gardening. A properly designed and operated hydroponic system allows gardeners to grow wholesome, pesticide-free produce when others are forced to subsist on store-bought veggies and entertain themselves with the latest seed company catalogs.

Outdoors, hydroponics permits gardening in areas with poor soil, or no soil at all, such as patios and rooftops. Recirculating systems conserve precious water and expensive fertilizers.

Hydroponics comes from the Greek words hydro, meaning "water," and ponos, meaning "labor." Hydroponics is the science of growing plants without soil, most often in a soilless medium. Unlike the soil grower, the hydroponic gardener can control two essential processes: nutrient intake and oxygen intake via roots.

In hydroponics, the inert soilless medium that provides support for the plants' root systems contains no nutrients of its own. Nutrition is supplied by the nutrient solution, a mixture of pure water and dissolved nutrients. With most hydroponic systems, the solution passes over the roots or floods around them at regular intervals.

Oxygen, essential to the health of roots, is either incorporated in the nutrient solution or drawn into the root area when the system is drained. Even the best soil rarely holds as much oxygen as a soilless hydroponic medium. The oxygen around the roots speeds the plants' uptake of nutrients. Plants grow faster hydroponically because they are able to assimilate nutrients rapidly and completely. Roots are able to take in food nearly as fast as the plant is able to use it.

Hydroponic gardening is more exacting than soil gardening. Soil works as a buffer for nutrients and holds them longer than the inert hydroponic medium. Still, hydroponically grown plants tend to grow faster with a little more lush foliage than plants grown in soil. When roots are restricted and growth slows in containerized plants, hydroponic plants are still getting the maximum amount of nutrients and growing strong.

System Types

Hydroponic systems are classified as active or passive systems, depending on how the nutrient solution is delivered to the root zone.

Passive systems rely on the capillary action of a wick and the growing medium. The nutrient solution is "wicked" from a reservoir to the root zone in much the same way as the wick of a kerosene lamp moves fuel up to the flame. The media normally used in wick systems are absorbent materials such as vermiculite, sawdust and peat moss.

The wick system has no moving parts. There is nothing mechanical to break, replace or malfunction. Wick systems also boast a low initial cost.

NFT SYSTEM

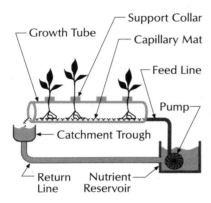

Growth Tube — Support Collar — Capillary Mat — Feed Line — Pump — Catchment Trough — Return Line — Nutrient Reservoir

AEROPONICS SYSTEM

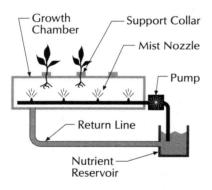

Growth Chamber — Support Collar — Mist Nozzle — Pump — Return Line — Nutrient Reservoir

The Growing Medium

Once set up and functioning properly, they require little work to maintain. Wick systems are perfect for slow-growing perennials such as African violets and rex begonias.

Active systems, as the name suggests, actively move the nutrient solution from a reservoir to the root zone. Examples of active systems are: flood and drain, top feed systems, and nutrient film technique (NFT).

The methods described here are active recovery systems. They work by moving a volume of nutrient solution into contact with the roots and returning it to the reservoir for later use.

In flood and drain systems, the water floods into the bed, usually from the bottom, pushing the CO_2-rich, oxygen-poor air out. When the medium drains, it draws new oxygen-rich air into the growing medium.

These systems tend to use media that will drain fairly rapidly and hold a lot of air, such as pea gravel, light pumice rock or crushed brick. The flood and drain method is used in many commercial hydroponic operations and home systems.

The top feed method, in which the nutrient solution is delivered to the media by way of pumps and tubing, is a little more intricate, but is widely used with excellent results. Top feed systems apply the nutrient solution to the base of each plant via small feeder tubes. The solution is aerated as it flows through the air. Additional aeration may be provided by an aquarium-type air stone placed in the reservoir.

NFT (Nutrient Film Technique) systems are one of the most productive available. They operate on a very simple principle: roots grow into a shallow mat located in a light-tight grow tube. Since there is no medium to hold moisture in the root zone, the nutrient solution flows over the roots continually. The majority of roots grow on top of the thin matting, which slows and distributes the solution in the growing tube.

Because nutrients are cycled constantly in the NFT system, it is highly productive and capable of producing impressive yields. In addition, there is no medium to buy or replace, reducing operating costs. On the down side, NFT systems are more susceptible to equipment failures and power outages. There is no medium to hold moisture and nutrients. Even a temporary interruption in the flow of solution can result in crop damage or death.

An even more exotic, "medialess" system is called aeroponics. In aeroponic systems the roots are suspended in air and misted with a nutrient solution. The light-tight misting chamber prevents algae from competing with roots. Due to their complexity, aeroponic systems are most often used in specialized commercial and research applications. They are especially useful where high oxygen levels are important, such as in rooting clones.

The purpose of the growing medium is to hold oxygen, water and nutrients and support the root system. As with soil, the texture of the soilless medium is of great importance. The texture should be one that lets the solution drain rapidly enough for the roots to get a good supply of oxygen. A fast-draining medium that will hold a small amount of water for a long time is ideal for active recovery hydroponic systems.

The size of the medium is important. The smaller the particles, the closer they pack and the slower they drain. The larger the particles, the faster they drain and the more air they hold.

Irregular materials have more surface area and hold more water than round ones. Avoid gravel with sharp edges that could damage roots. Round pea gravel; smooth, washed gravel; crushed brick; or some form of lava are the best media for growing flowers and vegetables.

Rock should be of igneous (volcanic) origin. This type of rock tends to have a neutral pH and will not break down under hydroponic growing conditions. Gravel is the most widely used hydroponic growing medium for flowers and vegetables. It holds moisture and nutrients without staying too wet.

The medium should be clean so as not to react with the nutrients in the solution. For example, gravel from a limestone quarry is packed with calcium carbonate and old concrete is full of lime. When mixed with water, calcium carbonate will raise the pH; concrete is toxic to plants. Other mixtures made of pebbles or anything found near the ocean could be full of ocean salt. If you suspect the medium is toxic, it may be easier to get another load than to try to flush away the salts.

Rockwool is an inert, sterile, porous, non-degradable growing medium that provides firm root support. This revolutionary new growing medium consists of thin strand-like fibers made primarily from limestone, granite or other rock. Rockwool is used in the production of about 50 percent of all Western European greenhouse vegetables.

Sterilizing

Instead of hauling copious quantities of soil in and out of the house, the soilless hydroponic medium is simply sterilized and reused. The reason for sterilization is to prevent disease causing micro-organisms from getting started in the garden.

There are many ways to sterilize hydroponic media. A simple method is to fill the reservoir with a solution of ordinary laundry bleach such as Clorox or Purex (calcium or sodium hypochlorite) or hydrochloric acid, the kind used in hot tubs and swimming pools.

Apply one cup of bleach for each five gallons of water. Flood the medium with the sterilizing solution for at least one-half hour, then flush with pure water. Use a lot of fresh water to leach and flush the entire system — beds, connecting hoses and drains. Make sure all the toxic chemicals are gone by flushing the entire system for at least one hour (two intervals of half an hour each) before replanting.

The Nutrient Solution

Always use the best hydroponic fertilizer you can find. Some are specifically designed for certain applications, such as rockwool, or for certain stages of plant growth. Read labels carefully and ask a lot of questions. All hydroponic fertilizers should have the necessary macro- and micronutrients. Fertilizers should be chelated, to help nutrient uptake by the roots. Chelated nutrients are soluble and immediately available to the plant.

Beware of bargains. Cheap fertilizers may contain insoluble nutrients or non-nutritive sludge that can build up, requiring more frequent cleaning of the system.

Like soil, hydroponic gardens can be fertilized organically or chemically. Filter organic teas to ensure that small pipes do not plug with residue and sludge.

For fast-growing annuals, change the nutrient solution at least every two to three weeks. It can go longer, but growth could slow and deficiencies result. Plants absorb nutrients at different rates, and some of the elements are depleted before others.

The best form of preventative maintenance is to change the solution often. Fertilizer is probably the least expensive necessity in a hydroponic garden. If you skimp on fertilizer, your plants may be stunted. The pH is also continually changing, another reason to change the nutrient solution frequently. The nutrients being used at different rates could create a salt (unused fertilizer) buildup. This problem is usually averted by using pure nutrients and flushing the soilless medium thoroughly with fresh, tepid water between nutrient solution changes.

Most flowers and vegetables grow hydroponically within a pH range of 5.8 to 6.8, 6.3 is ideal. Monitoring pH in hydroponic gardens requires some vigilance and a good pH tester. If the pH is not within the acceptable hydroponic range, nutrients may not be absorbed as fast as possible. Monitor the solution regularly and use a good quality "pH up" or "pH down" solution to correct imbalances.

The Reservoir

The reservoir is your buffer against short term changes in nutrient concentrations and pH. Therefore, it is helpful to have the largest reservoir that is practical for your system. The reservoir should contain at least 20 percent more nutrient solution than it takes to fill the beds, to compensate for evaporation and transpiration. The larger the volume of nutrient solution, the more buffering capacity, and the easier it is to control.

Plants use much more water than nutrients. Water also evaporates directly from the system. Water losses of five to 25 percent per day, depending on climatic conditions, the size of plants and whether the reservoir is covered, are possible. As water is lost, the concentration of nutrients in the solution increases, possibly to toxic levels.

More sophisticated systems have a float valve that allows more water to enter as it is used from the reservoir. Most systems have a full line on the inside of the reservoir tank to show when the solution is low. Add pure water as soon as the solution level lowers. That could be as often as every day, so check the reservoir regularly.

It is a big job to empty and refill a hydroponic reservoir with 20 to 60 gallons of water. To make the task easier, the system should be designed to pump the solution out of the reservoir. If the water must sit for a couple of days to let chlorine dissipate or to alter the pH before putting it into the tank, the system should pump water back into the reservoir. Using the pump in the reservoir to move nutrient solution will greatly ease your task as a hydroponic horticulturist. If you are unable to pump the used nutrient solution out of the reservoir, place the unit high enough for the solution to be siphoned or flow by gravity.

The used nutrient solution can be pumped into the vegetable garden outdoors where the soil's natural buffering capacity can handle any imbalances. Do not dump the nutrient solution into a septic tank. The fertilizer can disrupt the chemical balance of a septic tank. Do not use the unbalanced nutrient solution on other indoor plants.

The Irrigation Cycle

The irrigation or watering cycle will depend on the same variables found in soil gardening: plant size, climatic conditions and the type of growing medium. If the particles are large, round and smooth, and drain rapidly like pea gravel, the system should cycle more often: two to four times daily.

Flood systems with pea gravel are generally flooded two or three times daily for 15 to 30 minutes. The water rises to within half an inch of the top of the gravel and should completely drain out of the medium at each watering. Top feed systems are usually cycled for about 30 minutes and should be watered two to four times daily.

During the irrigation cycle, the nutrient concentration of the bed and the reservoir are at the same level. As time passes between irrigation cycles, the nutrient concentration and the pH gradually change. If enough time passes between watering, concentrations may change so much that the plants are not able to absorb nutrients.

As with soil gardening, experimentation and observation will probably tell you more than anything else about the condition of your garden. One gardener explained to me, "After a while you kind of get the feel for it." It took this hydroponic horticulturist nearly a year to find the right irrigation cycle for his system.

The temperature of the nutrient solution should stay between 65 and 75 degrees (18 to 24 C). In cool growing areas, heat the solution with a grounded aquarium heater or grounded heat cables. It may take a few days for the cables or heater to heat a large volume of solution. Never place heat cables in the soilless hydroponic medium. The heat from the cable could fry the roots when the medium dries out.

Replace lost nutrient solution with water that is at least 60 degrees (15 C). Cold water can shock plants. The new water could take a few days to warm up. In the meantime your plants could be stunted! Never let the water temperature get higher than 85 degrees (29 C).

Building Your Own

One option is to build your own hydroponic system. If you're handy with tools and like the feeling of doing it yourself, this is a workable option, but there are certain things that must be looked after for the system to work properly.

Sealing all joints and using few or no seams are two basic codes of hydroponic garden construction. Seal seams with waterproof caulk or use fiberglass resin and cloth to ensure no-leak construction. Drain holes or pipe connections must fit snugly with no leakage. Teflon tape (available at plumbing supply shops) is a good safeguard for threaded connections.

A large, covered reservoir is the easiest to work with. The size of the growing container is also important. The roots have to grow big enough to support a plant. In large bed systems, the roots form a mat of tangled roots. In smaller 1- to 3-gallon beds, roots could fill the container and grow out the bottom in two to six weeks. The size of the hydroponic container determines its buffering capacity.

Roots may clog the drain. Place a small mesh screen (quarter-inch or less) made from a non-corrosive material such as plastic over the drain. The screen should be easy to remove and clean.

Home Systems

Of course, the possibilities are almost limitless, but the following systems lend themselves well to home design and construction without sacrificing durability and efficiency.

Flood and Drain systems consist of a bed of growing medium that is flooded periodically to introduce water and nutrients and allowed to drain freely to draw oxygen into the root zone.

Dr. Allan Cooper developed the nutrient flow/film technique in England in the mid-1960s. The primary objective of NFT was to enable large-scale, low-cost crop production in regions where soil quality and the availability of water are inadequate for conventional soil farming. Dr. Cooper has participated in installations of such systems in a number of countries, including many in poorer nations of the Third World. The goal has been to keep it simple since it is often used in areas where the people who must do the day-to-day operations might lack education or experience.

NFT is a type of water culture in which plants are grown with little or no growing medium. Consequently, NFT systems offer the great advantage of minimal pH shifts in the nutrient solution. NFT costs little to set up since the plants are grown in a plastic envelope setting on the ground in outdoor settings, or on a slopping stand. The nutrient solution forms a thin film inside the envelope as it flows over the roots. The solution is collected in a reservoir at the lower end of the envelope for recirculation.

A common problem in outdoor settings is "pooling" where nutrient collects in small depressions in the ground under the envelope drowning the roots. This problem has been remedied by using concrete or some other rigid base beneath the envelope.

Other potential problems include: inadequate oxygen in the root zone can result in root dieback; large plants (including popular hydroponic crops such as tomatoes and cucumbers) require external support due to the lack of a supporting medium; and Pythium, a fungus, can travel quickly through the system, especially in warmer climates, resulting in total crop loss. Also, because the system requires constant circulation of the nutrient solution, power outages or mechanical breakdowns can cause extensive crop damage.

Dealing with these complications can entail a great deal of manual labor. Commercial operations do exist in several places throughout the world, but NFT is not yet widely accepted as a primary means for commercial production.

Dr. Cooper is currently doing experiments with highly concentrated nutrient solutions, so-called "hypertonic feeding." Two nutrient reservoirs are required; one called the "drink," and the other the "feed." The plants are irrigated constantly with the milder drink solution at approximately 600 ppm. For brief periods several times a day, they are switched to the feed solution, a very strong nutrient, up to 3000 ppm. Winter tests of the method on greenhouse tomatoes in England resulted in a successful crop, but hypertonic feeding remains experimental and little information is available. We can look forward to further breakthroughs from Dr. Cooper, one of the leaders in the field of modern hydroponics. — *Lawrence L. Brooke*

Excerpted from "Hydroponics: A Growing Technology for the '90s," first published in Volume 1 Number 1, page 21.

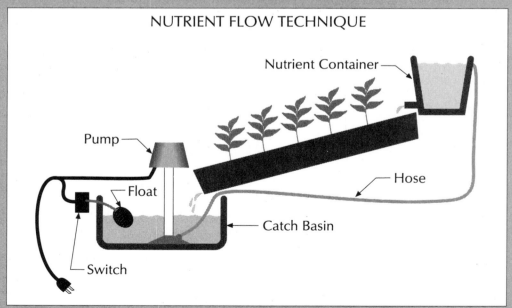

NUTRIENT FLOW TECHNIQUE

Nutrient Container

Pump

Float

Hose

Catch Basin

Switch

FLOOD AND DRAIN SYSTEM

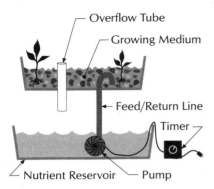

- Overflow Tube
- Growing Medium
- Feed/Return Line
- Timer
- Nutrient Reservoir
- Pump

TOP FEED SYSTEM

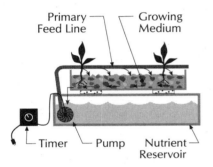

- Primary Feed Line
- Growing Medium
- Timer
- Pump
- Nutrient Reservoir

AIR PUMP SYSTEM

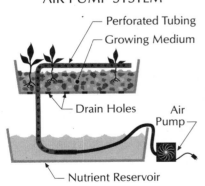

- Perforated Tubing
- Growing Medium
- Drain Holes
- Air Pump
- Nutrient Reservoir

A simple flood and drain system can be made from a 5-gallon plastic bucket filled with washed gravel that has a drain hole in the bottom. The hole is plugged with a cork. The nutrient solution, kept in another 5-gallon bucket, is manually poured into the bed. After 20 to 30 minutes, remove the cork and the solution drains back into the reservoir bucket.

This method is a little sloppy, to say nothing of tedious. It is, however, easy and inexpensive to set up and is a good way for the novice gardener to get his or her hands wet with a minimal investment.

Another slightly more sophisticated approach is to connect the two buckets with a piece of flexible tubing.

Once the basic concept behind flood and drain hydroponics is understood, it is pretty easy to envision an automated system. The addition of a submersible pump and a simple timer not only automate the system, but allow the use of a larger, more productive growing bed, and a larger, more stable nutrient reservoir. With automated systems, be sure to include an overflow tube in the growing bed to prevent accidental flooding.

Top Feed systems actively deliver nutrient solution to the top of the growing medium by way of pumps and tubes. Rather than flooding the bed, the solution trickles through and moistens the medium before returning, by gravity, to the reservoir. Half-hour irrigation cycles can be set for two to four times daily, depending on the crop and the medium used.

Top feed systems are reliable and offer greater flexibility than many other types of hydroponic systems. The snap-together feed tubes can be lengthened, shortened or removed to control the flow of solution to different parts of the growing bed. This permits the grower to cultivate plants of different varieties or at different stages of growth in the same growing bed. This is especially useful if the system is used to prepare starts for transplanting.

Media suitable for top feed systems include Geolite (expanded clay) and washed gravel. A top feed system filled with perlite makes and excellent nursery for seedlings and cuttings.

Air Pump systems may be of the top feed or bottom flood variety. The main difference is that the mechanical power needed to raise the solution from the reservoir to the growing bed is provided by a standard aquarium pump. As with the systems above, the nutrient solution returns to the reservoir by gravity.

With bottom flood systems, air is pumped into a sealed container full of nutrient solution. The pressure created by the pump forces the solution into the growing bed. After the solution is in the bed, the pump continues forcing air through the solution.

With the top feed air pump system, air is pumped through a small tube into the reservoir. The small tube is placed inside a larger tube connected to a "soaker" tube on the surface of the growing medium. Pressure created in the larger tube draws the solution up and into the growing chamber.

Both of these systems are easily automated with the addition of an inexpensive timer. They work great for people who will not be there every day to cycle the nutrients manually.

First published in Volume 3 Number 3, page 24.

Build Your Own Hydroponic System!

by Lawrence L. Brooke

Over the years a great many different types of hydroponic systems have been developed. Variations in environments, plant growth requirements and available materials have resulted in hydroponic methods which enable cultivation in regions which would otherwise be barren. The result is a great deal of confusion for the novice as to what method to choose for a hobby garden.

The classic hydroponic method is called "flood and drain," or "ebb and flow." To this day this method remains one of the most reliable and effective in almost any region and climate. It is "user friendly" both in construction and operation. Practically all types of plants that the hobbyist would be interesting in cultivating will flourish in these classic systems.

The method is very simple in concept, although an almost infinite variety of materials and layouts can be adapted. The plants are grown in a growing medium within a container. A reservoir containing hydroponic nutrient solution is located below the growing container and a pump, usually submersible, drives the nutrient up into the growing container to flood the growing medium. The pump is cycled on and off, usually with a timer. During the off cycle, the nutrient drains back by the force of gravity into the reservoir. The drain cycle pulls air down into the root zone enabling the roots to absorb oxygen.

The frequency of flooding varies with the growing medium used, the size of the plants (bio-mass) and temperature and humidity. In a typical system using clay pebbles as a growing medium and with average temperature and humidity (75 degrees at 70 percent humidity), flooding of 15 to 30 minutes duration followed by a drain cycle of two to four hours would be about right. If the environment is very hot and dry, it may be best to flood more frequently. In cool, wet climates, less frequent flood cycles may be best.

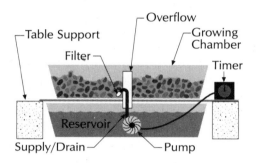

Materials

A variety of every-day items can be adapted to serve as growing containers and reservoirs. One of the best for the money is a child's wading pool. These plastic containers are generally about 5 feet in diameter, about a foot deep and cost about $10 each — an absolute bargain. Other plastic containers — tubs, trash cans, etc. — can also be used.

Another possible container is a concrete bowl that has been stained to look like terra-cotta clay. Look in the "garden ornaments" section. A piece of terra-cotta sewer pipe can be used to support the bowl and enclose the plastic reservoir. Connections between the pump, growing container and reservoir may be made with plastic pipe or tubing (PVC or polyethylene) and plastic fittings available at just about any hardware or irrigation supply store.

Pumps suitable for flood and drain systems will range in price from $25 to $75, depending on the overall size of the installation (a single module or multiple modules connected to a master reservoir) and whether economy or quality is the deciding factor. Little Giant is one of many well recognized manufacturers of pumps available nationwide.

The pump is controlled by an electronic timer which must be capable of several on/off cycles daily. Additionally, it is important that be able to cycle for a half hour at minimum; 15 minutes is even better as it would permit finer adjustments to the flood cycles. Prices for timers will range

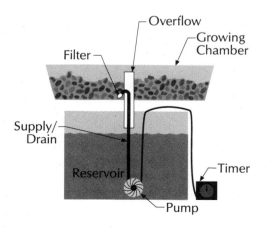

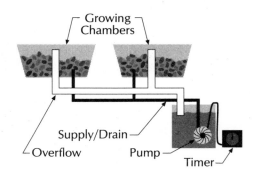

Growing Chambers

Supply/Drain

Overflow

Pump

Timer

from $10 to $50, depending on whether they are grounded (highly recommended) and whether they are electromechanical or digital. When shopping for this kind of hardware, look for quality. The failure of either the pump or timer can result in the loss of your crop.

The selection of the right growing medium is another important consideration. In traditional systems, non-calciferous gravel was used. (Calciferous media will dissolve, slowly releasing alkali compounds and causing nutrient pH to rise.) Modern media include rockwool and expanded shale.

Rockwool is a poor choice since it tends to absorb too much moisture and does not drain sufficiently. In addition, it must be replaced frequently and may pose a health hazard if dry rockwool particles are inhaled.

Expanded shale is produced by extruding clay into a furnace where it expands, somewhat like popcorn, resulting in uniformly shaped chocolate colored pellets. The construction grade variety of expanded shale tends to have a high pH unless it is pre-treated with an acid solution, followed by a thorough rinse before use. Hydroponic grade material, such as Grorox™, has a more stable pH and is currently available from hydroponic suppliers nationwide.

Expanded shale is recommended for flood and drain systems since it does not hold excessive water and drains freely, allowing plant roots to breathe. It is light in weight and does not tend to compact, is completely reusable and aesthetically pleasing. A good growing medium can make a big difference. Hydroponic grade expanded shale has been used for many years in Europe and is especially popular in Germany where it is used extensively for indoor ornamental gardens.

Construction

Tools required generally include an electric drill with appropriate hole saws to install fittings in the growing chamber and reservoir. A hack-saw or pipe cutter is helpful for cutting plastic pipe and tubing. Other tools may be required depending on the materials used.

Since it is essential that the growing container be located above the reservoir, you may either bury the reservoir in the ground below the growing container or build a support for the growing container over the reservoir. Another possibility is to place the growing container directly onto the reservoir, provided that the reservoir is strong enough to support the weight of the container, the growing medium, the nutrient solution during flood stage and the mature plants.

Instead of offering specific design and construction plans, this article has attempted to provide the conceptual information needed to build a working flood and drain system from a wide variety of possible materials. Too often, hydroponic systems have seemed cloaked in magic and marketed with the idea that you should purchase a complete system from a specialty manufacturer and not even consider building your own.

Purchasing a manufactured system could help you avoid many pitfalls and mistakes. Moreover, it is true that some methods, including various water culture systems — NFT, aeroponics and aero-hydroponics, are fairly critical in design and operation criteria. But even these systems can be made at home and ultimately work as well as the best commercially built equipment. The key is in understanding the principles of design, construction and operation.

First published in Volume 1 Number 4, page 24.

(Very) Basic Hydroponics for Beginners

Sometimes less is better. Would-be hydroponic growers are often put off by what appears to be a hopelessly complex technology with endless variations in design and technique, all shrouded in a jargon that only a few people in "the bizz" truly understand.

"What is a millimoho?" "What does NFT stand for?"

Add to that confusion the cost of purchasing a state-of-the-art hydroponic system, or the time and energy needed to build one. It is no wonder that many people who might be interested in hydroponic gardening content themselves with reading up on the subject and waiting for the day when they will feel knowledgeable enough or wealthy enough to set up a system of their own.

It is unfortunate. Stripped to the basics, hydroponic systems are not difficult to understand or operate. In fact, ease of operation and consistency of results are some of the strongest arguments for using hydroponics.

Described below are two very basic hydroponic systems suitable to the first-time grower. Both are easy and inexpensive to build and operate. Materials, with the exception of the growing media, nutrients and a good pH test kit, can be found at just about any hardware store.

While most growers would want to eventually move on to more powerful, automated systems, these systems offer the uninitiated an inexpensive way to get a taste for hydroponic cultivation without investing a tremendous amount of time and money. They are also excellent for classroom use where students could assist with both construction and operation.

Basic "Raft" Construction

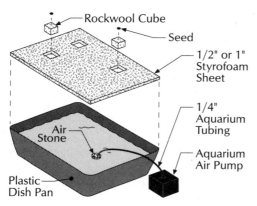

Rockwool Cube
Seed
1/2" or 1" Styrofoam Sheet
1/4" Aquarium Tubing
Aquarium Air Pump
Air Stone
Plastic Dish Pan

The basic raft system (also known as subaerated hydroponics) consists of a 1/2- to 1-inch thick Styrofoam sheet cut to fit inside of a plastic tub where it floats on top of the nutrient solution. Cut holes into the "raft" to accept rockwool starter cubes. The cubes should fit snugly enough to stay put, but loose enough to be pressed to the bottom of the raft. Space the holes 6 to 9 inches apart, depending on the plant variety to be grown.

The size and shape of the tub is not important, as long as it is large enough to hold 3/4 of a gallon of nutrient per plant; a plastic dish pan works well. Aeration for the system is provided by an aquarium pump connected by 1/4-inch tubing to an air stone placed in the tub. A small capacity air pump works fine for this system.

The basic raft system is great for growing basil, lettuce or any of a number of flowering plants. In general, look for plants that will mature in 40 to 50 days.

Basic 'Raft' Operation

- Fill the nutrient tank to within 1 inch of the top with tap water.
- Soak rockwool cubes completely. Make a hole in the top of the cubes 1/4 inch deep and insert the seeds. Press cubes into holes in raft.
- Place the raft on the surface of the reservoir.
- As soon as the seedlings appear, add a high quality hydroponic nutrient to the water at one-half the recommended strength. Correct the pH to 6.0 and keep the solution at about 70 degrees.
- Start the air pump and run continuously until the crop is finished.
- One week after the seedlings emerge, raise the nutrient solution to

full strength to encourage rapid vegetative growth.
- Check the tub regularly for solution level and pH.
- Change the entire solution every two weeks.

Basic 'Ebb and Flow' Construction

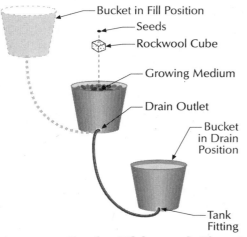

Bucket in Fill Position
Seeds
Rockwool Cube
Growing Medium
Drain Outlet
Bucket in Drain Position
Tank Fitting

Basic 'Ebb and Flow' Operation

The basic ebb and flow system uses gravity and muscle power to periodically flood and drain the growing medium. A plastic bucket with a bail handle works best for the reservoir container. The growing container can be another bucket or a tray; use poly or PVC only.

Use neoprene gasket type compression fittings to connect a flexible PVC line between the bottom of the reservoir bucket and the growing container. Other types of fittings installed with rubber sealants tend to leak.

Place a handful of 3/4-inch crushed rock around the outlet in the growing container to prevent clogging and then fill with a growing medium such as expanded clay, pea gravel, lava rock, perlite, loose rockwool, wood chips, vermiculite or peat lite mix.

The basic ebb and flow system requires a little brawn and a predictable daily routine (raising and lowering the bucket can get old pretty fast). But the system can be easily automated with the addition of a submersible pump and timer. It's a good system for heavier feeders such as tomato, cucumber, pepper and eggplant.

- Rinse the growing medium with tap water and drain.
- Completely soak 1 1/2-inch rockwool cubes. Make a hole in the top of the cubes approximately 1/4 inch deep and insert seeds. Place the cubes in a tray of water until seedlings emerge.
- Connect the reservoir bucket and place it in the lower position (below the bottom of the growing container). Fill with nutrient solution mixed to manufacturer recommendations.
- Place seedlings into the growing medium.
- Move reservoir bucket to upper position (place on a chair, table or shelf) and allow the medium to fill to within 1 inch of the surface.
- Allow solution to stand for about 20 minutes and return bucket to drain position. Repeat four to six times a day for pea gravel, expanded clay or lava rock. If any of the other media listed above are used, repeat two or three times a day.
- Keep a lid on the nutrient tank at all times.
- Keep solution at 70 degrees and at a pH of 6.0.
- Change entire solution every two weeks.

First published in Volume 2 Number 2, page 59.

Subirrigation on the Cheap

by Don Parker

In settings where cost and functionality are more important then good looks, or for the die-hard do-it-yourselfer, there are alternatives to expensive hydroponics systems. For growers who are as comfortable with a handsaw as they are with a trowel, homemade systems using simple wick technology may be an attractive alternative.

Containers

The basic wick system consists of two chambers, an upper chamber for soil or growing media, and a lower nutrient reservoir. Fortunately, such containers are easily had, sometimes for free, from restaurants and institutional kitchens. Food-grade, high density polyethylene (HDPE) tubs have several advantages for use in constructing wick growing systems. They are available in a variety of sizes and shapes. Round HDPE containers are usually found in 2-, 5- and 7-gallon sizes; square containers come in 2- and 4-gallon sizes.

Most of these containers are tapered slightly so they can "nest" for storage. Most also incorporate some kind of a "stop," an additional lip a few inches down from the top or a mount for a bail handle, that prevents them from nesting together permanently.

In addition, HDPE is a dense, stable plastic designed to be non-reactive with liquid substances over a wide pH range — from baby dills to baby food. As a result, food-grade HDPE tubs are less likely to contaminate irrigation water with constituent impurities or contaminants from previously stored materials.

There was a time when food-grade plastic tubs could be had for free at just about any restaurant. Today, many of the containers that used to find their way into the local landfill may be returned for a deposit or recycled. Ask around at a couple of local eating establishments. If they don't have any containers on hand, they may be willing to save a few for you.

You will need two identical containers with or without lids for one wick unit. Make sure that they nest together well and pull apart easily. Be certain that the containers have not been used to store hazardous materials. Restaurants purchase more than just food in plastic containers, such as industrial cleaners. Even a tub clearly marked as a food container may have had a second life as a mop bucket. If you are unsure, find out or find another container.

If all else fails, new food-grade containers can be purchased at most restaurant supply shops. You'll pay anywhere from $2 to $7, depending on the size and style, but there are some advantages to buying new. They are clean and ready to use. You may also have your choice of sizes styles and colors. Beyond any aesthetic considerations, some of the darker colored containers, blue, green, red or black, might reduce algae growth in the reservoir, a minor but irritating problem with systems placed in direct sunlight.

Other Materials

In addition to containers, you will need the following for a single unit:

- A length of 3/4-inch PVC tubing for the reservoir fill tube. For small systems, 1/2-inch tubing may be used, although it will make filling more difficult.
- PVC fittings to attach the fill tube to the base of the upper chamber. It is possible to use a single flange fitting to glue the tube in place, but screw fittings are inexpensive and provide a more positive connection. Screw fittings also allow the tube to be removed for cleaning. PVC tubing and fittings are readily available at hardware stores and plumbing suppliers.
- Polyester rope (sometimes called cable cord) for wicking material. Half-inch rope (#40) works well for larger systems. Remember, the wicking material is the heart of your system. Synthetic utility ropes will not provide sufficient wicking action and cotton rope tends to decay when in constant contact with water. Don't bother asking for

cable cord at the hardware store; it is available only at sewing centers and craft shops.

■ Silicon based adhesive to join the top and bottom halves of the growing chamber. Silicon aquarium adhesive, easily found at hardware stores and pet shops, is non-reactive when fully cured.

■ A piece of plastic rod or doweling for the level indicator and a cork or Styrofoam float.

Tools

No special equipment is needed to build the system described here. With the possible exception of the proper sized drill bits, the following tools should be found in any well-stocked garage:

■ A fine toothed, crosscut handsaw (10 or more teeth per inch) or a hacksaw can be used to cut both the PVC tubing and the upper container. A dull handsaw actually seems a little easier to control on long, straight cuts than a sharp one.

■ A variable speed electric drill allows for greater control when drilling plastics, but a single speed drill will work fine.

■ A 1/2- or 5/8-inch spade bit may be used for drilling entry holes for the wick material. A larger size spade bit or hole saw will be needed for the filler tube hole.

■ Medium and fine sandpaper are used to remove burrs and clean up saw cuts and drilled holes.

■ A utility knife or sharp pocket knife.

■ A laundry or similar indelible marker.

Design

The nesting feature of plastic food tubs is great for saving warehouse space, but it does pose a couple of problems for would-be wick gardeners. In the nesting position, the base of the growing chamber is too close to the bottom of the reservoir (lower container). Since it is necessary to maintain a minimum 1-inch air space between the bottom of the growing chamber and the maximum reservoir water level, that leaves very little space for water.

In addition, the upper chamber is too deep. Capillary attraction, the force the causes water to "wick" upward through the soil, dissipates with the vertical distance traveled. In other words, water from the reservoir will not be able to reach the upper portion of the growing chamber. That might be OK for established, deep-rooted plants, but it won't do for seedlings and smaller transplants.

The obvious answer to both problems is to shorten the upper container, a process that is simpler than it might sound.

The Growth Chamber

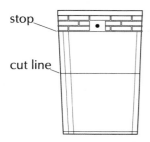

stop

cut line

Because they are designed to nest, plastic storage tubs are tapered from top to bottom. For the system pictured to the left, the upper tub was shortened approximately 3 inches by cutting it horizontally with a handsaw about midway between the stop and the base and inserting the bottom into the top.

Depending on the original size of the container and the degree of taper, it may be necessary to cut three pieces, fitting them together as before, to achieve the correct soil depth (assuming and inch or so space between the soil level and the rim) of 6 to 9 inches.

Before gluing the pieces together, sand the cut edges and test fit to

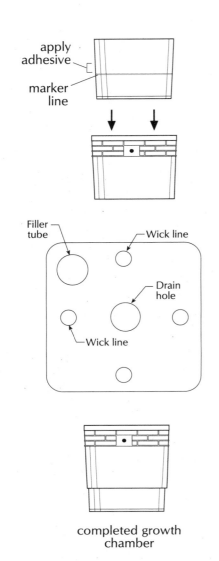

apply
adhesive

marker
line

Filler
tube

Wick line

Drain
hole

Wick line

completed growth
chamber

check for soil depth. Make certain that the pieces align on the vertical axis. If everything looks OK, use the laundry marker to draw a line on the lower section where the top section overlaps. This line will help you position the pieces when they are glued together. If you are using a round container, or if your saw cut was less than perfect, make a vertical mark on the top and bottom sections that will allow you to align the pieces later.

The pieces could be glued together at this point, but it is easier to drill the holes in the base first. The drilling pattern given at left is just a rough guide. The holes for the wicking material should not be too closely grouped to provide good contact between the wick lines and the potting medium. The larger hole for the fill tube should be sized to accommodate your PVC fittings and positioned so that the indicator float does not hang up on the side of the reservoir or get tangled in the wick lines. The center hole provides additional drainage and is especially important if the unit is to be placed outside where rainwater could collect in the upper chamber and drown the roots.

Carefully mark the position of the holes on the inside of the container. Place the container on a piece of scrap lumber to act as a backing. If you are using a variable speed drill, go slowly to avoid either melting or tearing the plastic. If you are using a fixed speed drill, press lightly and pull the drill up occasionally to allow the cutting blades to cool. Remove any burrs and smooth the holes with the sandpaper.

Now glue the pieces of the container together. Apply one or two beads of aquarium adhesive to the outside of the bottom section about 1/4 inch above the guideline. Don't be too stingy with the glue. This joint does not need to be watertight, but it does need to be strong enough to support the weight of the growing medium and the plant. If things get a little messy, relax, none of this will show when the unit is in operation. Carefully place the bottom section inside of the top section, making certain that the vertical marks on the top and bottom sections line up. Now pull the top section up to the guideline. Set the container on its side and allow the adhesive to cure for at least one hour before handling.

Fill Tube and Indicator

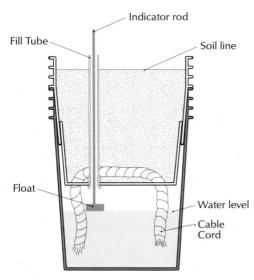

Indicator rod

Fill Tube

Soil line

Drain hole

Wick line

Float

Water level

Cable
Cord

Install the PVC fittings for the filler tube and tighten. This joint need not be water tight so no gaskets are needed. Cut the 3/4-inch PVC tubing with the handsaw so that the opening will be roughly flush with the top of the container. Take the worst looking end of the tube and press it into the fitting in the bottom of the container.

The filler tube doubles as a passageway for the level indicator. The indicator (as pictured at left) is simply a rod or dowel secured to a cork or Styrofoam float. The indicator used in the example was fashioned from a piece of a PVC coat hanger and a square of packing Styrofoam. There are, of course, other "found" items that would work as well — a bamboo skewer and a wine bottle cork, for example. Whatever you use, be sure to secure the rod to the float with a drop of glue before the final assembly.

The indicator rod should be long enough to reach from the bottom of the reservoir to the top of the filler tube with the unit assembled. To calibrate the "empty" level, place the indicator with float attached into the empty reservoir. Guide the indicator rod into the filler tube and lower the upper chamber onto the reservoir. With the laundry marker, make a line on the rod at the point where it emerges from the filler tube.

To calibrate the "full" level, make a mark on the outside of the reservoir 1 1/2 inches or so below the bottom of the upper chamber. It helps for this process to place the unit in front of a sunny window or strong light. Remove the upper container and fill the reservoir up to the mark. Again using the laundry marker, make a line on the rod at the point where it emerges from the filler tube.

If the unit is to be used outdoors, drilling one or two small drain holes in the reservoir at the "full" mark will prevent rain water from overfilling the system.

Finishing Up

For a more finished look, simply cut the center section out of one of the lids (Remember the lids?) with a utility knife or sharp pocket knife. Sand any sharp edges smooth and snap the rim in place. The other lid can be used as a drip catching base to protect fine floors and furniture from condensation that might form on the outside of the reservoir. Simply place the lid top-up on the floor and insert the reservoir container into the depression in the lid.

Any stray lines made with the laundry marker can be removed with rubbing alcohol and tissue paper. The black printing on the PVC line, at least the portion that will be above the soil line, can be removed with fine steel wool and then wiped with rubbing alcohol.

Dressing it Up

If aesthetics are important, you may want to build a decorative surround to hide the plastic containers from view. Since soil and water are wholly contained within the unit, you can take some liberties with materials and techniques. The materials used should be able to withstand an occasional spill during filling, but is not necessary to use rot resistant woods such as cedar or redwood unless the unit is to be placed outdoors.

Indoors, the possibilities are limited only by the dimensions of the unit and your imagination. Basically, an open bottomed box or cylinder wide enough and tall enough to enclose the system is all that is needed (see photograph on page 18).

Select design elements, materials and finishes to harmonize with the decor of the area in which the system is used. "Found" objects — terra cotta pots, redwood planters, pieces of clay flue liner cut to length — can also be used to enclose a wick system.

Start-up

Thoroughly wet the wicking material and insert through the holes in the bottom of the planter in a criss-cross fashion. The wicks should be long enough to just reach the bottom of the reservoir. Cable cord frays easily, so try to handle the material as little as possible.

To prevent potting mix from contaminating the reservoir water and to ensure good drainage, place a thin layer of rockwool in the bottom of the growing container, just enough to cover the holes and the wicks. A good handful of *water-absorbent* rockwool flock or a couple of crumbled rockwool cubes. (Always wear a particle mask when handling dry rockwool.) Rockwool is ideal because it does not degrade over time and, due to its high water holding capacity, it will distribute water more evenly through the soil.

If rockwool is not available in your area, a very fine mesh synthetic netting can be used. (Check at the fabric store when you go to pick up your cable cord.) Do not use pebbles, gravel or broken pots to line the bottom of the growth chamber. The large air spaces between these traditional pot liners will stop capillary action cold.

Whatever liner you use, wet it thoroughly and press it in around the cords to eliminate air pockets and improve contact between the wicking material and the growing medium.

Fill the growing container with a good quality potting soil and plant as usual. Take care to prevent the formation of air voids in the planting medium that could interrupt the upward flow of water. Soilless media may also be used with wick systems if a nutrient solution is added to the reservoir water. However, the need for flushing, monitoring and periodic changing of the nutrient solution eliminates some of the primary reasons for going with wick technology — ease of operation and low maintenance.

Before putting the system together, fill the reservoir to about half its full capacity with clean water. Place the growing chamber into the reservoir and top water to wet the soil. Once the upper chamber has drained completely, top up the reservoir through the filler tube until the indicator registers full.

Operation

Once the soil is thoroughly wetted, it should not need top watering again unless the system dries out. Until you get used to the system, check the indicator regularly. Gently press and release the indicator rod periodically to ensure that it is moving freely in the filler tube. It should bob up and down.

The system as described here should provide ample water for most houseplants and many vegetable varieties, even under warm, dry indoor conditions. However, some plants, some succulents for example, may find conditions too damp.

If you suspect a plant is getting too much water, remove the upper container, set it on its side and tie two of the wicks together to hold them up out of the water. Replace the growing chamber and monitor the plant for signs of stress.

Try not to let the system dry out completely. If it does, you will need to re-wet the soil and the wicking material to reinitiate the wicking action. Top water the system thoroughly until you hear water draining from the upper chamber into the reservoir. To avoid overfilling, allow the upper chamber to drain completely before refilling the reservoir through the fill tube.

Houseplants can grow for years in such a system with no more effort than an occasional topping up with water. For that reason, a good quality potting soil with a fine texture should be used. Fertilizers should be used sparingly, if at all, with slow growing houseplants. Use a good quality, water soluble fertilizer. Use organic fertilizers in the form of a very dilute tea, strained through a fine mesh screen or fabric to remove any solids.

In normal use, the system requires very little maintenance. Inspect the reservoir occasionally and clean if needed. Over time, roots may grow down through the drain holes into the reservoir. This is generally not a problem unless the mass of roots clog the drain holes, in which case the roots should be pruned back or the plant repotted.

First published in Volume 3 Number 2, page 36.

Aero-Hydroponics: The Hydroponic Method of the Future!

by Lawrence L. Brooke

The aero-hydroponic method was developed in Israel in the early 1980s. Dr. Hillel Soffer, senior researcher at the Volcani Institute at Ein Gedi developed the aero-hydroponic method to overcome the problems presented by the hot, arid conditions at Ein Gedi. The discoveries that followed the development of aero-hydroponics offer great benefits to all hydroponic growers.

During a two-year period from 1986 to 1988, Dr. Soffer performed extensive research using the aero-hydroponic method at the University of California at Davis, where he had received his Ph.D. in the early 1970s. The specific area of research was in quantifying the effect of various levels of dissolved oxygen on root growth, especially in the propagation of plants from cuttings.

The findings of his research were published in the *Journal of the American Society for Horticultural Science*, and *HortScience*. Both studies were co-authored with David Burger at UCD. In addition, Dr. Soffer presented his findings at the annual conference of the Hydroponic Society of America in 1988.

Aero-hydroponic Method

EIN GEDI MINI UNIT

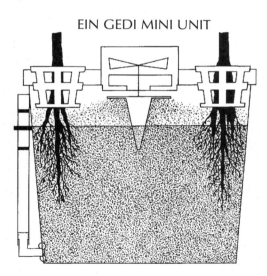

Aero-hydroponics is not a simple method to understand. The equipment required is somewhat more complicated than other hydroponic methods, but there is a great advantage in that once an aero-hydroponic system is set up, it will run almost indefinitely without additional investment in such disposable components as growing media and non-recirculating nutrients.

What is most surprising about aero-hydroponics is not how is works, but *why* plants grow better. The key is dissolved oxygen at the root boundary zone.

The essence of Dr. Soffer's work at UCD was in quantifying root growth in proportion to dissolved oxygen. Only the green parts of the plant can form oxygen from carbon dioxide — roots require a supply of oxygen for metabolism and growth. Plant growth in oxygen deficient conditions, such as those found in many soils, is limited. Dr. Soffer found the enhanced oxygen produced enhanced growth.

In aero-hydroponics, the nutrient solution is sprayed through the air in order to infuse the nutrient with dissolved oxygen. The method differs from classic aeroponics in that most of the plant's roots are not suspended in air and fed by a spray of nutrient solution; rather, the majority of the roots are submerged in oxygen-infused nutrient which is in constant motion in order to maintain high levels of dissolved oxygen at the root boundary zone where oxygen and nutrients are taken in by the plant.

The result is a propagating tool of unsurpassed performance. Dr. Soffer was successful in propagating varieties at UCD that had never been propagated before. He took particular delight in propagating varieties of conifers and even pistachio trees. Moreover, he found that cuttings could be rooted aero-hydroponically in purified water without using rooting hormones such as IBA or NAA. This is because plant tissue already contains the natural rooting hormone IAA (Indole Acetic Acid).

Aero-hydroponic Systems

Aero-hydroponic systems can be built using quite a variety of materials and in numerous design configurations. The Ein Gedi "Mini Unit" (see illustration on page 19) that was used at UCD for dissolved oxygen studies is a stand-alone module which supports four plants in 10 liters of nutrient solution. An electric motor mounted on the top of the unit spins a nutrient sprayer which lifts nutrient solution and sprays it onto the "aerial roots." Additionally, the rotation causes the nutrient within the unit to stir, moving constantly over the submerged roots.

Large scale aero-hydroponic systems follow the design of the commercial installation a Ein Gedi. These commercial systems consist of "canals" or growing chambers with plant sites on top. A pump provides the pressure to drive a system of sprayers to supply the aerial roots, while the submerged roots hang into the flowing nutrient in the canal much like a typical NFT system.

Both of these systems share fundamental characteristics that define the aero-hydroponic method. The plants are supported in cups. The roots hang down through an air gap in which nutrient is sprayed, then into the moving nutrient solution below the air gap.

The nutrient sprayed through the air gap is not so much intended to irrigate and feed the plant, but rather to infuse oxygen into the nutrient solution wherein the feeder roots remain constantly submerged. It is these submerged roots in oxygen rich nutrient that provide most of the nutrition and oxygen for the plant.

Home Installation

The "AeroFlo II," by General Hydroponics is a true aero-hydroponic system. It consists of a reservoir pipe measuring 10 feet long and 12 inches in diameter. The "canals" or growing chambers are supported over the reservoir pipe. Each of the chambers is 10 feet long and has 16 plant sites. Two of these assemblies are installed back to back and powered by a single pump. The entire installation occupies an area 10 by 22 feet and supports 384 plants.

The crop in the system pictured consists of several varieties of tomatoes, peppers and strawberries. Mixing crops like this is not always a good idea since the nutrient solution cannot be fully tailored to a given crop's needs. For this system a mixture favoring tomatoes has been blended.

The nutrient in this system is changed every two weeks and the pH adjusted to 5.5 to 6.0. Since there is no growing medium except a handful of "Growrox" at each plant site, pH remains very stable and only requires an initial adjustment when mixing fresh nutrient. The incoming water supply is approximately 200 ppm (parts per million) with a pH of 8.0 — fairly good water. The system is topped up with half-strength nutrient, or with plain water, to maintain 700 ppm indicated with a Hanna Dist-1 dissolved solids tester.

The aero-hydroponic method is without doubt one of the most advanced hydroponic methods developed to date. The cost of constructing and installing systems, plus the complications of obtaining licensing, have been deterrents to widespread commercial application. This is beginning to change as commercial growers, researchers and manufacturers become aware of the capabilities and value of aero-hydroponic technology.

First published in Volume 2 Number 1, page 25.

Plant Plane Hydroponics

by Fritz-Gerald Schröder

Among German farmers there has been a rapid spread in the use of hydroponic systems. The total greenhouse area is about 148 acres (60 hectare), especially for vegetables such as tomato, cucumber and sweet pepper.

Some inorganic substrates such as perlite, vermiculite and rockwool are used as solid media, as well as some organic substrates such as peat moss and rice husks. The most common aggregate system uses rockwool and drip irrigation. But the disposal of spent rockwool and waste nutrient solution are of growing concern.

In 1987 at the Institute of Vegetable Production at Großbeeren in what was then East Germany, we began investigations into a new type of hydroponic system we call plant plane hydroponics, in which fleece with different physical characteristics is used as a solid medium.

Tests covering 21,600 square feet (2,000 square meters) of greenhouse space were conducted with tomato, cucumber, sweet pepper, different varieties of lettuce, beans, radishes and ornamental plants such as chrysanthemum and carnations.

Plant Plane Hydroponics

The system is called "plant plane" because the nutrient solution flows across a flat plane rather than through a narrow channel. It can be used as an open or closed hydroponic system.

The growing medium is polyester fleece, although other flat, thin substances such as peat paper, viscose fleece or very thin layers of organic or inorganic waste material could be used.

The fleece material is sandwiched between two layers of plastic sheeting. The greenhouse floor is sealed off with the lower sheet. The top layer is made from white polyethylene or plastic and helps reduce evaporation of the nutrient solution, drying of the roots and the growth of algae. It also acts as a reflective surface.

A well prepared greenhouse floor with a slope of 1 to 2 percent is necessary to successfully applying the system. Due to the absorbency of the fleece, almost all of the solution will remain in the fleece for the plant to use, as long as a modest irrigation schedule is followed. Any surplus will drain out of the fleece and into the drainage channel.

Before seedlings are transplanted, the fleece is soaked with nutrient solution. The seedlings are started in small rockwool cubes. The cubes are inserted into slits cut in the top layer of sheeting and set directly on the fleece.

Nutrient solution is delivered via a pipe with irrigation rates adjusted to accommodate plant demand and environmental conditions.

Performance

Experiments with the system were carried out from 1987 to 1990. The first compared the growth, fresh weight and dry weight and vegetative shoot parts of cucumber plants. Later experiments compared the dry weight of roots and shoot growth of cucumber and tomato.

With cucumber, the increase in dry weight of roots and shoots was continuous (see graph on page 22). The plant plane system seems to have a positive influence on root growth and performance. On average, the shoot-root ratio was 3.1:1. With tomato, there were observed differ-

ences in the shoot-root ratio throughout the growing period (see graph, center, left). On average, the shoot-root ratio for tomatoes was 2.6:1.

Other types of vegetables and ornamentals were grown in plant plane hydroponics. The most relevant data from experiments in 1989 are presented in the table (below, left). High yields were determined for tomato with 35.3 kilograms per square meter, and for cucumber with 48.9 kilograms per square meter.

YIELD OF VEGETABLE (1989)

*Grams per plant

Crop	Plant-Harvest	Variety	Yield (Kilograms per Square Meter)
Tomato	1/6-11/7	Counter	35.3
	5/15-10/27	Counter	10.4
Cucumber	1/16-11/7	Corona	48.9
Sweet Pepper	2/21=11/7	Bell Boy	12.4
Lettuce	2/5-3/15	Carlo	110*
		Werina	111*

The experiments in 1990 involved the crops listed in the table above. One of the most important results of these trials is that none of the plants grown — lettuce, melons, roses, even radishes — presented any problems with nutrient delivery or disease control. Vegetative growth was excellent and the strong root systems of these crops appears to encourage early flowering, high production and good quality.

One reason for the strong root systems is that the oxygen level in the rhizosphere (root zone) remains high due to surface diffusion. The determined dissolved oxygen level of the solution in the root zone averaged more than 80 percent. Well known and expensive methods to oxygenate the nutrient solution were not necessary.

In addition, tests have shown that a mixed colony in the root zone includes saprophytic microbes. These mainly non-pathogenic microbes use a large amount of oxygen and produce CO_2. The CO_2 level at the root zone was about 60 percent. As a living community, the plant plane hydroponic system successfully mimics the biologically active environment found in organic soils. Other advantages of the plant plane system include:

- Construction and set up costs are reduced by at least 30 percent compared with traditional hydroponic systems.
- The quantity of growing medium is greatly reduced without sacrificing the high yield potential of traditional hydroponics.
- Materials, such as the polyester fleece, may be used for three to five years without replacement, reducing waste material.

Total dry weight of cucumber grown in Plant Plane Hydroponic System

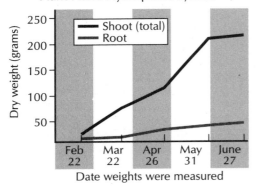

Date weights were measured

Total dry weight of tomato grown in Plant Plane Hydroponic system.

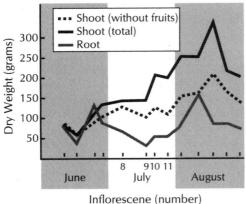

Inflorescene (number)

GREENHOUSE TEST CONDITIONS (1989)

Crop	Spacing (cm)	Plants per square meter	Area in square meters	Carbon Dioxide (ppm)
Tomato	80-60	2.1	77	600
Cucumber	90-60	1.8	77	800
Sweet Pepper	80-40	3.1	77	—
Lettuce	25-20	20	77	—

CROP PERFORMANCE (1990)				
Crop	**Variety**	**Plant-Harvest**	**Yield (Kg/sq m)**	**Plants /sq m**
Eggplant (Climbing)	Clasita	5/29-9/3	5.1	4
Bean	Melkim	7/24-11/15	1.5	4
Sweet Pepper	S. Golia Giallo	2/26-10/26	16.3	3.1
Melon	Pomilex	5/29-9/3	4.1	4
Lettuce (Iceberg)	Deutscher	5/29-7/20	1.2	—
Lettuce	Imperium	6/8-8/2	327*	13.5
Radicchio	Palla Rossa	6/8-8/2	348*	16
Lettuce	Karibu	6/8-7/5	184*	16
Radish	Cherry Bell	6/23-8/18	20**	—
Lettuce (Leaf)	Amerikanischer Brauner	6/8-7/17	225*	13
		*Grams per plant	**Bunches per square meter	

- The system works well with recirculating nutrient systems, reducing surface and ground water pollution.
- Installation is simple, requiring a minimum of skilled labor.
- The system is compatible with a number of existing nutrient supply systems.
- The structural characteristics of the polyester fleece ensures an even distribution of nutrient solution.
- The system permits crop rotation with varieties requiring different plant spacing, such as tomato, lettuce and chrysanthemum.
  More information is needed about plants and their surroundings, especially in the root zone. The future commercial use of plant plane hydroponic systems will be influenced by the advantages to be gained over the use of other types of systems.

First published in Volume 3 Number 1, page 52.

Hard Rock Gardening

by George Van Patten

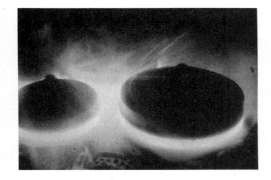

Rockwool is produced from rock alone or a combination of rock, basalt, limestone and coke. The best rockwools are produced from basaltic rock (diabase). These rockwools have a mineral balance that is inert and will not react with the nutrient solution. The high quality rockwools have uniform fibers, even distribution of the binder and very little shot (mineral pellets that have not been spun into fiber).

The rigid rock components are melted at temperatures exceeding 2,500 degrees. This molten solution is poured over a spinning cylinder. As the molten solution flies off the cylinder, it elongates and cools to form fibers. The process is very similar to the way liquefied sugar is poured on a spinning cylinder to make cotton candy.

A binder (phenol-based resin) is added to the rockwool immediately following spinning The rockwool is then compressed and cured into large uniform slabs or granular flock. The amount of pressure applied when forming the slabs dictates the density of the rockwool.

The blocks are rigid and easy to handle. They may be cut into just about any size desired. Granulated rockwool flock is easily placed into growing containers or used like vermiculite or perlite as a soil amendment.

The heat used to produce rockwool renders it sterile and safe to grow in. The length and thickness of the rockwool fibers are regulated by the speed of the spinning cylinder, the consistency of the molten rock mix and the temperature.

The grain or the direction the fibers run in the rockwool slab is important for water absorption. Most of the fibers run horizontally in slabs. The horizontal grain allows the nutrient solution to drain slower from the slab allowing good capillary movement and retaining even moisture in the slab.

Propagation and small cubes usually have vertical grain. The up and down grain is perfect for the fast draining required by seedlings and small plants. Larger rockwool slabs do not necessarily bring a higher yield. But a larger chunk of rockwool makes a larger reservoir for nutrient solution and is more reliable. Six-inch slabs are as good as 8-inch slabs for most hobby gardens and they are more economical.

Application

Even though rockwool will hold 10 to 14 times as much water as soil, it does not provide the buffering action available in soil. The pH or acid-to-alkaline balance of dry rockwool is about 7.8 to 8.0. pH down is added to the water solution to lower the pH to 6.5 to 7.0. An acidic fertilizer solution (about 5.0 on the pH scale) is required to maintain the actual solution at a pH of about 5.5. Errors made in the nutrient solution mix or with pH level will be magnified. Be careful to monitor both the pH and nutrient level.

According to Michael Dowgert, Ph.D., from Agro Dynamics, "Plants grown in rockwool do not suffer water stress until the rockwool is almost dry." But he also advises to never let rockwool dry out more than 50 percent. It is difficult to rewet properly and roots will not grow in the dry spots.

There are some tricks to handling rockwool. Like peat moss, dry rockwool can be abrasive and act as a skin irritant. Take extra special care if you have sensitive skin. Use gloves, goggles and a face mask or respirator when handling dry rockwool especially in enclosed areas. Once the rockwool is thoroughly wet, it is easy and safe to work with; it creates no dust and does not irritate the skin. Keep out of the reach of children and wash clothes thoroughly after prolonged exposure to rockwool as a safety precaution.

Rockwool mineral fibers consist of mono-filentous fibers. These mono-filentous fibers are impossible to split lengthwise to form even thinner fibrils. The physical characteristics of rockwool are different from asbestos. Asbestos fibers split lengthwise into super thin fibrils that the body has a very difficult time passing or breaking down after inhalation. Rockwool fibers are much thicker and break down cross ways to yield a short fat fiber the body can discharge easily.

Rockwool stays so wet that algae grows on surfaces exposed to light. While this green slimy algae is unsightly, it does not compete with plants for nutrition. However, harmless fungus gnats could take up residence.

Avoid the unsightly algae by covering the rockwool with plastic. The only time to be concerned about algae is if it starts to die off rapidly. This wholesale die-back robs oxygen necessary for nutrient uptake. There are several algicides that can be added to the nutrient solution to abate algae. If you decide to use an algicide, read the label carefully to ensure it is not toxic to plants.

Rockwool manufacturers offer slabs, cubes and granular flock. Cubes are wrapped with a sleeve of plastic and the ends are open. The rockwool flock usually comes in three grades: coarse, medium and fine. The flock may also be either water repellent (like the insulation that it is designed after) or water absorbent.

First published in Volume 1 Number 1, page 37.

Rockwool: Cube Gardens, Slab Gardens

by George F. Van Patten

Rockwool cubes can be used to start seedlings or cuttings and grow small plants. They can be watered by hand from above or flooded from below. In fact, cubes can even be used to wick nutrient solution up to the plants.

Making your own high performance ebb and flow rockwool garden is easy. The principle is simple: the nutrient solution floods into the garden bed, pushing the CO_2-rich, oxygen poor air out. When the rockwool drains, it draws in new oxygen-rich air.

Today, flood and drain systems, also known as ebb and flow, are used by many commercial hydroponic operations and in many home gardens. The growing bed can be almost any size or shape as long as it holds water. The table should be a little deeper than the cubes are tall to permit periodic flushing every week or two. A growing bed or table with 4-inch sides and large, flat ridges for drainage along the bottom is ideal for 3-inch cubes. Many gardeners report that complete submersion is not necessary, perhaps not even desirable, with cubes and grow healthy gardens in beds with 2-inch walls.

Plant roots must not sit in stagnant water; water must drain freely instead of pooling or puddling up. The table should drain completely when level or be set at a slight incline. Cubes can also be set on a shallow grate above the water "puddles."

Rockwool that shifts to the lowest point in the growing bed will always be waterlogged unless the drain outlet is situated at this point. Low spots create soggy, wet conditions that promote rot and fungus. A carpenter's level can help you position the table for proper drainage. Ideally, the high performance growing table has broad ridges on the bottom that allow the rockwool to lie flat while the narrow gutters carry the runoff toward the drain hole.

On flat bottomed tables, perlite placed under the blocks would allow better drainage, but it's so light that it floats to one end of the table or washes down the drain. Washed gravel or expanded clay work well to create an air space under the cubes and do not wash away. The most critical point to control in a rockwool garden is the root zone. The root zone must stay evenly moist.

Growing Tips

Use a mild nutrient solution (quarter to half strength) on small seedlings and young cuttings. The tender plants can not endure a heavy nutrient concentration.

Start seeds and cuttings in 1-inch rockwool cubes. Lay small seeds on top of the rockwool and insert larger seeds into the pre-drilled holes. Push loose rockwool over the hole so that the seed stays in contact with the rockwool to remain moist. Larger seeds, such as melon, peas and cucumbers, will fit easily into the hole while smaller tomato and lettuce seeds are best started by broadcasting and gently pressing down into the rockwool. When roots emerge from the bottom and sides of the cubes, transplant into pre-drilled, 3-inch or larger cubes.

To harden off for outdoor planting, set the entire flat or garden in the shade outdoors for several hours each day. Leave the garden outdoors in a cold frame or greenhouse all night when the last chance of frost has past.

Rockwool cubes are very durable, but the roots they contain are very frail; take care during transplanting. Transplant shock will result if the roots are broken off and not gently returned to the medium. After careful transplanting, cycle the nutrient solution through the garden so the roots are saturated.

Unwrapped 1-inch cubes are the best size to transplant in soil. The composition of soil and rockwool are different and each holds water at different rates. Moisture held in the rockwool is drawn away by the soil. The larger the cube, the more difficult transplanting will be because of this change in surface tension. It is OK to transplant larger cubes if large clusters of roots are dangling from the bottom. Remember to remove the plastic sleeve before transplanting cubes into soil.

Salt Build-up

Top off the reservoir containing depleted nutrient solution with water just before the weekly draining. Plug the drain port and flood the bed with the now dilute nutrient solution. Completely submerge all the cubes for a minute or two before draining back into the reservoir. Do not let the dilute nutrient solution set for more than 30 minutes. If the stems stay too wet, they could dampen off or rot.

If the nutrient solution is recirculated over one week, flowers and vegetables may grow more slowly. Salts can build up that may retard nutrient uptake. Some water supplies contain more sodium (Na+) ions than plants can use. After a few weeks, sodium may build up in the rockwool. This can happen with other salts or nutrients as well, but the problem is usually associated with sodium.

Even with over-watering by 20 to 30 percent, there might still be a build up of other elements. By flooding the cubes completely once a week, the ion balance will be retained. Without flooding, the upper half of the cubes may be deficient in nutrients.

Slab Gardens

After seedlings get too big for a small rockwool cube garden or you have developed an insatiable appetite for fresh vegetables, a larger slab garden will bring you higher yields.

Rockwool slabs are designed for greenhouse flower and vegetable production. They will also hold a great kitchen or a patio garden. A slab will hold nutrient solution much longer than soil and will support lush growth.

To make a simple slab garden, just place a 6- or 8-inch by 3-inch by 3-

foot slab in a garden bed with good drainage. Slabs perform best in areas that provide consistent drainage such as a concrete floor, patio or greenhouse. Plastic sleeves envelop the slab to form a garden bed, a plastic grate placed under the slab will improve drainage. Once the slab is set in place, soak thoroughly.

Slabs can be elevated at one end (tilted) so that gravity carries runoff back to the reservoir. Set the slabs on a flat surface that is sloping approximately two percent from end to end. A two percent slope is a drop of about one-half inch from one end of a 36-inch slab to the other. Slabs set at ground level can also use gravity to deliver the nutrient solution via drip tubing.

Set the slabs up in an appropriate floor plan, side by side or around the perimeter of a patio. Once the slabs are in position, let the water drain out by cutting two to six slits in the sides and bottoms of the slabs for drainage.

After the drainage holes or slits have been cut, slip one wet slab after the other into the plastic sleeves or set into a growing bed. Make sure that there is enough sleeving at the end to channel for drainage. Seal the other end of the sleeve with duct tape or fold shut and secure with clothespins. The sleeving must be dry before sealing with tape. If sleeving is unavailable, cover exposed slabs with two-ply plastic sheeting, black on the inside to stop algae growth and white on the outside to reflect light.

The use of sleeves is important to producing strong plants. Roots grow out the sides of the slabs into the moist environment between the rockwool and the plastic. This space is perfect for root growth.

To transplant a three or four-inch cube onto a slab, cut a hole through the sleeve that is about the same size as the cube to be transplanted. The cubes can be moved from a smaller garden and set directly onto the slab.

Rockwool slabs are very efficient when irrigated by a drip system. Drip systems deliver the nutrient solution to the base of each plant with a small emitter. First the emitter is placed in the cube, in one or two weeks as the roots reach down into the slab, it can be placed next to the cube. This will help keep the water where it is used and reduce the growth of unwanted algae.

GERMINATION IN ROCKWOOL

While the water holding characteristics of rockwool have been largely responsible for the medium's rise in hydroponic circles, Dutch researchers have concluded that it may be too much of a good thing, at least for delicate tomato and sweet pepper seeds.

Experiments carried out at the Glasshouse Crops Research Station in the Netherlands into the recurring problem of seedling failure in rockwool starting cubes suggests that excessive water — or more accurately, a lack of oxygen — in rockwool cubes inhibits germination in most of the cultivars tested, even if the cubes were allowed to drain freely after watering. Increasing the oxygen available to seeds by simply squeezing out about 25 percent of the water improved germination.

Of the other variables tested, water quality and nutrient concentrations also appeared to play a role in successful germination. The study confirmed the belief that plain water is superior to fertilized water for germinating seed. But in an unexplained finding, tap water produced better results than rain water collected from greenhouse roofs. — *by Don Parker*

Setting Up

Lay out a half-inch drip supply tubing along side the rockwool slabs and cut the tubing to length. Set stiff drip tubing in hot water to make it more pliable and easier to work with. Lay the larger supply tubing out flat and secure in place with plastic ties or conduit tie downs. Use a hole punch, nail or electric drill to make holes in the half-inch supply tubing to accept the drip spaghetti tubing.

The spaghetti feed tubing should be long enough to reach each plant easily (12 to 24 inches), but remain out of the way. Cut the tubing at a 45 degree angle and insert it into the hole in the half-inch tubing. Attach the other end to the drip emitter.

Secure the emitter so that it drips on the rockwool cube or slab. Take care so that the water does not run out on the plastic sleeving and spill on to the floor. One dripper should be sufficient for each plant. If not, add another or go to a higher volume emitter.

Commercial growers are starting to recycle the nutrient solution for conservation and ecological reasons. When no nutrient is recovered, complications and labor are reduced, but the environment may suffer if large amounts of nutrient are dumped on soils or in waterways. Non-recovery gardens can work well for commercial greenhouses and outdoors where the runoff can be channeled away safely and efficiently. For home growers, the run-off solution makes a great fertilizer for your outdoor garden.

For systems where the nutrient solution is recovered, make certain to change it every week or two. Changing the nutrient solution on the same day of the week, such as Saturday, makes it easy to remember.

To drain the reservoir, install a "Y" in the supply hose. One end is connected to the pump and the drip system, the other to a male threaded end cap that fits a garden hose.

Cleaning and Maintenance

Flush supply lines between crops or every two to three months with an algicide/bactericide like Phaisan, hydrogen peroxide, bleach or potassium hydroxide (pH up). Run it through the reservoir and the supply lines. Install a valve on the end of each pipe so the solution flows through the lines and back to the reservoir. Be careful to rinse the system with fresh water before putting the garden back in use.

Scrub out the reservoir and garden bed with a sponge and a mild bleach solution to remove accumulated algae or sludge.

Reusing Slabs

To reuse rockwool slabs, remove the small cubes and discard. Remove the slab from the plastic sleeving. When all of the plastic is removed, set the slabs up on end and turn a fan on them so that they dry completely. Scrape the old, dry roots from the sides and bottom of the slabs.

If you are concerned about virus, fungus or other diseases, discard the slabs or sterilize them. A wall paper steamer can be rented and used to raise the temperature to 212 degrees (100 C) in the entire slab to kill all insects, nematodes, fungi, bacteria and viruses.

Turn the dry slabs over, bottom side up, and insert them into clean sleeves or place on a clean bed. Condition the slab as above before use, then replant. Reused slabs are more prone to diseases and other problems.

First published in Volume 2 Number 3, page 25.

An Orchard of Lettuce Trees

by James B. DeKorne

People often ask me about the optimum size for an attached greenhouse to provide them with both winter heat and fresh produce. I always suggest that they construct the largest greenhouse they can afford. If they are as addicted to growing as I am, they will never have enough space for the constantly proliferating plants in their lives.

Under fantasy conditions, I guess I'd have many thousands of square feet under glass, but here in the real world I must make do with only 320 square feet. That makes for fairly crowded conditions most of the time, and I'm always looking for ways to increase my effective growing area.

One method is to exploit more of the vertical space in your greenhouse. We are so used to raising plants "horizontally," as in nature, that we seldom consider the idea that there is usually nothing to prevent us from going vertical to take advantage of all those cubic feet above the floor.

Certain plants lend themselves to this more than others, of course, and one of the best uses of vertical space I have ever seen is to plant an "orchard of lettuce trees."

Nutrient Flow Technique

I was first introduced to this idea over 14 years ago when I met Dr. P.A. Schippers of the Long Island Horticultural Research Farm operated by Cornell University. Dr. Schippers pioneered the development of many unique hydroponic growing systems, one of them being the lettuce tree, an outgrowth of his experiments with what he calls the Nutrient Flow Technique (NFT). Like most elegantly clever forms of technology, this one is extremely simple.

Essentially, the Nutrient Flow Technique consists of a series of shallow troughs filled with gravel or perlite to serve as root support for the plants. These troughs are inclined just enough to provide for an adequate runoff of hydroponic solution. At the high end of the module is an elevated container from which this nutrient fluid drips at a adjustable rate (via a manifold of faucets or drip-irrigation fittings) into each trough.

The excess solution not absorbed by the plant roots flows into a catch-basin at the low end of the system. There it accumulates until an ordinary toilet float activates an electric pump switch, returning the excess fluid back to the container from which it originated.

And that is essentially it — the method is a closed-loop, continuous-flow hydroponic system that will operate indefinitely on gravity plus an insignificant amount of electricity. Of course, water must be added to replace that lost to the plants and evaporation, but even that can be automated via another float valve in the nutrient reservoir connected to your water supply.

I've never bothered to insert this last element into any of the systems I've built because it is easy enough to top off the nutrient container every day or so with water from a bucket. For best results, it's a good idea to change the hydroponic solution every one or two weeks anyway to prevent nutrient imbalances from developing.

The NFT system I've just described is a "horizontal" system, using

Building Your Own

troughs laid out on the greenhouse floor or on benches. The system can be easily adapted to a vertical configuration by replacing the horizontal troughs with 1 1/2-inch PVC pipe "tree trunks."

Each length of pipe (sized to the height desired for your application) has a series of square holes about 1 1/4 inches wide by 2 inches long cut into it at 6-inch intervals. These are designed to accommodate a standard Jiffy-7 peat cube which usually expands to about 1 1/2 inches square — making for a snug fit in the 1 1/4-inch holes.

With the use of pipe "trunks" we have shifted the horizontal troughs to a vertical axis, gaining an incredible amount of growing space. An orchard of lettuce trees can produce a quantum level more food than a horizontal garden plot in the same way that a skyscraper contains far more office space than its ground floor alone.

The way it works is simplicity itself. Each hole in the south-facing plane of the pipe trunk snugly holds a Jiffy-7 and lettuce seedling. The nutrient solution drips into the pipe trunks from above via a "manifold" (that is, a strategically perforated length of 1/2-inch black plastic pipe) located above each upper pipe opening.

I use a standard drip irrigation fitting at each perforation with a short length of 1/4-inch plastic hose attached to securely guide the solution into the pipes.

As the hydroponic fluid slowly drips down the pipe, it is soaked up by each Jiffy-7, which in turn drips its excess solution down onto its down-stairs neighbors. Once all of the peat cubes have been thoroughly saturated, the remaining nutrient solution will stabilize at a relatively constant volume which is returned to the reservoir and recycled through the system.

A somewhat more sophisticated module could be made using elbow and tee fittings to avoid the open trough at the bottom (see illustration, left). This would prevent evaporation as well as protect the nutrient solution from debris and algae growth.

Such modules could be made in virtually any length to accommodate large growing areas. I even envision greenhouse lettuce trees growing in long rows, like corn plants. If they were staggered, each plant should get its full share of sunlight even in a densely planted greenhouse.

Readers with a talent for plumbing could easily tie the rows together into one system serving the entire growing structure with a single nutrient container and pump. Just remember to slant the pipes enough to provide for proper run-off into the catchment basin.

You also might think of shielding the nutrient solution from exposure to light that can encourage the growth of algae. This has sometimes been a problem with open tanks in my greenhouse. Your cover need be nothing more complicated than some pieces of black plastic sheeting or plywood scraps strategically covering open containers.

In terms of growing a lot of produce in a limited amount of space, Dr. Schippers' NFT method is the most efficient and easy-to-build hydroponic growing system I've ever encountered. If a better one exists, I haven't seen or heard of it yet. After 14 years of growing and experimentation, that's a pretty strong claim. Whether you try the horizontal or vertical NFT system, I'm willing to bet that you'll soon be as sold on the concept as I am.

First published in Volume 4 Number 2, page 52.

BASIC LETTUCE TREE

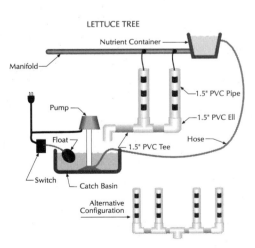

1/2" Irrigation Hose
1/2" ABS Pipe with drip irrigation fittings
End Cap
1 1/2" PVC Pipe
1 1/4" Holes for Jiffy-7's
110 VAC
Float
Cooler Pump
Nutrient Tank
Wooden Framework
Switch
Holding Basin

LETTUCE TREE

Nutrient Container
Manifold
Pump
Float
Switch
Catch Basin
1.5" PVC Pipe
1.5" PVC Ell
Hose
1.5" PVC Tee
Alternative Configuration

Since there is no medium to hold moisture in NFT systems, the circulating pump operates continuously. According to Dr. Howard Resh in his 1991 book "Hydroponic Home Food Gardens," continuous flow NFT systems can present a problem, especially with mature plants.

"The greatest problem facing NFT systems has been root dieback caused by inadequate oxygen in the nutrient solution immediately around the roots. The problem is associated with large root mats developing in the bottom of the NFT trough which impede the flow of water. This stagnation of water allows plant roots to use up all the available oxygen in that area and with a slow exchange of water a shortage of oxygen develops."

One possible solution to this problem involves aerating the nutrient solution in the reservoir or just before it is delivered to the roots. This approach can at best produce only 8 percent dissolved oxygen in the nutrient solution, compared to the approximately 21 percent available in the air.

The problem of water stress only arises when the plants have developed thick root mats in the trough. One approach would be to reduce the flow into the trough as the root mat develops. But to do so without risking damage to the plants would require constant monitoring. The system described here would achieve the same result with less monitoring, the only investment being a simple electronic timer attached to the pump.

Cycling NFT System

The test used a GE-24 (Garden of Ease), Aquaculture's smallest NFT system. It uses a 4-gallon reservoir and 80-gallon-per-hour pump to supply four 3-foot long PVC troughs. The troughs are 2 inches deep and have a cover that eliminates light and maintains high humidity in the root zone. It was assumed that humidity levels in the trough would be even more crucial with a cycling system to prevent drying of delicate roots.

Two of the troughs were run on the continuous pump and the other two on a pump connected to a timer set for alternating half-hour cycles — 30 minutes on, 30 minutes off. Both pumps drew from the same reservoir to supply identical nutrients to both the test and control plants.

The nutrient solution averaged 940 parts per million (ppm) with a pH of 6.8 and a temperature of 71 degrees (22 C). Light was provided by a 400-watt metal halide lamp. The photoperiod was maintained at 15 hours per day.

A variety of plants — cabbage, lettuce, kale, nasturtiums, string beans and radishes — were planted in both systems. The plants were treated identically from germination through transplanting. Each type of plant was placed in a corresponding site within the systems to ensure that they received equal amounts of light.

Results

During the first two weeks there was little visible difference between the two groups. Examination of the roots, however, did reveal a difference. The roots of the plants in the cycling system were larger with more root hairs.

By the third week, the plants in the cycling system were visibly larger and more robust. There was still no puddling in the troughs and no root dieback in the control group. The solution level had risen from about 1/8 to 1/4 of and inch.

It is significant that there appeared to be a benefit to cycling the nutrient solution even before root dieback came into play. The plants were grown for 31 days and then pulled and separated for examination of the root systems and to measure overall growth. The most noticeable difference was seen in nasturtium, lettuce and cabbage.

The reason for this increase in growth appears to go beyond the elimination of the problem of puddling in NFT systems. The nutrient depth and flow rate did not change significantly in the continuous flow system. One possible explanation is that the roots of the plants grown in the cycled system develop more root hairs early on, increasing their surface area and their ability to take up nutrients. — *by Russell J. Antkowiak*

Plant	Cycling System*	Continuous Flow System*
Nasturtium	.49	.15
Lettuce	.38	.33
Cabbage	.66	.48

*Fresh Weight in Pounds

Chapter 2
Nutrients

Hydroponic Nutrient Management

by Chuck Erikson

Choosing the right commercial nutrient solution for your application can be a bewildering and frustrating task. Sorting out the competing claims of manufacturers and the biases of various writers on the subject — some justified and some not — often leaves the beginning grower more confused than enlightened.

Unfortunately for the neophyte grower, simply making the "right" choice is no ticket to successful hydroponic gardening. Yes, a quality, balanced nutrient solution is essential to getting the most from your high-tech garden. But in the long run, it is how you manage that solution and the system that will determine success or failure.

Nutrient Monitoring

Beginners should always use nutrients according to the manufacturer's suggested dosage, usually one or two teaspoons per gallon. Experimentation has its place, but if you are just starting out, resist the temptation. The freshly mixed solution should contain between 1300 and 1500 parts per million (ppm) of total dissolved solids (some writers recommend a more dilute mix). These are the scientifically correct terms for the measurement of the actual strength of your nutrient and you should become familiar with them.

Many gardeners have found it necessary to change nutrient every three or four days to sustain flowering or fruiting plants; some have probably even tried changing formulas. Both of these methods have been widely used with varying degrees of success and failure. If, however, you are serious about hydroponics, and really do want to enjoy twice the yield as soil growers, you must take one more simple step ahead in technology. You should purchase any one of a number of nutrient testing devices and start monitoring your nutrient solution.

You will still need to change the entire solution every two or three weeks to remove any excess plant wastes and allow you to keep your storage tank clean. It is also a good idea to rinse your growing medium thoroughly every time you change nutrient. This one simple step ahead in the science of growing will assure better results in every size and type of hydroponic system. If your current supplier of hydroponics can't help you find this equipment, locate one who will.

Nutrient Solutions

All hydroponic systems have one thing in common: the need for a complete and balanced nutrient formula. This, of course, brings us back to where we started. Your nutrient solution must contain all of the following: nitrogen (N), phosphorus (P), potassium (K), calcium, magnesium, sulfur, iron, copper, manganese, boron, zinc, molybdenum, and cobalt.

Because of federal and state regulations, nutrients are sold and labeled according to the standard "NPK" three-number designation, such as 8-6-12. To the science of hydroponics these numbers have less significance than you might think. What really makes a nutrient formula correct is the balance, or ratio, of the different elements to each other and the solubility of the compounds.

While nutrient balance and interaction is beyond the scope of this article, it is important for the fledgling grower to at least be aware of these nutrients and their function in the growing process. Listed below are 11 key elements and some typical deficiency symptoms for each. It is important to note that a number of these symptoms, stunted plants for example, are listed under several different nutrients. Only careful monitoring can tell you for certain the condition of your solution.

Nitrogen

Nitrogen is a key element affecting plant growth and crop yields. It is absorbed by plants primarily in the nitrate form (NO_3) and is used by plants to synthesize amino acids and form proteins. It is also required by plants for other vital compounds such as chlorophyll and enzymes. Too much nitrogen will produce lush plants with dark green foliage with few blossoms and poor fruit set. Nitrogen is a mobile element which means any deficiency symptoms will appear first on the older leaves.

Nitrogen deficiency symptoms include:
- Slow growth and stunted plants.
- Foliage becomes yellow (chlorotic)
- "Firing" (browning) of tips and margins of leaves

Phosphorous

Phosphorous stimulates early growth and root formation and is absorbed by plants as PO_4. It is used by plants to form nucleic acids, DNA and RNA, and is very important to the plant's energy transport system. It can hasten maturity and promote seed production. Phosphorous is also a mobile element and is greatly affected by temperature. Too much phosphorous will interfere with the normal function of other elements such as iron, manganese and zinc.

Phosphorous deficiency symptoms include:
- Slow growth with thin stems and small leaves
- Purplish coloration of foliage on some plants
- Dark green coloring with the tips of the leaves dying
- Delayed maturity with poor fruit production

Potassium

Potassium is taken up by plants in the form of potassium ions (K+) and tends to remain in ionic form within the cells and tissue. It is essential for translocation of sugars and for starch formation. High potassium levels are required for protein synthesis and fruit production. Potassium is another mobile element in plants. Too much of it can induce a calcium or magnesium deficiency.

Potassium deficiency symptoms include:
- Older leaves develop marginal burning
- Weak stalks
- Slow growth
- Forward curling of leaves

Calcium

Calcium is absorbed by plants as the calcium ion (Ca++). It is essential for the formation and structure of cells. Calcium is non-mobile in plants which means that any signs of deficiency occur first in the newer leaves.

Calcium deficiency symptoms include:
- Shoot tips yellow and die back
- Abnormal dark green foliage
- New leaves distorted

- Premature shedding of blossoms and buds
- Root tips die and acquire black spots

Magnesium

Magnesium is used by plants in the form of the magnesium ion (Mg^{++}). It is contained in the chlorophyll molecule which means it is essential for photosynthesis. It is also required for activation of many enzymes involved in the growth process.

Magnesium deficiency symptoms include:
- Yellowing of older leaves
- Withering of leaves
- Upward curling of leaves along margins

Sulfur

Sulfur is used by plants as SO_4. It may also be absorbed from the air. Sulfur is a constituent of amino acids which means it is essential for protein synthesis. It is also present in the oil compounds that are responsible for the characteristic odor of plants. The deficiencies appear similar to nitrogen except that the symptoms appear in the new leaves.

Sulfur deficiency symptoms include:
- New leaves appear light green to yellowish
- Small spindly plants
- Retarded growth and delayed maturity

Iron

Iron is required by plants for chlorophyll synthesis. It activates biochemical processes such as respiration, photosynthesis and nitrogen fixing. Iron can easily combine with other elements and should be provided in a chelated form for hydroponic nutrient solutions.

Iron deficiency symptoms include:
- Yellowing between the veins of newer leaves
- In severe cases, death of entire limbs may occur

Manganese

Manganese serves as an activator for enzymes and aids iron in forming chlorophyll. It also helps produce oxygen from water during photosynthesis.

Manganese deficiency symptoms include:
- Yellowing between the veins of leaves near the tip of the plant
- leaves may turn brown and drop off

Boron

Boron is used to regulate the metabolism of carbohydrates in plants. It is a non-mobile element and a small but continuous supply is required at all growing points of the plant.

Boron deficiency symptoms include:
- Dieback of shoots and root tips
- Young leaves appear thick and curled
- Reduced flowering

Molybdenum

Molybdenum is required by plants for the utilization of nitrogen. Plants cannot transform nitrate nitrogen into amino acids without it.

Molybdenum deficiency symptoms include:
- Yellowing of older leaves moving into newer leaves

- Stunted, slow growing plants
- Some cupping or rolling of leaves

Copper   Copper is an activator of several enzymes and also plays a role in vitamin A production. A deficiency interferes with protein production.

Copper deficiency symptoms include:
- Stunted growth
- Poor pigmentation
- Wilting and eventual death of leaf tips

The hobby gardener must remember that these symptoms were discovered under ideal conditions. There are many other simpler factors that affect plant growth. These other factors include:

- **Ventilation** is probably the most overlooked problem in controlled environment growing. Plants absorb nutrients when the water in which the nutrients are dissolved is respirated (evaporated) from the leaves. The better the ventilation, the higher the respiration rate is and therefore the rate of nutrient uptake is also higher.
  Remember that ventilation means changing the air, not just blowing it around the grow room. You need to have an equal amount of fresh air blowing in as you have used air blowing out. The average commercial greenhouse can completely change the total volume of air every minute. This may or may not be possible in an indoor grow room.
- **pH** should be maintained in the range of 5.8 to 6.5. Too high or too low of a pH value in the solution (or in soil for that matter) can restrict nutrient uptake.
- **Temperature** of the nutrient solution should be in the range of 70 to 80 degrees at feeding time. Many nutrient elements, most notably nitrogen and phosphorous, are greatly affected by temperature and may not be available at all if the nutrient is too cold.
- **Light** — the higher the light level, the bigger the harvest.

First published in Volume 1 Number 1, page 53.

The Chemical Dynamics of Hydroponic Solutions

by Lawrence L. Brooke

Successful hydroponic crop production requires an effective system to support plants and deliver nutrients and oxygen. A hydroponic system is, by definition, nutritionally sterile. Therefore, the chemistry of the nutrient solution is the primary factor in plant growth.

Plants consume very specific chemical elements: the macronutrients, nitrogen, phosphorus and potassium; secondary nutrients, calcium, magnesium and sulfur; and the micronutrients, iron, manganese, zinc, copper, boron, molybdenum, cobalt and chlorine. To this list we should add carbon, which is absorbed as carbon dioxide from the air, and hydrogen and oxygen supplied by water.

In soil, plants derive these elements through complex biological processes. For example, bacteria break down nitrogen to make it available for plants to consume. With hydroponic cultivation we are able to provide the nutrients in a more direct and pure form.

The key here is "availability." A common problem is that many of the chemicals used to make plant nutrients are not compatible in strong concentrations and can bind together causing nutrient lock-out. Calcium and phosphorus, for example, may join together to form calcium phosphate which plants are unable to use. Phosphorus can also combine with magnesium to form magnesium phosphate — again this is not available to the plant.

Selecting and combining chemicals to produce a "fully available" nutrient for plant growth is an art form. In hydroponics, where the nutrient solution is the only source of food for plant growth, availability is critical.

H2+O+?

Bad water can cause big problems. Pure water is often not available to hydroponic growers. Almost all domestic water supplies contain certain "dissolved solids," minerals that cannot be filtered out in the way that particles can. Generally these conditions won't cause too much trouble. A simple pH adjustment will usually correct an imbalance caused by "hard" water.

However, there is a limit. In some areas the amount of total dissolved solids or of specific elements in the water supply can combine with elements in the nutrient solution resulting in nutrient lock-out. This may occur when well water is used to mix nutrient solution or where the municipal water supply is very hard. Water containing more than 50 parts per million (ppm) of calcium and magnesium (called "total hardness") can create serious problems. Other common elements that may be present in hard water include various carbonates, sulfur, sodium, iron and boron.

Your municipal water supplier can provide you with an analysis of your water supply. If you are using well water, there are many laboratories that can provide you with an analysis if you send them a sample. If the news is bad, it may be necessary to collect rainwater (a good idea wherever possible), install a reverse osmosis filtration system, deionization system, steam distillation system or use purified water (not mineral or "spring" water).

More or Better?

Dissolved solids (ppm) can be measured by using an instrument called a conductivity meter. Pure water will not conduct electricity. The higher the amount of dissolved solids the solution contains, the higher its conductivity will be. Thus, the conductivity meter can measure the electrical conductivity in the solution and interpret that measurement as ppm.

Generally this method is the best available to the home grower to measure water quality before nutrients are added and to identify dissolved solids (ppm) after adding the nutrient mix.

It is critical that the nutrient solution not exceed the plant's tolerance for dissolved salts. That tolerance can range from extremely low for some plants such as orchids, to a very high for salt-tolerant crops such as barley. Unless you know the specific tolerance of a given crop, it is best to use a nutrient between 800 and 1,200 ppm.

When in doubt, remember that it is always better to apply too little nutrient than too much. The typical "dose response" curve of plants to variations in nutrient concentration (see chart at left) shows three

DOSE RESPONSE CURVE

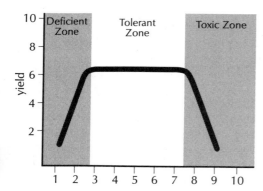

The Dose Response Curve shows the effect of solution concentration on plant yield.

Source: Dr. Wade L. Berry, *Proceedings of the 10th Annual Conference on Hydroponics*, Hydroponic Society of America, May 1989.

distinct and sharply defined zones: a "deficient zone" where there are insufficient nutrients for healthy plant growth; a "tolerant zone" in which sufficient nutrients are available; and a "toxic zone" where nutrient concentration is too high (too strong) for healthy plant growth. Notice that the portion of the curve within the tolerant zone is nearly flat; there is no advantage in yield from using a stronger or weaker solution.

A complicating factor in determining nutrient strength is that not all salts give equal electrical conductivity readings at specific concentrations. For example, monopotassium phosphate, a common salt used in the composition of plant nutrients, offers very poor conductivity and is practically invisible to conductivity meters. Nutrient solutions containing high monopotassium phosphate levels will appear to be much weaker than they actually are. It is important to be aware that this type of nutrient is stronger than it appears to be, based on your readings.

Always follow the manufacturer's recommendations for mixing nutrient, then measure the conductivity of the resulting solution. This will tell you what "indicated ppm" should be for that particular nutrient solution when mixed with your water supply, although "actual ppm" is probably higher. (See table at right for the indicated ppm of several common hydroponic salts.)

As plants consume nutrients and water, the nutrient strength will change in the hydroponic reservoir. In hot, dry regions it is common for plants to transpire lots of water; if you measure the ppm you may find that it rises. It will be necessary to top off the reservoir with water and bring the indicated ppm down to a reasonable level. In cool, humid environments you may find that the ppm drops; this is because the plants are consuming nutrients and not transpiring lots of water. It will be necessary to top up the reservoir with nutrient solution in order to bring the indicated ppm up to its proper level.

A fast growing crop can consume huge amounts of nutrients. If you have a small reservoir it is important to change the solution frequently. Depletion of the solution will result in slow, spindly growth and sickly

NUTRIENT MANAGEMENT

One difference between hydroponic nutrients and common soil fertilizers is the balance of elements. In soil, plants will find the nutrient elements that are missing from a supplemental fertilizer. Hydroponic crops depend on the nutrient solution for virtually all of their nutrient needs. Thus, hydroponic solutions must supply all the above nutrients in a balanced mix.

Another difference is the quality of the compounds used to make the fertilizer or nutrient mix. Common soil fertilizer is made with cheap "technical grade" chemicals including urea, ammonium phosphate and other inexpensive and impure ingredients. Soil will absorb impurities and protect the plants, at least until it is poisoned by repeated applications.

Because the delivery of nutrients is so efficient, hydroponic crops require less fertilizer than many soil crops, but they will not tolerate poor quality, unbalanced or impure mixes. The roots are constantly bathed with the nutrient solution and impurities or excesses will damage crops in a hurry.

Due to transpiration and evaporation, nutrient solutions can become more concentrated in hot, dry environments. It is easy to damage a crop with a nutrient solution that is too strong; it is nearly impossible to damage plants with a very mild solution. In general, it is best to mix the solution milder than recommended if you are in doubt. — *Lawrence L. Brooke* plants. A large reservoir in proportion to the total bio-mass will not have to be changed as often. Small plants, or naturally light feeders will deplete nutrients more slowly.

What Flavor?

Different types of plants have differing nutrient needs. The composition of nutrient solutions for all types of plants will contain the same elements as the list at the beginning of this article, however, the ratio of these elements can differ greatly. These variables can be striking when the nutrient needs of one type of plant are compared with the needs of another.

For example, orchids prefer a nutrient that is not only mild (low ppm) but also of a different NPK ratio in comparison to a high metabolism plant such as a fruit producing annual which must complete its entire life cycle within one growing season — from seed germination, through seedling, vegetative growth, flowering, fruit and seed production. Moreover, the fruiting annual which is going through this high-speed metamorphosis in less than one year will also have greatly differing nutrient needs during the various stages of its life cycle.

During rapid vegetative growth a plant can use lots of nitrogen, but a flowering or fruiting plant needs more phosphorus and magnesium. Hydroponic cultivation enables the grower to provide different diets for the crop at different times during the growth cycle. One of the great advantages of hydroponic over soil cultivation is the ability to manipulate nutrient concentrations for enhanced plant growth.

There are many nutrient formulations on the market that provide the same NPK combination throughout the plant's life cycle. The best of these are crop-specific formulations. Many manufacturers produce a particular product for orchids, another for tomatoes and perhaps another for indoor ornamentals.

These products will provide reasonable nutrition for the particular crop for which they are designed. However, since it is not possible to alter the NPK combinations during the various phases of growth, it is not possible to perform "nutrient manipulation" with general-purpose products. A multi-stage nutrient that permits adjustment of total ppm *and* NPK ratios will help you gain the full advantage from your hydroponic system.

First published in Volume 1 Number 2, page 47.

Water Should Taste Good to Plants

by Dr. Cal C. Herrmann and Lawrence L. Brooke

Taste, as we all know, is something personal. Pure water, containing no dissolved solids whatsoever, tastes completely flat and offers no nutritional value to either plants or animals. Spring water may be delicious to people, containing dissolved minerals which help build strong bones and teeth. The same water offered to plants, on the other hand, may not provide balanced nutrition and indeed may lock-out essential minerals if, for example, calcium or magnesium are present in sufficiently large quantities.

One of the advantages of hydroponics is that adjacent growth chambers with varying temperatures, humidities, light levels and nutrient solutions can suit very different species. To achieve balanced mineral nutrition we must start with an understanding of the water source content and the effect that it will have on the nutrient requirement of our plants.

Water qualities are measured by several properties, all of which effect the growth and health of plants. Let's list them first and then examine their effects on plants and what we can do about them to improve water quality. Keep in mind that the hydroponic environment is active; the grower controls nutrient composition while the plant removes both water and solutes.

FACTORS IN DEFINING WATER QUALITY:

pH

Water hardness. Carbonate content in some regions, sulfate in others.

Salinity

Iron content

Sulfide content

Extraordinary metals such as selenium

Chlorine and the products of chlorination

Biological contaminants

Taste and odor

pH Most municipal water sources are significantly basic with a pH of 8 to 9 to protect iron pipes from corrosion. On the other extreme, water that has passed through decomposing vegetation such as forest run-off and water that has passed through mining areas tend to be significantly acid. The phosphate content of hydroponic nutrient solutions makes a good buffer to ameliorate all but the most extreme variations in source water pH. However, for acid loving plants, preferring a pH of 6 or lower, phosphate is a poor buffer; it has little ability to furnish or absorb excess hydrogen at nutrient concentrations.

Water originating in limestone regions, for example in the Appalachian Mountains of the Eastern United States, has an advantage in that carbonate is an effective buffer in this range. It is necessary to add acid carefully to your nutrient solution and it will generally hold for several days before another adjustment is required. It is those gardening in the rest of the world, those with fine, soft rainwater, who need help.

Fortunately, the better commercial hydroponic nutrients are well buffered, but there is a limit to the amount of buffer that can be put into a concentrate or soluble solid fertilizer. A common agricultural pH buffering additive is dolomitic limestone, a slightly soluble carbonate rock which also contains useful amounts of calcium and magnesium. Usually a bit of silica mud remains from impurities found in agricultural grade dolomite. Another carbonate source could be common blackboard chalk, or calcium carbonate. Both of these are better for plants than the sodium bicarbonate (baking soda) that we might choose for digestive difficulties.

A word of caution is in order when talking about pH. Making pH adjustments based on faulty measurements is worse than ineffectual. It is important to calibrate pH meters frequently since the electrodes respond poorly after heavy use.

Hardness Water hardness tends to come along with carbonate content except in places like California's Central Valley where calcium and magnesium sulfates have accumulated, rather than the carbonates originally laid down elsewhere as ocean coral. Since calcium, magnesium and sulfates are important nutrients, hardness can be a good thing as long as you know what is there and adjust your nutrient concentrations accordingly. The calcium or magnesium content of hard water, when added to that supplied by your nutrient solution, may exceed the optimum for healthy plants. (Note that calcium is generally expressed by analytical services as parts-per-million of calcium carbonate, so actual calcium content is only

40 percent of the values reported. The same is true for total hardness — calcium plus magnesium.)

While they may work OK for softening wash water, beware of water softeners. They work by exchanging "good" calcium and magnesium for "bad" sodium.

If you are in a region with high sulfate concentrations, you need to know how much is present. Plants need sulfate and can tolerate a considerable excess, but nutrients prepared with sulfates, added to high-sulfate water and then subjected to concentration by evaporation and transpiration, as can occur in the Southwest, can become higher in sulfates than many plants can tolerate.

Salinity

Salinity is something that can be easily measured with a conductivity meter. The problem is that the conductivity meter will not tell you *what* salts are present and their true concentrations.

The recommended maximum salinity for drinking water, 500 ppm, is a substantial part of most plant's salinity tolerance and can be reached or exceeded in some areas by a combination of dissolved salts of nutritive or negative values. Fortunately, most municipal and regional water departments do a good job of analyzing their water throughout the year and are quite happy to share their detailed reports. County agricultural agents often have typical analysis of local surface and underground water. If all else fails, there are analytical service labs that specialize in water testing; $100 can get you quite a bit of information.

Iron

Iron discolors water but has limited solubility It tastes better to plants than it does to you! With pH at near neutral, ferric iron is quite in-soluble. Ferrous iron is more soluble but is readily oxidized by air, making a precipitate that could clog filters if present in large quantities. In any case, it is likely to be unavailable to the plants. Iron in the water can be an inconvenience and does not significantly decrease the amount of iron chelate needed by most species. A good fertilizer is necessary to provide hydroponic crops with "available" iron.

Sulfides

Sulfides are readily recognized by the rotten-egg odor they produce when acid is added. One might hope that sulfides in water would be a source of sulfur. Sadly, several other nutrients form insoluble sulfides, zinc, manganese and copper, for example. Sulfides in your supply water should be taken seriously. Serious nutrient deficiencies can occur in crops grown using high-sulfide water even when the finest fertilizers are used.

Activated carbon has been reported to do a very good job of removing sulfides but its carrying capacity is limited to about three percent of the weight of the carbon used. Other methods of sulfide removal exist using chemical extraction processes.

Extraordinary Metals

In a few areas of the country extraordinary water contaminants exist. Selenium, for example, has been a recent concern in California. Boron is found in excess in some other locations and other contaminants may be found by chemical analysis of local water.

These contaminants require individual attention. The first question to ask is whether they are harmful for your plants, or likely to contaminate your produce. Some water plants happen to be excellent for removal of some contaminants. Water hyacinths and others have been used to improve waste-grade waters before further treatment.

Chlorination

Most municipal water supplies are chlorinated. While tiny amounts of oxidant chlorine can have a beneficial effect on some plants, frequent, excessive chlorination of source waters leads me to suggest aeration; an air stream bubbled through source water will purge most of the chlorine and the products of chlorination.

Biological Contaminants

Biological contaminants — the bugs that the chlorine was intended to kill — are likely to flourish in the hydroponic environment. This is a good argument for cleanliness in setting up systems, operation and when handling nutrient solutions. It is also a good argument against "topping-up," rather than changing, nutrient solutions and against maintaining solutions in reservoirs for long periods of time.

Taste and Odor

Tastes and odors in water are most likely to come from humus residues in rural water supplies, assuming that sulfides are not present. These organic residues are easily removed in municipal treatment facilities by flocculation: a process that must be carefully controlled and is not convenient of individual installations. Alternatively, activated carbon is excellent for cleaning up contaminated water but, again, has a limited capacity.

Purification

When the water supply contains unacceptable contaminants it is necessary to purify the water. A variety of methods have been developed for a variety of different applications:

Distillation is the method that first comes to mind. Except for the most advanced multistage distillation technology found in large installations, it is quite energy intensive. In addition, distillation produces a product that for our purposes is unnecessarily pure. Indeed, for most municipal

PPM EXPLAINED

In most hydroponic literature measurements are given in parts per million, or ppm. The term often induces an unnecessary case of science anxiety in beginners who may be more used to measuring nutrients in shovel fulls or truckloads. How do you measure something as tiny as a millionth part, especially as a solid dissolved in a liquid solution?

Actually, ppm is less frightening than it sounds. One gram of table salt, for example, dissolved in one liter (1000 grams) of distilled water will produce a solution containing 1000 ppm of salt, roughly the strength of a typical hydroponic nutrient solution. Assuming that your water supply is relatively pure, it is a simple matter to mix up a hydroponic solution of the correct concentration, especially if you are using a commercial mix in which the measurements have already been converted to more familiar teaspoons and gallons.

use, distillation plants allow a partial bypass so that the output is not totally devoid of salts.

Solar distillation deserves consideration, especially in tropical and arid regions where high salt content can make water unsuitable for use by plants without purification and where plentiful solar energy can be used.

Laboratory deionizers also produce unnecessarily pure water for hydroponic purposes, are difficult to regenerate and fairly expensive.

Reverse osmosis (RO) shows more promise. At the University of California Water Technology Center we conducted a series of research studies on the process, though significant early development was at UCLA and other labs. RO is a workable option for home hydroponic use where the waste water can go on to the outdoor garden but is rarely needed for water of average quality.

Dehumidification

There is another source of very good water — your greenhouse. Plants transpire quite a lot; it is their method of imbibing nutrients. Almost all of the water taken up by the roots is released to the atmosphere as humidity.

Dehumidification within the greenhouse offers several advantages. By lowering humidity in the greenhouse, plants are encouraged to transpire more water and thus take in more nutrients. In regions of water scarcity, recycling transpired water can significantly reduce the water required for operation. Additionally, water recovered from dehumidification contains no dissolved solids and is thus practically pure.

Dehumidifiers operate quite efficiently since the heat removed by the cooling coils from the air inlet stream is rejected to the air exit stream, with some increase in temperature. The fan power can be used as a part of your greenhouse ventilation scheme. The theoretical energy cost to cool and condense humidity is about 2.6 kilowatt-hours per gallon of water; at 75 percent efficiency that would be 3.5 kilowatt-hours per gallon. To reduce this cost requires a source of "cold." Temperatures cool enough to help condense humidity might be found underground or in nighttime air.

Waste Water

Hydroponic discharges include used nutrients and, when water purification systems are used waste might include RO or other brines and resin regenerate wastes. Discharge might be to the homeowner's garden or septic tank or to a municipal sewage system.

A first consideration is the corrosion of piping by acids. This is controlled in industry by passing acid wastes through limestone gravel as a convenient neutralizing agent.

Most sewage systems have very low tolerances for pesticides and bactericides. One solution might be the evaporation of waste water to a solid residue that can be bagged for disposal. The evaporation pond became favored in California's Central Valley for large quantities of agricultural wastes when recycling was abandoned.

Discharges to the land require your careful consideration of what is in the water and who is going to use it next. Some RO brines, for example, are really quite good water. One might not want to drink it, but it can be used for washing or irrigation.

First published in Volume 1 Number 4, page 39.

Organic Hydroponics for the Home Gardener

by Don Parker

In a sense, nearly all agricultural history up to this century has been the history of organic culture. It has only been during the 20th century that the understanding of basic plant nutrients has combined with advances in chemistry to bring us that thing, at once revered and reviled: chemical agriculture.

On a scale that includes the domestication of wheat and the invention of the plow, chemical agriculture may represent a revolution in humankind's relationship with the environment, or an insignificant blip — the historical equivalent of the hula hoop and the pet rock. Is chemical agriculture the "wave of the future" as so many slick chemical company salesmen in the '30s and '40s undoubtedly put it, or is it already becoming a thing of the past? And if the latter is, at least in part, true, where does that leave high-tech, cutting-edge agricultural techniques like hydroponics?

It was the realization spawned by the pioneering work of Justus von Liebig in the mid-1800s that much of what plants take from the soil, especially the big three: nitrogen (N), phosphorous (P), and potassium (K), were simple chemicals that launched the science of chemical agriculture. By burning plant matter and analyzing the residues, Liebig was able to identify the basic soil components needed for plant growth. Though Liebig failed to carry through with his discovery, he began what might be called the demystification of soil fertility and plant growth, a process that in the intervening years has transformed the farmer from the part work horse, part artist and part shaman of centuries past, to the serious businessman and chemical engineer of today.

Hydroculture as we know it today came into being as an offshoot of this ongoing work in chemical agriculture. Early experiments with soilless, high-tech growing were not intended to demonstrate the efficiency of such systems, but to prove the emerging theory that nutrient uptake in plants was a knowable and controllable process. Once it was established by Julian von Sachs in 1860 that a simple soup of synthetically produced NPK and a dozen or so micronutrients dissolved in water could produce vegetative growth in the lab, the progression to commercial applications of that knowledge became a simple matter of economics.

Given that historical background the chemical bias of most hydroponic gardeners is understandable. To some, "organic hydroponics" is almost a contradiction of terms. It is often though that the lack of precise control inherent in organics negates some of the most impressive results offered by hydroponic technologies. Dumping an organic nutrient mix into a high-powered hydroponic system, so the argument might go, is like putting fuel oil into the gas tank of your new Porsche.

Most of the widely noted failings of organic hydro systems — the difficulty of precise nutrient control, the possibility of contamination by undesirable organisms, higher nutrient and labor costs, the smell, undissolved solids clogging drip emitters and in general gumming up delicate components — remain speculative only because so little serious research, or even casual experimentation, has been done on the subject.

Likewise, proponents of organic hydroponics, either as an existing technology or a goal for the future, are forced to rely on anecdotal evidence or the circular argument that organic nutrient solutions are "better" because they are, well, organic.

Fortunately, it is not necessary to wax poetic about the unknown "life force" of living systems or the synergism of organic nutrients and biological agents to appreciate the possibility that organic hydroponics offer an alternative to chemical nutrient mixes. Such systems do exist, after all. The question is not whether it can be done, but why bother.

The possible advantages for traditional field agriculture of organic materials and methods are still the subject of some debate, but several are well known and widely accepted:

- Chemical fertilizers, especially when heavily applied, tend to strip soils of beneficial organisms, from earthworms to bacteria. Organic fertilizers not only feed plant roots, but also the community of organisms in which they live. Organic methods generally improve soil texture, long-term fertility and water retention characteristics.
- Water run off from chemically fertilized fields is increasingly recognized as presenting an environmental danger to surface and ground water supplies and to downstream ecosystems. The buildup of toxic salts in some soils is another potential drawback to chemical cultivation.
- The non-availability and increasing cost of inorganic salts and compounds make organics, at least as a supplemental measure, an attractive option in some applications. This is especially true of lesser developed regions where the choice is often made between expensive chemical fertilizers, and cheap or free indigenous substitutes.

All of these concerns are more or less addressed by traditional chemical hydroculture. Obviously, problems of soil erosion, fertility and toxic build up are unlikely to arise with a soilless culture. In addition, the closed nature of most hydroponic systems and the ability to efficiently deliver plant nutrients can drastically reduce the cost of fertilizer inputs per unit of production, while at the same time protecting rivers and streams.

The Wave of the Past

But there are other reasons to "go organic," not the least of which is the widely held perception that organically grown produce is superior in taste, eye appeal and nutrition.

Flavor and appearance are important considerations for the home grower and the commercial operator. Both involve a subjective judgment and are unlikely to yield to consensus in the foreseeable future. The question of nutrient content, on the other hand, lends itself to objective evaluation. But here, too, a lack of conclusive evidence one way or another makes it nearly impossible to settle the issue.

Some studies show that organically grown foods may be more nutritious, while others find little or no difference. Variables like crop variety, soil quality, weather and others limits the usefulness of much research. Suffice it to say that proponents of either growing method should be able to find at least one or two studies supporting their predetermined position.

While hard-headed commercial producers are unlikely to make decisions based on such sketchy information, consumers can and often do. In the tangled logic of the market, perceptions have a way of becoming reality. A product that is perceived to be superior, rightly or not, will always fetch a higher price. For organic produce, that advantage can be 10 to 50 percent at the retail level. And that market is growing at a rate of 8 to 15 percent a year, depending on your definition of "organic" and

NITRATES IN GREENHOUSE GREENS

High concentrations of potentially harmful nitrates have been found in winter glasshouse crops in Europe. In a study of winter-grown produce between 1984 and 1986, it was found that nitrate levels rose beginning in October to peak in January. Levels declined from January to April. The highest concentrations were found in leafy greens such as lettuce and water cress.

The New Alchemy Institute has developed a new technique that can dramatically reduce nitrate concentrations in winter-grown lettuce. Soaking lettuce roots in pure water for 36 hours after harvest reduced nitrate concentrations by an average of 32 percent compared to a group of control plants in one test conducted on January 10. Unfortunately, the effectiveness of the technique appears to decline rapidly as the season progresses. Plants harvested on March 22 showed only a nine percent difference in nitrate content.

who's doing the counting. The recent scare over Alar tainted apples is a dramatic example of a heightened concern about chemical pesticides and, to a lesser extent, chemical fertilizers in agriculture.

For the hobby gardener who prefers organically grown foods, organic hydroponics can mean a substantial savings over the high-priced produce available at the local co-op or health food store. For the commercial grower, it might someday mean a product that will demand a higher price, in season or out, than the products of the "chemically dependent" giants of agribusiness. This is especially true of high-end produce, a category that includes "pesticide-free" hydroponic as well as "organically grown" produce.

For the foreseeable future chemical nutrient mixes are certain to remain the mainstay of most hydroculturists, especially for commercial applications. But for the home hobbyist of today and perhaps the commercial grower of tomorrow, organic hydroponics should not be dismissed without further investigation into the possibilities.

Home Sweet Home

Hydroponics consists of the application of nutrients dissolved in water directly to plant roots to maximize nutrient uptake and plant growth. Generally plant roots are housed in a medium, rockwool, gravel or soilless mixes. The purpose of the medium is to allow contact between roots and the nutrient solution while at the same time ensuring sufficient oxygen is made available to the roots. It is the balance between nutrients, water and oxygen that makes hydroponics such a dynamic method of cultivation.

With organic hydroponics, the chosen media must serve an additional function — housing the micro-organisms needed to release nutrients bound in the organic nutrient solution. Most chemical gardeners would shrink at the thought of encouraging biological activity in the medium or nutrient reservoir, but that activity is as central to the absorption of organically derived nutrients in the greenhouse and grow room as in the backyard garden spot.

Given that limitation, several popular media would appear to be out of the question for organic cultivation. Any system in which roots are simply suspended in an aerated solution or, as with aeroponics, in air would not be a first choice for organic culture. Likewise many nutrient film technology (NFT) systems would suffer from the same flaw, although one home gardener has reported a successful organic experiment using rockwool cubes placed in NFT tubes with the capillary mats removed. That example notwithstanding, rockwool in bats or cubes might present some difficulty for the organic grower because of its tendency to raise the pH of the nutrient solution, already a potential problem with organic mixes.

The ideal medium for organic hydroponics should be chemically inert, porous enough to provide space for microbes to thrive, yet loose enough to provide adequate drainage and oxygen exchange. Lava rock, Geolite, perlite or pea gravel in some kind of flood or top-feed system are probably the safest choices for the home gardener.

Feed Me

In a sense, the term "organic nutrients" is a misnomer, at least from the plant's point of view. Regardless of the original source, nutrients are absorbed by plants as inorganic salts dissolved in water — the definition of a chemical nutrient solution. Organically derived nutrients must be reduced to this form, mostly by biological activity in the soil, compost pile or medium, to be taken up by growing plants. Thus, organic nutrients are made available to plant roots gradually over time.

This self-modulating characteristic of organics accounts for the relative stability of organic crops in soil. It is difficult to burn organically grown crops with too much fertilizer; plants are also less susceptible to damage from the temporary depletion of certain nutrients.

For the organic grower this stability involves a trade off, some would call it a deal with the devil. Something less than the maximum yield per unit of time and space is undoubtedly the price that must be paid for that stability. While to the commercial producer time and space represent costs that must be measured against possible marketing advantages, there are still circumstances in which it may be possible to get the better of the devil in the exchange.

The obvious example is our hobby gardener with a taste for organically grown mid-winter tomatoes. The not-so-obvious example is in settings, especially in lesser developed nations and some rural areas, where time and space are less at a premium than are chemical salts and the expertise needed to use them to advantage.

In a 1985 supplement to his book "Advanced Guide to Hydroponics," James Sholto Douglas notes that organic hydroponics systems have been producing successful crops in several Third World countries for decades. On the Indian subcontinent where inexpensive labor and cheap natural fertilizers make the practice profitable, organic hydroponics approaches an art. Though an advocate of chemical hydroculture, Douglas admits that the systems allow the people of these areas to reap many of the benefits of hydroponics — the efficient use of resources, especially land and water — without expending precious capital on imported chemicals.

The formulae at left, the first from India and the second from the East African country of Burundi, illustrate the use of indigenous materials to create a balanced nutrient solution. Both are dumped into fine weave sacks and steeped in clean water for one week to produce a nutrient tea.

Clearly, few growers in the industrialized world would have the time or inclination — or the necessary livestock — to whip up any of these concoctions. They are included here mostly to show the application of appropriate technology to local conditions. Anyone interested in experimentation along these lines, however, is directed to the above source.

ORGANIC MIX FOR FOUR TO FIVE GALLONS OF WATER:

430 grams hoof and horn meal

228 grams bonemeal

171 grams ground chalk

513 grams ground magnesium rock

570 grams fresh wood ashes

120 grams mature oilcake (compressed and aged flax or cottonseed)

10 grams of scrapings from a rusty nail

ORGANIC MIX FOR 100 LITERS OF WATER:

16 kilograms bloodmeal

7 kilograms bonemeal

5 kilograms fishmeal

8 kilograms wood ashes

6 kilograms well rotted compost or farmyard manure

50 grams Epson salts

450 grams lime

Several rusty nails

PERCENT CONTENT (AVERAGE)

Fertilizer Type	N	P₂O₅	K₂O	CaO	MgO	SO₂
Poultry	2-5	2.5-3	1.3-1.5	4	1	2
Sheep	2	1.5	3	4	2	1.5
Goat	1.5	1.5	3	2	-	-
Horse	3-6	1.5	2-5	1.5	1	0.5
Cow/Bull	2	1.5	2	4	1.1	0.5
Dried Blood/ Bloodmeal	13	2	1	0.5	-	-
Bone ashes	-	35	-	46	1	0.5
Bonemeal	4	22.5	-	33	0.5	0.5
Hoof and Horn Meal	14	1	-	2.5	-	2
Dried locust/ grasshopper	10	1.5	0.5	0.5	-	-
Fishmeal	9.5	7	-	0.5	-	-
Woolwaste	3.5	0.5	2	0.5	-	-
Wood Ashes	-	2	5	33	3.5	1
Cottonseed ashes	-	5.5	27	9.5	5	2.5
Ground cocoa pods	2.5	1	2	1.5	0.5	-
Pulverised cotton seed	7	3	2	0.5	0.5	-

Douglas' book includes average analysis for major nutrients found in a number of organic fertilizers (see table at left), and a handy procedure for making your own organic nutrient solution from ingredients on hand.

Fortunately it is not necessary to don rubber boots and gloves to set up a home-sized organic hydro system. Concentrated nutrient solutions made from organic sources are clean, easy to use and widely available.

One of the most popular for this purpose is guano, fossilized bat or seabird droppings. Combined with earthworm castings and a trace mineral supplement, the mix is packed with readily available nutrients in a form that if handled properly is clean and virtually odor free.

An organic hydroponic demonstration system using a flood and drain system (Hydrofarm Solo) with Geolite proved the value of such a mix by cranking out herbs, peppers and cabbage for nearly a year.

The fertilizer mix was a liquid concentrate containing bat and seabird guanos and sifted earthworm castings marketed by Humboldt Composting Co. as Simeon's Super Tea. The concentrate was combined with water at a rate of 1 tablespoon per gallon and supplemented with Maxicrop liquid seaweed concentrate at 1/2 tablespoon per gallon. The 4-gallon reservoir was changed and the system flushed every month or so. (Some growers recommend a chelated iron supplement be added to the mix, in addition to a general micro-nutrient supplement.)

Since a liquid mix was used, there was no need to strain the solution before it was placed in the nutrient reservoir. If dry mixes are used, and/or the system employs drip emitters that might be clogged by undissolved particles, the solution should be strained through a fine cloth.

Overall performance of the organic hydro set-up was roughly on a par with similar chemical systems in terms of yield and overall plant performance. The cost of operation was roughly the same as a similar sized system using ready-mix chemical nutrients.

In addition, the system seemed to display some of the stability and resistance to shocks that characterize organic cultivation in soil. In one instance, the system was accidentally left unplugged for four or five days. While growth came to a halt, the plants didn't wilt and quickly recovered once the system was restarted.

I use a similar mix (see chart, next page) in my home system, a timer-controlled top-feed system with a 25-gallon reservoir and a perlite medium with similar results. In more than two years of continuously turning out tomatoes, peppers, herbs and ornamental plants, the system has shown a surprising stability, despite occasional periods of neglect.

Monitoring and pH Control

Nutrient monitoring and pH control present the organic hydroponic grower with a unique set of problems, or opportunities, depending on your point of view.

A long-time advocate of the latter position, Simeon Murren, president of Humboldt Composting Co., says that one of the major benefits of organic hydro systems is that they are so stable, requiring fewer flushes, fewer nutrient adjustments and less fooling around with in general. Nutrient "monitoring" consists of regular nutrient changes and keeping an eye on the condition of the plants, rather than relying on expensive metering equipment.

Developing such a relationship with your system is more than just an aesthetic ideal; it's a practical necessity. Traditional monitoring of the organic solution for parts per million (ppm) nutrient concentrations is virtually impossible. Since organic nutrients are often locked into more complex compounds, ppm readings tend to be lower than chemical mixes. Readings from the system above averaged about 300 ppm.

Some growers have attempted to meter the ppm of fresh solutions to establish a baseline against which subsequent readings could be gauged. Unfortunately, experimenters have been frustrated by unexplained fluctuations that have no visible effect on the plants.

Visual monitoring of the plants, of course, lacks the precision of electronic monitoring, but organic systems seem to provide the grower with enough latitude that it is easy to get the hang of it. With my own system, I top up the reservoir with fresh water when the weather is warm and plants are transpiring heavily, and with a dilute solution when the

ORGANIC HYDROPONIC SOLUTIONS

There has been little research on the subject of organic hydroponics, but the experience of several innovative growers and a three-year test project by *The Growing EDGE* suggest that none of the problems normally associated with organic nutrient solutions are insurmountable for the hydroponic grower.

High quality powdered nutrients — worm castings, bat and bird guanos, purified fish products and seaweed extracts — are easy to store and mix and produce a solution with a mild earthy smell, similar to a good quality houseplant soil. Clogging of small openings with undissolved particles can be a problem if your system uses drip emitters, although it is not a concern with most hydroponic systems. If clogging occurs, try straining your mix through a fine cloth before adding to your system.

It is true that standard hydroponic monitoring equipment, electrical conductivity and pH meters, are useless for monitoring organic solutions. On the other hand, organic systems may not need the type of monitoring recommended for traditional systems. The system at *The Growing EDGE*, a timer-controlled top-feed unit with a perlite medium, has gone for up to a year between nutrient changes, just an occasional topping up with water or dilute solution, with no sign of macronutrient deficiency. Micronutrient deficiencies are headed off with foliar applications of seaweed extract.

Monitoring of organic systems is much more intuitive — keeping an eye on the plants, being aware of changing conditions. Good records — planting dates, the types and quantities of nutrients added, general comments on plant health and performance — can do a lot to enhance intuition.

The following recipes have been used with success in *The Growing EDGE* system. No doubt there are other ingredients and combinations that would work as well:

Vegetative/General-Purpose Mix
- 5 gallons water, warmed to room temperature
- 2 tablespoons dried earthworm castings
- 4 tablespoons bat guano or 3 tablespoons bat guano and 1 tablespoon fish flour*
- 5 drops Superthrive™ hormone and vitamin supplement (optional)
- 1 teaspoon soluble seaweed powder such as Maxicrop™

* Fish flour is included for extra nitrogen. Do not use liquid fish emulsion products found at most garden centers, unless you plan on wearing a gas mask around your hydroponic system.

Flowering/Fruiting Mix
- 5 gallons water, warmed to room temperature
- 5 tablespoons seabird guano
- 5 drops Superthrive™ hormone and vitamin supplement (optional)
- 1 teaspoon soluble seaweed powder such as Maxicrop™

Premix all ingredients in about one pint of water (a second-hand blender works great) before adding to the remaining water. Allow the mixture to stand for 24 hours, stirring occasionally, and strain (if needed) before use. — *Don Parker* weather is cool. Every few months the system is drained and fresh nutrient added, although it has gone as long as six months between complete changes with no apparent ill effect on the plants.

Temperature is also important to promoting and controlling biological activity in active and stored organic nutrient solutions; low temperatures can stunt plant growth, while excessive heat can lead to an explosion in biological activity that can be harmful to plants and offensive to the nose. Murren says that a well developed sense of smell is a valuable "metering" device for organic solutions. The telltale scent of rotting eggs means the solution has gotten too warm and/or is in need of a change. Murren advises against storing mixed solutions for too long or in too warm an environment. Ideally, organic nutrient mixes should be prepared only at the time of use.

Two Steps Forward

In light of what is known, or more importantly, what remains to be discovered, about organic hydroponics, commercial applications of the technology are at best far in the future. Too many questions in the critical areas of systems control, effect on yield and operating costs have yet to be answered.

Even among devotees of organic foods, there may be some who are simply not comfortable with the intuitive approach to monitoring and control necessary with organic systems. The inability to meter organic nutrient mixes means developing a new kind of relationship between plants, system and gardener, a relationship that depends more on keen powers of observation and some amount of faith than on high-powered equipment and the latest techniques. However, for the home hobbyist interested in nothing more than a steady supply of off-season, organic produce, organic hydroponics is an option worth exploring today.

First published in Volume 1 Number 1, page 25.

Foliar Feeding: Fast Food for Plants

by Kathleen Yeomans

A plant's vital life processes take place in its leaves. Each leaf converts the solar energy, carbon dioxide from the air, water and minerals into carbohydrates — the fuel of life. Leaves are made up of cells that receive sunlight and gases from the atmosphere. Chlorophyll cells use the sun's energy to fuel the plant processes. Leaf pores, called stomata, exchange carbon dioxide, oxygen and other gases with the atmosphere. Veins in the leaf make up the plumbing system that carries water and nutrients to the leaves during the day, and then back to the roots at night. Using energy from this food factory, the plant builds more roots, stems and leaves — the plant grows.

Bypassing the root-vein-leaf system with a foliar spray that penetrates the stomata adds an extra boost to plant growth. This delivery of vital ingredients directly to the energy conversion part of the plant produces a quick response to nutrients.

The root is a plant's anchor and main food source. Without a constant supply of water and minerals from the roots, a plant cannot survive. But

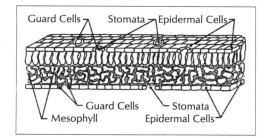

Guard Cells   Stomata   Epidermal Cells
Guard Cells   Stomata
Mesophyll   Epidermal Cells

roots can absorb water and nutrients only under certain conditions and these conditions are not always met.

Cold soil can slow root activity enough to starve a plant. Frozen, or waterlogged soil can kill roots, and fragile root hairs can be injured by rocky soils. Some soils bind nutrients, making them unavailable to plant roots. In these cases, a "booster shot" of nutrient spray, applied directly to the food-converting leaves can save an ailing plant.

Radioisotope research has shown that at least half of the nitrogen in fertilizer enters the leaf directly within a few hours after application and that phosphorus and potassium are also absorbed in this manner.

At the Montreal Botanical Gardens where young African Violets, yellow and sickly in appearance, were given a foliar feeding, the response was almost immediate. Leaves turned a healthy dark green and the plants started growing again within a few days. Foliar feedings cannot take the place of root feedings, but they are a useful supplement.

The process of feeding plants through their leaves was developed in 1950 by researchers at Kansas State College. Until that time, it was used infrequently by experimental gardeners. After work at Kansas State showed that wheat protein content could be increased when nitrogen additives were applied directly to plant leaves, commercial growers began using this new technique.

Foliar feeding has been of particular interest to researchers in areas that lack ideal growing conditions. For instance, in the USSR this method of application has developed because it is vital in the Arctic regions where permafrost retards root growth and nutrient uptake.

Some plants can assimilate nutrients through their leaves more readily than others. Absorption is most efficient through the undersides of the leaves where the stomata are found. Leaves with thick cuticle layers and heavily waxed leaves absorb nutrients poorly. You may need to experiment to see which plants in your garden benefit most from foliar sprays.

Fruit trees, such as apples, peaches, and citrus can receive as much as 75 percent of their nitrogen fertilizer and about 50 percent of their phosphorus and potassium by foliar spray. The pineapple is another crop plant that is commonly fed by means of foliar spraying.

Soybeans, celery and potatoes and other vegetables benefit from foliar applications of fertilizer. Greenhouse plants, such as African Violets, anthuriums, orchids, bromeliads, philodendrons and ferns show an amazing response to properly applied foliar feedings.

Micronutrients

Although the main plant nutrients, nitrogen, phosphorus and potassium can be applied by foliar spray, it is best used for delivering micronutrients. The greatest problem in supplying nitrogen, phosphorus and potassium is that, if sprayed in adequate amounts to feed the plant, these ingredients can cause chemical burns on plant leaves. Micronutrients, on the other hand, are necessary in such small quantities, that therapeutic doses do not cause plant injury.

Micronutrients include iron, copper, boron, molybdenum, chlorine and zinc. They are needed by plants in extremely small amounts. Too much is often as harmful as not enough. Micronutrient deficiency is common in plants because so many soils either lack specific micronutrients, or contain them in forms that make them chemically unavailable to plant roots. Often a micronutrient deficiency is due to pH imbalance. High pH soils in low rainfall areas cause chlorosis in soybeans. Spraying with iron has been 80 percent effective in overcoming this problem.

Plants absorb many nutrients better through their leaves than through their roots. Leaf sprays of zinc seem to be more efficient than soil applications for fruit trees such as citrus or peach. Manganese sprays are often recommended for new soybean crops on problem soils and pineapple growers regularly spray their crops with iron because soil applications are ineffective. Blossom end rot of tomato plants has been successfully controlled with calcium chloride sprays and soil moisture increases.

Micronutrients should not be used indiscriminately, however. Since the difference between need levels and toxic levels is so small, deficiencies should be diagnosed before therapeutic spraying is started. Soil tests and plant examination can help determine which supplements to use.

In addition to conventional nutrients and micronutrients, there are other types of sprays that enhance plant performance. New products to boost plant growth and production are being developed every day. Many of these "magic potions" are foliar applications that claim to stimulate growth, improve the soil, and increase crop yields and quality.

Enzymes

Enzymes are protein-like substances, made up mainly of amino acids. They act as catalysts to speed up chemical reactions and make plant nutrients available to roots. Without enzymes, plant activity would virtually grind to a halt. Without enzymes, microbe activity would cease and therefore, soil, formed mainly by these microscopic organisms, would no longer exist. Enzymes are naturally present in varying amounts. Organic soils are rich in enzymes while low humus soils are enzyme-poor.

A Hawaiian orchidist first used enzyme material as a plant growth stimulator 25 years ago. When he sprayed a by-product of a local enzyme factory on his orchids, their growth was extraordinary. This product was found to contain small amounts of the enzymes amylase, protease, lipase and a bacteria that produces enzymes. Similar reports were heard from California growers.

Enzyme products, combined with nutrients and humic acids, can be applied as foliar sprays and are commercially available.

Seaweed

Seaweed and other sea products are rich in micronutrients and growth hormones. Enzymes, vitamins and over 70 minerals are claimed to be available from kelp extracts. A special constituent of seaweed is alginic acid, an active soil conditioner and microbial stimulant.

Fish fertilizers, high in nitrogen and phosphorus, are often used in combination with kelp sprays to enhance their performance. Almost immediate "greening up" can be seen after foliar application of fish emulsion. A little odoriferous at first, the fishy smell of this seriously organic fertilizer dissipates after a day or two. Take your houseplants outdoors for a couple days after spraying with these products if the scent of the sea is too intrusive.

It's been suggested that these sea products are so effective because they contain not only nutrients and hormones, but possibly other compounds that are unknown yet necessary to stimulate plant growth.

Seaweed gets kudos and high praise from diverse authorities. The organic gardener and the more chemically inclined suppliers of bio-technological products agree that it is a totally safe and effective plant health promoter.

Seaweed contains plant vitamins, minerals, growth hormones and beneficial enzymes; its carbohydrates help plants absorb otherwise unavailable trace elements. Drought, disease and insect resistance are also cited as some of its virtues. According to some, seaweed extract prevents disease by restricting spore reproduction.

It is reported that spraying plants with seaweed extract stimulates leaf bacteria that are thought to increase the rate of photosynthesis. Other benefits include increased yields, reduced transplant shock and prolonged fruit production.

Humic Acids

Humic acids are complex organic molecules formed by the breakdown of organic matter in the soil. They are not considered to be fertilizers, per se, but soil enhancers and improvers. Humates are said to biologically stimulate plant growth, chemically change the fixation properties of soil and physically modify the soil. Some claims for humic acids include:

- Builds a more substantial root system.
- Helps soil absorb more water and hold moisture longer.
- Enhances results from fertilizers, disease and insect control products.
- Helps plants produce more abundant foliage, flowers and fruit.
- Promotes healthier, thicker lawns.
- Gets seedlings and transplants off to vigorous start.
- Enhances flavor, color and shelf-life of fruits and vegetables.

Humus products are commercially available in a variety of forms and mixes. They come combined with essential plant nutrients as a complete fertilizer, or combined with micronutrients as a supplement to regular fertilizer programs. Liquid and wettable powder solutions can be sprayed directly on the plant leaves to improve growth and maturity.

Humus products are compatible with most fertilizers, micronutrients, and pesticides except those with a low pH. Read labels for specific instructions.

Chelating Agents

Chelating agents increase the solubility of metals, making metallic nutrients, such as iron, copper, zinc and manganese available to plants. Chelates can be applied either to the soil or to plant leaves by spraying.

Many soil fungi yield by-products that behave as chelators. Sprays that contain microbe stimulating properties, such as the humic acids and seaweed extracts, assist chelation by increasing the microbial populations.

Hormones

Hormones are substances that regulate plant growth and development. Commercial growers commonly apply them as foliar sprays to alter many plant processes. Some of the more commonly used for foliar applications include:

- **Auxins** are naturally occurring growth-promoting plant hormones. Auxins affect growth patterns, cell enlargement, leaf and blossom drop, fruit set and sex expression in some plants. Their influences are so diverse they are sometimes referred to as "master" hormones. Auxin containing compounds are sprayed on plants to promote rooting and fruit set, control fruit drop, and to thin fruits with a minimum of labor.
- **Gibberellins** affect cell enlargement and cell division. Gibberellins are

so powerful, they can stimulate growth in genetically dwarfed plants. Gibberellins increase plant size, stimulate seed germination, and manipulate seed stalk and fruit development. Applied to barley in the malting stages, gibberellic acid increases the enzyme content of malt. In Japan it is used to induce seedlessness in grapes and in California, gibberellins are sprayed on vines to enlarge the berry size of Thompson seedless grapes.

- **Cytokinins** stimulate shoots and cell division. They impact leaf growth, light response and aging. Cytokinin-gibberellin compound sprays control fruit shape in apples, and are commonly used to accentuate the characteristic elongated shape of the Delicious apple.
- **Ethylenes** have been long used to induce fruit ripening and latex flow in rubber trees. In addition, ethylenes encourage fruiting and bring about fruit drop at harvest time.
- **Abscisic Acid** is a natural inhibitory compound that affects bud and seed dormancy and leaf drop. It can also promote flowering in some short-day plants. This effect is vital to those who produce seasonal plants such as poinsettias for holidays.

Hormone sprays are of greatest use to the commercial grower, but home gardeners can reap some of the benefits of these horticultural developments. Naturally occurring hormones, such as those found in kelp extract and humic products are a safe and easy way to give your plants a jet-fueled boost.

Other Sprays

Other foliar sprays are constantly being introduced. Here is a sampling from current literature on the subject:

- **Plant growth and stimulant combinations.**
- **Growth inhibitors** that shorten ornamentals, retard ripening, and improve transplant durability.
- **Blue-green algae sprays** to reduce the effects caused by ozone layer depletion.
- **Plant shields** to protect against wind chill and frost damage.
- **Daminozide containing sprays** that speed recovery from drought-induced stress.
- **Amino acid-enzyme-polysaccharide blend** mentioned in *Avant Gardener* that is reported to have produced a world record of 415 bushels of corn per acre. (Dr. Bargyla Rateaver, 9049 Covina Street, San Diego, CA 92126)
- **Micronutrient complex** that "acts as a biocatalyst," is said to result in high yields and increased growth. (Spray-N-Grow, 8500 Commerce Park Dr., Houston TX 77036)

The Case for Foliar Spraying

- Foliar spraying produces more rapid absorption of nitrogen than soil applications.
- Foliar sprays can help prolong active growth in short season areas where cool soil temperature delays nutrient movement from the roots to the leaves.
- Foliar sprays are easy to apply.
- Where soil quality is poor, foliar feeding is a necessary supplement to conventional fertilizing.
- Foliar nutrients can be combined with most pesticides to save labor.
- Foliar sprays can help "unlock" unavailable nutrients.

- Foliar feeding can aid fast-growing plants, such as vegetables, whose growth can outstrip available plant food.
- Under many circumstances, spraying fertilizer on the leaves of plants may be three to five times more effective than root application.

The Case Against

- Repeat applications are necessary to maintain optimum growth.
- Foliar application of macronutrients, NPK, can cause chemical burn of leaves if used at high strength.
- Foliar sprays can be more expensive than dry products.
- Timed-release products are not available.
- Foliar sprays must be used with regular, soil applied fertilizers.
- Careful mixing and proper application can be more time-consuming and require more precision than simply broadcasting granular fertilizers.

Application

Foliar food can be applied by dusting, spraying or overhead sprinkling. Any spray equipment that mixes accurately can be used. Droplet size affects plant response; the smaller droplets are more easily absorbed. Choose a sprayer that gives you a fine mist. A simple, recycled pump-spray bottle can be used for houseplants. Since some plant sprays don't "age" well, mix only what you need, or avoid storing the mixture for more than a few weeks.

Most plants respond better to foliar feeding during the morning hours when the plant is most active. Early spraying also allows time for the leaves to dry before nightfall when many plant fungi take advantage of wet leaves to spread disease. Be sure to thoroughly cover the undersides of the leaves; they are the most absorbent part.

Environmental factors, such as temperature, humidity, and light intensity affect the rate of absorption. High humidity assists leaf absorption and conditions that promote plant activity; warm, sunny days, also enhance assimilation. So, for best results, spray during good weather.

Foliar sprays, applied just before and during bloom and fruit set can greatly increase fruit yields and quality, so time your sprays accordingly. For the best results, most growers suggest foliar feeding every two weeks during the growing season. Many start with two or three weekly feedings, then follow a maintenance schedule of monthly feedings.

Mix solutions carefully, high concentrations of some nutrients can cause foliar burn. If you are tempted to experiment (and who isn't?), try new combinations and strengths on only a few plants to see if any damage occurs. Some growers add sucrose to foliar sprays to reduce damage caused by urea and phosphorus.

A spreader-sticker, such as those derived from coconut oil or non-detergent soap can help enhance the efficiency of foliar sprays. You can save time and effort in the garden by adding insect-repellent herbal extracts, insecticidal soap, or fungicides to nutrient sprays.

As horticultural research advances and new plant products become available, foliar feeding will continue to enhance crop yields and plant production. Farmers and gardeners alike are finding that convenience, ease of use and rapid action make these "fast foods of the plant kingdom" a useful adjunct to conventional fertilizing practices.

First published in Volume 2, Number 3, page 30.

Chapter 3
Pest Control

- Integrated Pest Management for the Home Gardener
- Hydroponic IPM
- Dishpan Pest Control
- Pest Controls for the Greenhouse
- Homemade Yellow Sticky Traps
- Poison Plants
- Thirst Aid for Plants

Integrated Pest Management for the Home Gardener

by Justina Marie Kelliher

Gardening practices have changed through the years to reflect current technology and the culture of the times. Since World War II we have had at our disposal a number of chemical tools to control garden pests. The usefulness of many of these chemicals is limited, however, by adverse environmental effects, pest resistance and increasing government regulation of their use. Now more than ever we need to be responsible for the choices we make in dealing with pests, weeds, diseases and other problems.

Often we wait until pest and disease problems reach a crisis state before we begin to think of solutions. At this point what is needed is quick action and a cool head. Unfortunately, this approach to pest management tends to encourage over-reaction. Overuse and misuse of chemicals often happen when disease and insects get out of control. It is important to first work on prevention before resorting to remedial measures.

Mapping a Strategy

The gardener has several strategies to choose from. The most common choice is to reach first for the chemical solution — chemical fertilizers, herbicides and pesticides. The contrasting choice is the organic system, using only naturally occurring substances like manures and ground rock for fertilizers, biological control agents, extracts of plants and physical labor for controlling pests. Both choices involve certain tradeoffs.

With a chemically based system you have the obvious disadvantage of increased environmental pollution. Chemical fertilizers can cause nitrogen burn and salt damage. Pests can become resistant to pesticides. Most chemical gardeners spray by the date on the calendar rather than for a known problem or a known potential problem. This is referred to as a preventative spray. This practice has its place in trying to grow difficult and endangered plants, but it can sometimes mean that a chemical was used when there was no problem or that the wrong chemical was used since the problem was not accurately identified.

When using an organic system one chooses to limit the products available for use. The successful gardener limits the plants grown to ones that are well adapted to the indoor or outdoor environment. This is the choice I have made for my home gardens and cacti and succulent collections. This has meant that I must eradicate sick plants that may transmit diseases and pests to the rest of my collection. Gardening organically requires more physical labor and planning. The fertilizers weigh more and hand weeding takes a lot more time than simply spraying a chemical herbicide. Prevention by maximizing the vigor of your plants is the key to successful organic gardening. But remember, botanical insecticides are dangerous chemicals and need to be treated with the same care as chemical preparations.

Integrated Pest Management

The third choice is the integrated pest management system. It is really not a separate choice, but a system of planning that can be used by either style of gardener. In my consulting business I try to meet the grower where they are and try to come up with a system that best suits their needs. That could be a chemical management program aimed a minimal use and prevention.

Integrated pest management combines all the different components of the growing system to allow the grower to make educated decisions about pest control. Some of those components include the crop species, environment, economics, pathogens (insects, diseases and weeds), fertilizers, irrigation and safety for both the consumer and the grower. The same basic system that commercial growers use can also be applied in the home garden.

Indoor growers face unique problems since they have a closed system. The timely management of problems indoors is critical. In indoor systems fungal diseases and insects can become major problems very quickly.

Information is the heart of an integrated program of pest control—information on the species to be grown, the possible pathogens and the unique characteristics of the system. Thus, keeping simple garden records is essential to a successful program. They can be kept in a notebook with planting dates, varieties planted, weather, what varieties did well and what varieties did poorly, where things are planted, when plants flowered and were harvested, when and how much water and fertilizer were used, any disease, insect, or other problems and, of course, when and how much chemical sprays were applied and whether or not they were effective. It is important that all control measures are implemented as a conscious educated decision and that must be based on information that only you can provide.

It does not take a scientist to jot down a few notes on how the garden is doing this week and what the weather has been like. A few years of records from your own greenhouse or garden spot are more valuable than a lot of book knowledge since it tells you how your particular site reacts to changing conditions.

Define Your Goals

The first step is to look at the whole system and define what you are trying to accomplish. In the home situation this can be fruits, vegetables, flowers, a nice landscaped environment or personal enjoyment.

In many ways this is the most important step in the process as all subsequent decisions will have to be made in the context of your particular goal. For example, if your garden includes rare or expensive plants, you may be willing to use a chemical spray before resorting to the final solution, eradication of an infected plant. If, on the other hand, a chemical-free environment is more important to you, you should realize now before a crisis develops that it may mean pulling up and destroying a favorite plant.

Define Potential Problems

The next step is to define problems or potential problems. The possible problems can include a diverse number of things including insects, diseases, weeds, pet droppings, good relations with neighbors, the environment, both the large scale local environment and the microclimate of your particular site, and safety.

Trapping for early detection of insect problems can be a useful tool. This can be done with a simple yellow bar covered with a sticky substance. The yellow color attracts aphids and whiteflies. Correct identification of a problem is critical and help identifying problems is available from your fellow local gardeners, the extension office, books, magazines, university personnel, libraries and private consultants.

Choose a Solution

Look at all the possible solutions to the problems identified in step two. The solutions can range all the way from doing nothing, to a full-blown chemical control plan, although some point in between is much more likely.

Choosing a solution is one of the most important steps in the process. Just remember that it is OK to decide that no remedial treatment is needed. Personal preferences, economics, chemicals legally available, weather and many other factors need to be considered, all in the context of the goals defined in step one.

A plant that one really enjoys or is unusual, for example, will be worth more time and expense than some other plants. A sick and diseased plant may need to be destroyed rather than stay and have the infestation spread to other healthy plants. This is especially true when there is a virus involved. Insects can spread viruses when they are feeding, so control efforts need to be more effective.

The amount of tolerable damage will vary according to individual preferences. An example of this is cucumber beetle damage on beans. The home gardener can often cut out the damaged portion of the beans, a solution that would not be acceptable to a commercial cannery.

Implementation

When using any insecticidal spray — organic or inorganic — proper care needs to be taken. Protection for the spray applicator — you — is important. All precautions on the label need to be followed. Protection to the consumer needs to be provided by washing sprayed food before consumption, by following the instructions on the label, by waiting the correct amount of time before harvest and by using only chemicals that are registered for use on food crops. Staying out of the garden after applying a chemical more than the recommended time provides better safety for the gardener. I cannot stress enough the importance of reading the label carefully and following its instructions.

Protection of bees and other beneficial insects is also important. Some protection can be provided by spraying in the evening after bee flight has stopped or in the morning before bee flight. During hot summer nights sometimes the bees will spend the night hovering just outside the hive so special care needs to be taken. At your local extension office there is a list of which chemicals are most toxic to bees.

Chemicals, organic or not, should only be used when needed. Timing is crucial with many insecticides to ensure effective control and to avoid overuse. It is best for safety and environmental reasons to use as few chemicals as possible; it saves money, too. If you have young children who might eat sprayed plants or a family member who is in poor health or has allergies, a chemical spray may not be a good idea at all.

Evaluation

After implementation the program needs to be evaluated for effectiveness. This is one of the feedback loops of the system. Evaluation is an important part of the system since you do not want to continue to invest in a program that is ineffective.

Again, garden records are important. They can also help you plan your garden by looking at past years and tell you if you are being unrealistic about what can be grown on your site. Over the winter you can go over your records and evaluate your garden as you plan for next year. It helps at this point to go back to step one and see how well you stuck with your original goals and how you might do it differently next year.

The integrated pest management system is dynamic and requires constant reevaluation and change. The chemicals available for use change from time to time. The environment changes both in major weather patterns and in the garden microclimate. Gardening is a dynamic, changing system and one must not get fooled into thinking that just because something worked once that it will always work.

Prevention

The indoor grower faces unique problems. There is no natural biological control indoors so insect populations can really explode. Prevention by careful inspection and isolation of newly diseased plants is important. The dry leaf conditions that occur under lights provides ideal conditions for spider mite infestation. The lack of rain and wind results in softer leaves and stems that are more susceptible to some insect and disease problems.

Prevention is preferable to active control measures. Some preventative measures include planting resistant varieties, applying dormant sprays for known problems, trapping pests, removal of garden debris that can provide a breeding place for pest and disease organisms, timing plantings to avoid problems and using protective covers to protect plants. Crop rotation, starting with clean healthy plants, maximizing the vigor of plants with proper fertilization, irrigation, and soil preparation, interplanting to interrupt the travel of diseases and pests and using plants that are well adapted to the environment are other measures that can reduce reliance on chemical sprays.

Resistance

Insect, weed and disease resistance to control measures is becoming more of a problem. The home gardener can develop resistant pests in the home system just as commercial growers do. The massive use of DDT in the '50s is a classic example of the development of insect resistance to chemical control.

There several ways insects can defend themselves from chemical sprays including changing their behavior so they are not exposed to the chemical, developing a thicker coating so the chemical does not enter sensitive tissues, or chemically altering the substance internally so it is no longer toxic.

Weeds can also develop resistance to control measures in similar ways. Even cultural (non-chemical) control measures can cause a resistance response. An example of this is the dandelion which has developed a very strong root that readily resprouts, an adaptive response to constant hand pulling.

Resistance is developed because the survivors of any control measure are reproduced at greater frequencies than the original population would have allowed since they now have more access to the food source.

The home gardener can take measures to help keep resistant pests

60

from developing. One is to rotate the chemicals used. An example of rotation could be aphid control in an organic system in which insecticidal soap and rotenone are rotated. The inorganic system rotation for control of aphids could be between diazinon (an organo-phosphate) and resmithren (a synthetic pyrethrum).

Effective spraying of the infested plants—good coverage, the right dosage applied at the right time for maximum kill—also helps slow the development of resistant pests. Repetitive, ineffective, lower dosage applications speed the development of resistance. Preserving the insect predators and parasites helps slow resistance since they are not selective for the insecticide in their predation.

The basic concepts of integrated pest management are applicable to the small scale gardener. The first and one of the most important steps is the maintaining of garden records. A garden or landscape that is planned will be closer to the original goal than one that is just planted. I feel that the satisfaction of a healthy garden outweighs the extra effort of planing and record keeping. May we all enjoy a successful garden.

References

My most valuable resource has been all the people who over the years have opened their garden, greenhouses, research and minds to me.

The Ortho Problem Solver, Ortho Publishing Corp., 1975.
Pacific Northwest Pesticide Handbooks: Insect Control, Oregon State University Extension Service, March 1989.
Resistance Crisis, World Resources Institute, 1984.
The Bug Book and Encyclopedia by Helen and John Philbrick, Garden Way Publishing, 1974.

First published in Volume 1 Number 3, page 30

Hydroponic IPM

by John McEno

In a nutshell, practitioners of Integrated Pest Management (IPM) closely monitor both plants and pest populations, and use a variety of controls — chemical, cultural or biological — to keep crop damage below economic levels. A rose gardener may find damage caused by a single Japanese beetle economically intolerable. In other crops, such as field corn, IPMers forbear quite a number of pests.

Hydroponic environments share many problems with soil-based indoor systems. Pest control is complicated by year-round plant cultivation and continuous heating. Crops are often grown in monocultures. Pests introduced into these optimal conditions encounter no natural enemies to slow their population growth.

On the other hand, certain aspects of hydroponic IPM are unique. Of course, soil insects such as white grubs pose no problem in hydroponic systems. But diseases caused by water molds can quickly shut down an entire hydroponic system.

Hydroponic cultivators have more control over fertility and pH than soil-based gardeners. If properly used, hydroponic technology can rapidly produce vigorous plants able to fend off fungal diseases and insect pests. Improper handling, however, will increase the incidence of "abiotic" or noninfectious plant diseases such as nutrient deficiencies and mineral toxicities.

To illustrate the use of IPM in hydroponically based systems I would like to review one disease and one pest common to hydroponic systems — water molds and spider mites. For every pest or disease problem, the grower should become familiar with signs of the causal agent and symptoms expressed by the plant.

Water Molds

Water molds grow via long threadlike filaments called hyphae. Hyphae absorb water and nutrients for the parasites. They penetrate plant roots and secrete digestive enzymes and toxins causing the symptoms of water mold disease. Since these "molds" reproduce by strongly swimming flagellated spores, some scientists consider the organisms more protozoan than fungal.

Three species cause most of the water mold problems in hydroponic systems. They include *Pythium aphanidermatum*, *Pythium debaryanum* and *Pythium ultimum*. These species are differentiated by the size and shape of their reproductive structures. All three water molds attack a wide variety of plants, although some crops are more susceptible than others. Commercial hydroponic production of spinach, for instance, is currently limited by *P. aphanidermatum* (Zinnen).

Pythium species cause "damping off," the destruction of small seedlings. "Pre-emergent" damping off kills seeds before they even sprout. Faced with this symptom, many growers blame their seed company. "Post-emergent" damping off is more evident, attacking seedlings shortly after they become upright. Symptoms begin with a brown watery soft-rot of roots. Seedlings usually topple over and die.

Sometimes symptoms are "subclinical," not visible to the eye. Zinnen describes a 50 percent yield loss in hydroponic lettuce: "Even when growers produce an apparently healthy crop, with rot-free, white roots, they may be losing half their yield potential to a pathogen they cannot see..."

If you suspect a subclinical water mold problem, lightly grasp a seedling root between thumb and forefinger and pull away from the stem. If the outer layer of the root (epidermis and cortex) slips away leaving only a thin inner cylinder (endodermis and stele), you have a Pythium problem.

Thanks to the high humidity and succulent plant growth of hydroponic systems, mature plants may also suffer Pythium damage. Symptoms include a nondescript yellowing, browning and wilting of leaves.

Detecting the presence of water molds is difficult. Often the only visible sign of these parasites is a small fluff of hyphae around stricken plants. Pythium species can be identified under a microscope by their milky-white wide-diameter hyphae, which contain lipid droplets but conspicuously lack septa (hyphal cross-walls).

Harvey invented a successful pest-monitoring technique in 1925, using seeds as a "bait" for water molds. Steam-sterilized seeds are suspended in the hydroponic solution and frequently checked for signs of colonization. The bait will sport a white fuzzy ring of hyphae, warning of water mold presence before plants show symptoms.

The most powerful method of controlling water mold disease is to keep the parasites out of your growing area. All equipment used in hydroponic systems should be washed in a sodium hypochlorite (bleach) solution. Seeds, too, should be soaked in bleach or a fungicide solution. Unfortunately, even with the best precautions, exclusion can fail. Pythium may be transmitted via internal seedborne infection.

Once introduced, water molds are nearly impossible to eradicate. Chemical control is hampered by a lack of registered fungicides. Metalaxyl (Ridomil™) and benomyl (Benlate™) control water molds but are not registered for commercial use. Similarly, water mold-resistant crops are not commercially available. Seed companies have little incentive to develop hydroponic-friendly varieties, since the market is so small.

The fungus *Trichoderma viride* antagonizes many Pythium species, and may serve as a biocontrol organism. Unfortunately, *T. viride* is a soil fungus, and adapts poorly to hydroponic environments.

Optimizing conditions for crops will reduce disease losses — rapid root growth permits plants to partially "escape" damping off. Strong full-spectrum lighting inhibits water molds and benefits plants. Nutrient solutions must be carefully balanced; too much nitrogen will increase losses. Solutions near a neutral 7.0 pH inhibit fungi.

Crop temperature is critical — *P. aphanidermatum* prefers warmer temperatures, above 73 degrees (23 C), while *P. ultimum* occurs at cooler temperatures, 68 to 68 degrees (16-20 C).

Spider Mites

These insidious arachnids are the most common and destructive pests of greenhouse-grown crops. Luckily, spider mites cause less damage in hydroponic systems, thanks to the high humidity. Spider mites attack hundreds of different plant hosts and occur around the world. They normally congregate on the undersides of leaves, sucking plant sap.

The two-spotted spider mite, *Tetranychus urticae,* is most commonly encountered in North America. At optimum conditions for development, 86 degrees (30 C) with low humidity, new generations can arise every eight days. Females lay as many as 200 eggs.

Red spider mites, *Tetranychus cinnabarinus,* are less common but equally destructive. Red spider mites enjoy a higher optimum temperature than two-spotted spider mites, thriving at temperatures above 95 degrees (35 C).

Symptoms of spider mite infestation are not initially obvious. Leaves eventually droop as gray-white speckles appear on upper surfaces. With more loss of chlorophyll, these parched areas enlarge and the leaf turns chlorotic, then necrotic and dies. In severe infestations the whole plant may dry up.

Inspection of lower leaf surfaces reveals silk webbings, eggs and the mites themselves. *T. urticae* adults appear green with two brown-black spots on their dorsal surface. As mites feed on chlorophyll-rich plants, these spots may enlarge to nearly cover their backs. Female mites average 0.4 to 0.5 millimeters in length. The males are slightly smaller, with a wedge-shaped posterior. Their spots may not be as evident. Eggs are spherical and 0.14 millimeters in diameter. Eggs originally appear translucent to white, turning to a straw color just before hatching. They are laid singly on undersides of leaves or in webs spun by adults. Hatching larvae are not much larger than eggs, with six legs and two tiny red eye spots. Protonymph and deutonymph stages are eight-legged and light green.

T. cinnabarinus eggs and immature stages are indistinguishable from those of *T. urticae*. Adults, however, become bright to brick red with dark internal markings. In cooler periods when the adults are not actively feeding, they turn a darker shade of green and are difficult to distinguish from two-spotted spider mites.

Quick action must be taken to keep spider mites in check. Once established, they are nearly impossible to eradicate. Spider mites can be carried into growing areas on people, pets or transferred plants (including houseplants). Once introduced, a grower's best efforts only serve to keep populations low, not eliminate them.

Like water mold problems, spider mite damage is minimized by keeping plants happy. The optimal temperature for most crops is cooler than most spider mite's liking. High humidity causes all spider mite stages (larvae, nymphs, adults) to stop feeding and enter a quiescent period. Maintain plants in a balanced nutritional solution.

Much attention has been focused on biocontrol with predaceous mites, which have been commercially available since 1968. *Phytoseiulus persimilus* is a popular mail-order mite. Both nymphs and adults feed on spider mites. This predator first gained attention in West Germany, via plant material imported from Chile in 1959. From a "founder population" of less than 10 females, today over 500 million mites are raised per year (van Lenteren & Woets).

P. persimilus remains active at a higher humidity than most mites, but becomes inactive with warmer temperatures, above 80 degrees (27 C). Strains of *P. persimilus* resistant to organophosphate insecticides (e.g., malathion, diazinon) are now available.

Several other predatory mites are effective under a variety of conditions: *Metaseiulus occidentalis* controls spider mites in orchards and other outdoor cool-weather crops. *Amblyseius californicus* does well in moderate humidity and reproduces rapidly in temperatures up to 86 degrees (30 C). A new South American import, *Phytoseiulus longipes*, thrives in temperatures up to 100 degrees (38 C).

To be effective, predatory mites must be introduced in early stages of spider mite infestations. Life cycles of predatory mites are twice as fast as those of spider mites. But if pests have too great a head start, damage will occur before the predators catch up. Predatory mites must be placed near infested areas, not randomly scattered around the greenhouse. Manually transplanting predatory mites from healthy leaves to infested plants is effective. Predatory mites can sail on lengths of spun web;

DISHPAN PEST CONTROL

Growers who have thrown everything but the kitchen sink at pesky whiteflies, aphids and spider mites, might try looking inside the sink for the answer. Researchers at the USDA's Phoenix, Arizona, facility report that a mixture of soybean oil, dish washing detergent and water can rid plants of these common pests.

Make a base solution of 1 tablespoon of detergent to 1 cup of soybean oil. Dilute at 1 1/2 to 2 1/2 tablespoons per cup of water before use. The mixture can be applied about once every 10 days, depending on the severity of the infestation. Test the mix on a few leaves first to ensure that it won't damage plants. Although it may not keep your hands soft and lovely, the mix is said to be easy on the environment and tough on bugs.

oscillating fans placed in growing areas help them move about the greenhouse in search of new populations.

Predators thrive in a ratio of one per 20-25 spider mites. The two populations establish an equilibrium, keeping the pests below crop-damaging levels. Sometimes the predators nearly annihilate pest populations, then die out themselves. When pest populations revive, it is time to buy a new vial of predators. Maintaining a mite colony on a "banker plant" of African violets is an alternative to buying new vials — predators may be transferred to the plant area as needed.

Avoid insecticides, miticides and even fungicides while using predatory mites. Allow previously applied pesticides two or three weeks to break down before introducing predators. Some metal halide bulbs emit a light spectrum insufficient for predatory mites. Adding a sodium light source to the greenhouse will correct this.

Turning to spray-gun therapy, the most innocuous agent used to control spider mites is a stream of cold water. As with all sprays, direct it at undersides of leaves. Mites will be knocked off and their webbing destroyed. Spray several times each week or until your leaves are shredded by the treatment.

A spider mite deterrent developed at Purdue University mixes 4 cups whole wheat flour and half a cup of buttermilk in 5 gallons of water. Strain through cheesecloth and spray on plants, repeating in a week. Spider mites become stuck in this gooey mixture and suffocate.

Spraying plants with a tree nursery product, Wilt-Pruf™, will also suffocate spider mites. Although Wilt-Pruf is approved for use on edible crops, I don't like the idea of eating Saran Wrap (polyvinyl chloride, same stuff).

Many entomologists recommend malathion for controlling spider mites. Every mite population I've sprayed is resistant to this insecticide. Pentac™ (dienochlor) still knocks 'em dead. Although Pentac was introduced in the early 1960s, spider mites have remained uniquely susceptible to this miticide.

For IPMers who believe in "limited chemical warfare," Pentac is less toxic than malathion and decomposes under direct sunlight, ultraviolet light or at temperatures above 130 C. Kelthane is an alternative and very effective miticide, but decomposes slower than Pentac.

Avoid using systemic insecticides (e.g., Systemic™). Systemic sprays should only be used on ornamental plants, not crops destined for human consumption. They contain extremely poisonous substances (e.g., methyl demeton) and remain in plant tissues without breaking down. Several greenhouse growers successfully control spider mites by hanging No-Pest Strips indoors. Again, the safety of this product is questionable.

Selectivity

I would like to end with two concepts: Biological controls vary in their efficacy from one crop to another, but rarely damage plants. Pesticides, in sledgehammer fashion, work equally well on nearly all crops but are phytotoxic to some plant species.

The IPM cornerstone for applying pesticides is selectivity. Optimally, a pesticide selectively kills pests and not beneficial organisms. Use selective timing to optimize the effectiveness of pesticides. Finally, you should selectively spray only the most seriously infested plants, not the whole greenhouse.

Sources Harvey, J.V. 1926. A study of the water molds and pythiums occurring in the soils of Chapel Hill. *Journal of the Elisha Mitchell Scientific Society* 41:151-164.

van Lenteren, J.C. & J. Woets. 1988. Biological and integrated pest control in greenhouses. *Annual Review of Entomology* 33:239-269.

Zinnen, T.M. 1988. Assessment of plant diseases in hydroponic culture. *Plant Disease* 72(2):96-99.

First published in Volume 1 Number 3, page 35.

Pest Controls for Greenhouse Growers

by Justina Marie Kelliher

Year-round gardening offers many benefits, providing fresh food and spices in winter, creating your own tropical paradise, or allowing you to get a jump on spring planting. More and more people are building and using small greenhouses to expand their gardening options. Of course, greenhouse gardening requires some special skills. The ability to control the growing environment offers some unique opportunities and presents some special problems, especially in the area of pest control.

Some greenhouses are as simple as a wooden frame covered with plastic. Others are complex systems integrated into the design of the home. There are many small, free-standing greenhouses and easy-to-assemble kits on the market. Even a small window box greenhouse or bay window provide opportunities to expand your gardening horizons.

Greenhouses have many uses, depending on the goals and expertise of the gardener. Winter cultivation of exotic perennials is my passion. And my greenhouse lets me to grow things that the cool, damp climate of Oregon's Coast Range would not otherwise allow.

In my simple attached glass greenhouse and sunroom I am able to grow succulents including *Lithops, Conophytum, Aloinopsis, Fenestraria, Faucaria, Frithra, Crassula, Echeveria, Bursera, Haworthia* and cacti. I start most of my plants from seed and they are very small and sensitive for a few years. Success requires a carefully controlled environment.

The popularity of attached home greenhouses presents some unique pest control problems. The closeness to the dwelling area generally means that as higher level of control is desired, since pests can fly or crawl into the living area. In addition, any treatments used have to be safe for the people and pets living in the home. The choice of plant material needs to match the temperature, humidity and light regimen of an environment that also serves as human habitat. Healthy plants are better able to deter insects and resist disease; the first step in controlling insect and disease problems is to match your plants to their environment.

Physical Barriers

Since a greenhouse or solarium is a closed system, the next step is to prevent pests from entering the structure in the first place. Pests can enter the greenhouse in several ways, so your efforts will have to be consistent and cover all of the possibilities.

Insects such as scale, whitefly and mealybugs usually enter the greenhouse on living plants. Other pests can catch a ride in infected soils or on gardening tools. Always inspect new plants and soils carefully before bringing them into the greenhouse. Eggs and some immature insects can be difficult to see with the naked eye so it is helpful to have a quarantine area for new plants. I use my sunroom as a transition area for new plants and as an infirmary for sick plants from the greenhouse.

Arthropod pests such as aphids, spider mites, slugs and sow bugs can fly or walk into the greenhouse from outside. Screens and barriers are the first line of defense, but some pests will still enter through cracks or hitchhike on people. Chickens and ducks allowed to run outside of the greenhouse can reduce the number of slugs, but they can cause damage to plants if allowed inside of the building. Placing plants up on benches can slow down slugs and sow bugs.

Even with regular inspections and the use of physical barriers, pests may still enter the greenhouse in infested soils. Fungus gnats, symphylum, thrips and wire worms often enter the greenhouse in soil. Soil sterilization is effective against this type of pest, but it also kills microbes that are beneficial to plants. One alternative is to sterilize soils and then add a commercial microbial inoculant before use.

Greenhouse conditions can allow insects and other pests to reproduce at high rates. Higher, more consistent temperatures, the absence of wind or rain, lush plants and the lack of natural predators encourage insect outbreaks. Major insect problems in my greenhouse include fungus gnats, whiteflies, spider mites, mealybugs, thrips, sow bugs, aphids and slugs.

Fungus Gnats

Fungus gnats (including many species of small flies) often reproduce well in the greenhouse. Our tolerance for them is even lower when they are in a solarium that is part of the house. I have had gnats drown in my morning coffee, even when population levels were relatively low.

The key to dealing with these pests is in understanding their life cycle. The eggs are laid in the soil and hatch in about four days. There the immature fly develops and lives for about two weeks on organic mater, root hairs and seedlings. They pupate three or four days in the soil and the adult fly emerges to mate and reproduce for about a week.

Adult fungus gnats are annoying, but it is the larvae that cause most of the damage and are a major cause of seedling death. Since I maintain greenhouse temperatures above 40 degrees (4 C), fungus gnats breed

HOMEMADE STICKY TRAPS

Aphids? STP to the rescue! You know, the motor additive. Besides protecting your engine it may help your plants if they are having their juices sucked by aphids.

The idea is to use STP as the stickem for a yellow sticky trap. Start with four-ply "railroad board" cardboard (4 by 11 inches). Paint it with two coats of bright yellow alkyd semi-gloss paint. The paint not only provides the sirens-song yellow that lures aphids to their doom, but also waterproofs the cardboard. Finally coat the trap via a paint brush with STP.

Check the traps after a heavy rain since the STP can be washed off. However it does not drip, make a mess or catch larger insects if you are using ladybugs as a biological control for instance.

POISON PLANTS

Gardeners making room for "poison petunias" and "killer carnations" may have to wait a little longer for the genetically engineered pesticidal plants. While scientists prepare to test plants designed to produce their own pesticides, regulators are considering changes that would slow testing and marketing of the plants.

The federal EPA has proposed treating pesticidal products produced by genetically altered plants as chemical pesticides for the purposes of testing and registration. The change could push approval time—now one to two years—to as much as a decade and at up to 20 times the cost to developers.

The gene for the production of the toxin found in the bacteria *Bacillus thuringiensis* (Bt) is the most commonly used for the procedure. When inserted into plants, the gene triggers the production of the toxin that disrupts the digestive process of the invading pest. Although in use as a biocontrol agent for nearly two decades as the bacteria Bt, the toxin when produced by plants would be considered a chemical control.

Another approach to the use of genetic engineering to enhance plant resistance has already been successfully tested by a Maryland firm, Crop Genetics International. Rather than inserting genetic information into the plant, CGI researchers have inoculated plants with a genetically engineered bacteria capable of producing chemicals that can kill or deter insect and fungus pests.

The product, which will be marketed under the brand name InCide, uses a common bacteria, *Clavibacter xyli* subspecies *cynodontis.* The bacteria can live only in the plant xylem and cannot be transmitted by contact or through seed. The gene for the insect toxin found in Bt is inserted into the bacteria and the genetically altered result is injected into seeds prior to planting.

year round. In the solarium, where temperatures are even higher, they reproduce even faster.

Excluding fungus gnats from the greenhouse can be difficult. Adults are active and can fly into the greenhouse. Their small size allows them to enter through the smallest openings, even through some screens. To control these pests it is necessary to implement control measures at all of their different life stages.

I monitor the insects in the greenhouse with yellow sticky traps. The smaller cards, about three by five inches, work better inside as they are less obtrusive visually and easier to work around. Fungus gnats, aphids and whiteflies are all attracted to yellow sticky traps. Place traps horizontally for fungus gnats. I inspect the traps every time I am in the greenhouse and change them every other week. They are one of the best tools for early detection of these insects.

In the fall I apply parasitic nematodes on all of the plants and the pumice floor of my greenhouse. This reduces the number of larvae in the soil. A few days before applying the nematodes, I often spray down the plants with an insecticide (soap, oil, or pyrethrum) if my traps show there is a large adult population. I want to reduce the population to as close to zero as I can to prevent them from overwintering.

There is a Bt (*Bacillus thuringiensis*) insecticide and an insect growth regulator (metheprene) that are effective on the larvae in the soil. I use these in the spring and summer only when the traps show an increase in population. I do not use these products in the fall because I want the nematodes to have enough food to last the winter. The metheprene prolongs the larval stage in which the fungus gnats do the most damage, so I prefer the Bt against the larval stage. In the summer, the population naturally declines as reduced humidity and higher temperatures cause the soil surface to dry out.

Whiteflies

After fungus gnats, the greenhouse whitefly (*Trialeurodes vaporairiorum*) is my major concern. The parasitic wasp *Encarsia formosa* is an excellent whitefly control when greenhouse temperatures are closer to 70 degrees (21 C). Since I allow wintertime lows of 40 degrees (4 C) in my greenhouse, parasitic wasps are impractical as a biological control. At lower temperatures the whiteflies reproduce faster than the wasps.

Whiteflies generally enter the greenhouse on infected plants. They lay several hundred eggs in circles on the undersides of plant leaves. In five to ten days, the eggs hatch and over the next three or four weeks several larval stages develop. While still on the leaf, the insects pupate and the flying adults emerge within a week. Adult whiteflies can reproduce without mating.

Since whiteflies spend most of their lives on the undersides of leaves, it is easy to introduce them to the greenhouse by accident. Careful inspection of the leaves of new plants is essential in the control of the greenhouse whitefly. Susceptible plants like fuchsias, verbena, coleus and tomatoes are the first places to look for eggs in established plantings.

Yellow sticky traps placed vertically can catch adult whiteflies once they are in the greenhouse. Early spot treatments with soap or summer oil sprays of infected plants can keep this pest under control. Releasing generalist predators like lacewings in your greenhouse in the summer can keep populations low. Sometimes treatment with stronger pesticides is warranted if trapping indicates that populations are getting out of control. When insecticide treatment is necessary, taking plants outside is a good idea.

Aphids

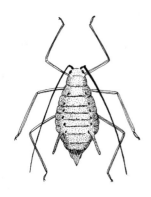

Control and treatment of aphid problems is similar to those described for the greenhouse whitefly. Too much fertilizer and water will encourage aphid populations. Aphids, like whiteflies, can reproduce without mating. Yellow sticky traps are a good monitoring tool for this pest as well. Spot treatment of infected plants with soap sprays is sometimes needed. As with whiteflies, aphids reproduce quickly in the protected greenhouse environment and early detection and treatment is the key to effective control.

Mealybugs

Although the citrus mealybug (*Planoccus citri*) is often the bug seen in greenhouses, there are many species of mealybug that can cause problems. Mealybugs usually enter the greenhouse on infected plant material. Separating new plants out and watching for this pest is important. Mealybugs look like small tufts of cotton on the surface of plants. They tend to develop where the petiole, or leaf stalk, of newer leaves joins the stem, or on the undersides of leaves.

There are several biological control agents on the market for this pest. One is a small beetle called the mealybug destroyer (*Cryptolemus momtrouzieri*). Generalist predators like the green lacewing are also effective against mealybug. There is also a parasitic wasp (*Leptomastix dactylopii*) available for use against mealybugs. When mealybug populations are low, the best treatment is a cotton swab dipped in alcohol.

Most of the mealybug's life cycle is spent on the surface of plants. The adult female lays about 500 eggs in a cottony mass that covers most of her body. Nymphs hatch in about a week and migrate on the plant until they find a favorable spot where they feed on the sap. The nymphs that develop into males encase themselves in cottony filaments while feeding for a period of about a month and then develop into winged adults in about two weeks.

Root mealies are a type of mealybug that feed on the roots of plants. Check all plant roots at transplanting for this pest. I transplant all new plants upon arrival so that I won't accidentally introduce this pest. When root mealies have been identified, dip roots in insecticide before repotting and hand crush all of the pests you can see.

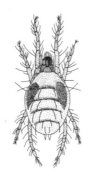

Mites

Mites often walk into the greenhouse during the summer. Misting of leaves discourages this pest. Beyond that, predatory mites can control populations. Several releases of predatory mites are usually needed. The predators appear to reduce the mite population to such a low level that they either die of starvation or migrate out of the greenhouse.

Mites, which resemble tiny spiders, are very hard to see with the unaided eye. Often the first sign of a mite infestation is drying leaves and a fine webbing on the plants.

Thrips

As with mites, the first sign of a thrips infestation may be a damaged plant. Infected plants look like the plant is drying out from the bottom up. Careful inspection of the leaves should reveal dark specks of frass excreted by the thrips.

The adult female deposits several hundred eggs into the tissue of the plants. Depending on conditions in the greenhouse, it takes from a week to several months for the eggs to hatch — faster under warmer temperatures. Thrips feed on plant sap for two larval stages and then drop to the soil for the prepupal and pupal stages. The adults emerge from the soil to infect new tissue.

Soil sterilization is a good way to control thrips in the early stages. Acute infestations may require insecticidal sprays. Large thrips populations can slow the growth of plants and cause much leaf damage so control of this pest is important.

THIRST AID FOR PLANTS

It is well established that severely drought stressed plants are more vulnerable to insects pests and diseases, but recent research suggests that slight stress caused by intentional underwatering may actually improve resistance in some plants.

A 1988 study at the University of Virginia found that oak lace bugs preferred well watered oak saplings over their slightly parched siblings. And a later test of Mexican bean beetle larvae on soybeans yielded similar results.

One reason that insects may find water-stressed plants less appealing is that the leaves contain less water (11 percent less in the soybean test) and may be harder to penetrate. To test this notion researchers fed the larvae leaves from water-stressed plants that had been doused just before harvest to bring water levels up to normal. Yet the resistance characteristics continued to protect the leaves.

What's more, the larvae forced to eat the leaves took longer to mature, gained weight more slowly and suffered a 10 to 15 percent higher mortality rate than those feeding on normal well-irrigated plants. Analysis of plant tissues reveals that mild water stress can induce plants to step up production of certain waxes, resins and oils that may play a role in resistance to diseases and insects.

Slugs and Sow Bugs

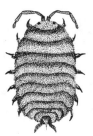

There are a few other pests that seem to find their way into greenhouses despite valiant efforts to stop them. Slugs and sow bugs are always on the outside of the greenhouse just waiting for a chance to get in. Barriers are the first step in the control of these pests. A good foundation that is well sealed from the outside will keep out many of these pests. Good plant shelves with slug barriers can keep slugs off of plants. Slug traps and hand picking can also help. Always inspect the drainage holes and the bottoms of pots for slugs and sow bugs and hand pick them before bringing them into the greenhouse.

Early detection and a carefully thought out response is the key to keeping your greenhouse and solarium pest free. The lifecycle of the pest dictates where and how to monitor and treat infestations. There are biological control agents that can be used even if you have only a small area. Biological controls, monitoring, and early spot treatments can keep your need for pesticides to a minimum, perhaps even more important in the indoor or greenhouse environment than it is outdoors. Keeping healthy plants without poisoning ourselves or our pets is certainly an attainable goal.

Acknowledgments

Thanks to William Koch and William McKewan for their support of my greenhouse dreams over the years.

First published in Volume 4 Number 1, page 39.

Chapter 4
Environmental Control

Environmental Dynamics in the Grow Room

by Erik Ackerson

Maintaining proper conditions in an indoor grow room can be difficult without an understanding of the dynamics of that unique environment. One field in particular helped me get a better handle on comprehending the interaction of humidity and heat in indoor spaces — passive solar building design/energy efficient construction. Just how useful some of the concepts and techniques were did not occur to me until I began to develop plans for an energy-efficient passive solar studio/greenhouse.

The goal was a small work space that would double as an abode for a year-round vegetable garden. The siting of this structure would tuck it snugly in the forest but position it where it could still be graced by the sun — especially on those cold but clear days here in the Pacific Northwest when passive solar design makes good sense.

One of the main advantages of an indoor growing space is control of the plant's growth cycle regardless of the season. I planned to use a 1000-watt metal halide lighting system to provide that inner glow in which my plant guests can bask and flourish. Rather than give the cucumbers the impression that their sun is standing still in the sky like in some biblical story, the light would be mounted on a 6-foot light track so that it runs back and forth so the plants at the end of the rectangular 9- by 13-foot growing space would not think they got the worst seats in the house. It would also mean that the leaves that happen to be behind other leaves will not be kept in perpetual gloom — a depressing situation if you are a plant in search of your full potential.

Light and Heat

The connection between light and heat is an important consideration in the greenhouse or grow room, as it is for the passive solar structure. Aside from the fact that this energy is the driving force for photosynthesis, some of the energy from this lighting system will be converted into heat. The amount of energy depends on the location and the nature of the surface the light strikes.

This has design implications for the grow room. It is first necessary to determine just what we are trying to accomplish, at what place, and at what time. For example, take our studio/greenhouse located half way between the North Pole and the Equator (45 degrees north latitude) during late December — the shortest days of the year.

Although the sun is at its lowest point in the sky, and the day-time temperatures hover around freezing, the days are often clear and sunny and our solar structure should be absorbing and storing heat. How? The design of the cabin, including its particular placement on the site, has been adjusted for optimal seasonal control of solar radiation. The leaves of the deciduous trees that shade the cabin from the summer sun will have fallen off and the roof overhangs along the south face of the cabin that warded off the summer sun now allow the low angle light of winter to pass through the glass surfaces along the south wall.

Once inside the structure, the light will strike various surfaces converting some of its energy to heat. The darker the color of the surface, the greater the conversion to heat. The radiation that passes through the glass on its way into the structure does not get out so easily once its wave length has been shifted by striking the surfaces inside the cabin. This is the "greenhouse effect," which in the earth's atmosphere is caused by CO_2 and other gases acting in a manner analogous to the glass. In your car on a sunny day, the "greenhouse effect" can produce an oven, especially if it has a dark interior.

Since we don't want to overheat this space and we do want to save some of this heat for the night, we need some kind of "heat sink." An example would be a dark tile floor over a cement slab. The dark surface would optimize the conversion of light energy to heat energy. The high density of the tile and the cement would retain more of the heat imparted to it than would a less dense material like wood. The heat sink is also a buffer against temperature extremes — it can absorb heat that would overheat the air, and then at night radiate that heat back to the room. A heat sink not only diminishes the need for energy, it also helps equalize the temperature over time.

A traditional heat source like a wood stove, a gas or electric heater could be used as needed to supplement the energy supplied by the sun. Insulated window coverings could be used, not only at night but also during cloudy days. (A general rule of thumb in solar design is that if you can see the sun even faintly through the clouds then there is solar gain potential.) Without insulation or at least some sort of curtain, the heat the building has absorbed during periods of solar gain would radiate through the window. What comes in can go out. Insulation is like a reverse heat sink; it does not retain heat very well — its low density means it retards the passage of heat. This building is planned to allow an extra depth of insulation (framed with 2-by-6 rather than 2-by-4 lumber) to better retain any heat gained through solar input and whatever heat source is used to supplement that provided by the sun.

The dark soil of the planters will also function as a heat sink, increasing heat storage capacity and buffering against overheating. If hydroponics is your preference, water makes a good heat sink. You could use a dark container as a preheater for your nutrient solution.

A common method for building in sufficient mass for solar heat sinks is a cement slab integrated into the overall foundation. The slab/foundation is insulated so that it retains as much heat as possible rather than transferring it to the earth. Duct work may be incorporated into the slab so that fans can better distribute the heat to warm the structure at night or even vent it to the outside so that it can help buffer against overheating during hot weather. Unfortunately in this situation, the topography of our hill-side building site would place the greenhouse floor several feet above grade, making a concrete heat sink impractical.

One solution might be a "floor sandwich," something I had seen used in another building to soundproof a music studio. The sandwich consists of two layers of plywood separated by 2-inch furring strips. The cavities between the layers were filled with dry sand (be sure to check out local building codes for floor-load requirements).

In my structure a dark colored floor covering will absorb heat and transfer it to the denser sand. The floor joist spaces beneath the heat sink are insulated so the sand will not radiate heat below the building.

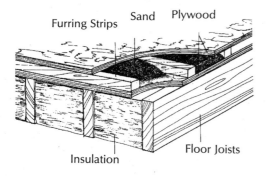

Furring Strips Sand Plywood

Insulation Floor Joists

Humidity

The interrelation of environmental factors shows up again in humidity, actually relative humidity — an expression of the ratio (percentage) of moisture in the air based on how much it can hold at that temperature. Since the capacity of the air to hold moisture increases with temperature, doubling with each 20-degree rise, humidity and temperature manipulations should always be considered together.

For example, our supplemental lighting has an overall drying effect by elevating the temperature which drops the humidity because the same absolute amount of moisture in a given volume of air of a higher temperature takes less of that temperature's capacity to hold moisture. Meanwhile the air which now has less relative moisture can receive more from any source — living or non-living — so that wet surfaces will dry more quickly and plants will transpire at a greater rate.

The winters in the area are humid and unless you have a good wood stove (or other dry heat source) you may end up sharing the space with mold. Since the plants are allergic to mold but would not like to share their intimate space with a wood stove, I needed another way to control temperature and humidity. The energy efficient design helps retain the heat gained from the light and ballast, but with all the water around in the soil, the plants, and the air, humidity build-up could be a problem. Venting, bringing in outside air to replace inside air, can lower the humidity but it also lowers the temperature requiring the extra expense of providing supplemental heat, not to mention undesirable temperature swings.

Air-to-air Exchangers

Since tightly enclosed spaces retain the staleness in the air, as well as the heat, designers began designing in ventilation controls such as air-to-air exchangers. These devices baffle incoming and outgoing air across shared surfaces so that 60 to 80 percent of the heat in the air going out is transferred to the air coming in. The incoming and outgoing air share a common surface that acts as the heat transfer membrane while the currents of air do not mix. This affects both the temperature and the humidity of these two currents of air.

Understanding how that happens is worth a digression into an explanation of "dew point" which will help in understanding the relationship between heat and humidity.

Remember the beads of moisture that formed on the outside of your iced tea on those hot summer days? This is an example of dew point. It happens whenever the temperature of the air is lowered to the point that it can no longer hold the amount of moisture it did at the higher temperature. The higher the humidity and the greater the temperature drop — air hitting a cooler object or another mass of air — the more dewing out occurs. Thus air going out of the structure through the air-to-air exchanger will lose some of its moisture content given a sufficient temperature differential. The humidity of the incoming air is lowered to the extent that it is heated by the warmth of the heat transfer membrane.

Remember that a 20-degree rise in temperature doubles the capacity of the air to hold moisture. The end result of flushing inside air and replacing it with outside air through the mechanism of an air-to-air exchanger achieves just what we would want, given a cold, damp outside climate. Fresh, dehumidified, prewarmed air.

But there must be a rub, and there is. These spiffy machines don't come cheap. In evaluating the costs and benefits for residential use, *New Shelter* (January '84) concluded that it would take a long time for an air-to-air exchanger to pay for itself in saved heating costs unless the house was in a fairly cold climate and the fuel used for heating that house was fairly expensive.

For example, if an air-to-air exchanger cost $700 and saved $70 in heating costs per year, then its payback period would be 10 years. In *New Shelter's* evaluation, using Minneapolis as an example, it would take from six to ten years to pay for the various air-to-air exchanger models (installation included) they tested, given a 12,000-cubic-foot house heated by electricity, but 19 to 250 years if heated with less expensive gas. Unfortunately, *New Shelter* did not conduct its evaluation with criteria based on the special and unique requirements for an indoor grow room.

Besides maintaining the optimal environment for plant health, the air-to-air exchanger or other methods of humidity control can help prevent moisture damage to the building itself, another factor to consider when looking at the cost/benefit.

Vapor Barriers

Since a building acts as a membrane separating inside and outside air, energy efficient design usually employs vapor barriers, plastic sheeting placed beneath the final finishing material on walls, floors and ceilings that border unheated spaces. The sheeting acts as a barrier to air, and also as a barrier to moisture.

In the old, leaky uninsulated house, the air that you take the trouble to heat doesn't stick around long. In fact the total air in the house may experience as many as 10 air changes per hour (ACH). This happens partly through leaky doors and windows and partly right through the walls. Or almost through the wall in the case where there is a layer of paint on the outside of the house.

This is an inadvertent vapor barrier. Not only will the paint slow the passing of the moisture at this point, but it will also precipitate that moisture out of the air right into the wall cavity because that paint layer will often be cold enough, relative to the heated air, to reach dew point. The result being wasted energy, water in the wall and blistered paint.

The well insulated house has a vapor barrier on the inside where it will work to retain heat (reducing air flow to around one ACH and perhaps even down to .5 to .1 ACH when combined with caulking and other measures). What about moisture? When the heated air hits the moisture barrier in this position it is not hitting a colder surface because the insulated space intervenes between it and the cold outside air.

In places of high moisture, like the bathroom or the kitchen, the air can become so saturated with moisture that it does not take much of a temperature drop for a slightly cooler surface to dew that moisture out. In these areas of potential moisture problems, the response has been to provide extra ventilation, especially fans that vent to the outside, and to provide special surfaces like tile and water resistant dry wall (blueboard).

Thus the strategy in dealing with moisture in the air is not to let it haphazardly vent itself out along with the heated air but to control ventilation, particularly in critical spots. This would apply to the indoor grow room where watering, misting and plant transpiration can easily peak humidity to heights that are hospitable for mold but not for many plants or for the structure.

This does not mean that you should necessarily tile your grow room like your bathroom shower enclosure, but a properly installed plastic vapor barrier and/or a vapor barrier wall surface paint would be a good idea. If the inner surface of the grow room is to be dry walled, using the blueboard variety of dry wall designed for bathrooms would be a good idea as well.

Too tight?

Once it was discovered that tightly sealed houses had potential inner air pollution problems, some states adopted building codes that required that the house be able to maintain from .5 to .7 ACH (accomplished via vent fans or air-to-air exchangers).

This standard provides a handy reference to evaluate the need for fresh air in the grow room. If we assume that the same range of air renewal is adequate for plants, it is interesting to note that the average house built to code has an air exchange rate of around 1 ACH that happens just from air leakage around doors and windows as well as plumbing and electrical penetrations. This should be adequate for most grow rooms (assuming that air within the room is well circulated by an oscillating fan) except that humidity and heat during warmer weather will probably build up beyond "safe" levels.

The standard approach for controlling grow room heat and humidity is a vent fan with a CFM (cubic feet per minute) capacity adequate to exchange the total air volume in about five minutes. (A 10- by 10- by 8-foot room which equals 800 cubic feet vented with a 200 CFM fan would accomplish a total air exchange in four minutes). Thus, aside from any need to provide supplemental heat during cold weather, the grow room climate can be regulated by two control elements: a humidistat and a thermostat wired "in-line" to a vent fan. (Plug-in humidity/temperature controllers are now available from several manufacturers).

The humidistat is a device that is analogous to the thermostat except that it responds to a preset humidity level. When *either* the temperature *or* the humidity exceeds the level set on the corresponding control, the fan will be turned on and run until the set level is reached. A simple timer may also be necessary in case the grow room needs a periodic flush to renew the air if venting to control heat and/or humidity does not kick the fan on often enough.

If you are venting with a fan and you have to renew the air several times an hour to keep the humidity in check then it might be worth investing in a dehumidifier which, at around $200 to $250, may be a savings in the long run if you are providing supplemental heat from an expensive source like electricity.

Like the air-to-air exchanger the cost effectiveness of a dehumidifier can be evaluated by its payback period. Even if you plan to use an air-to-air exchanger, it would still be necessary to use a vent fan (for warmer weather when you do not want to recover the heat in the outgoing air) as well as the monitoring controls (thermostat and humidistat) to assure that heat and humidity do not exceed that desired for your garden.

You can establish the basic ventilation system and then evaluate the need verses costs of a humidifier and/or air-to-air exchanger based on your experience. The same control devices connected to run the vent fan could be connected to run the air-to-air exchanger.

The dehumidifier has it own built-in humidistat, but will usually have a minimum operating temperature of around 65 to 70 degrees (18 to 21 C). It "extracts" moisture from the air by dewing it out, that is by running it past a cool surface. Thus the warmer the air and higher the humidity, the more efficiently it works.

Other strategies for dealing with interior humidity come from standard construction practices. Most are relatively inexpensive and easy to do, especially during the construction or remodeling process.

In buildings with a crawl space, for example, a polyethylene vapor barrier placed on the ground will prevent the migration of soilborne

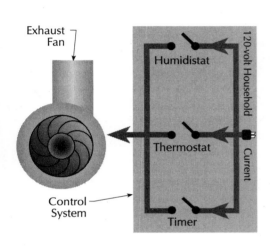

Exhaust Fan

Humidistat

120-volt Household

Thermostat

Current

Control System

Timer

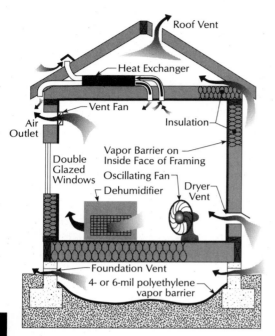

Roof Vent

Heat Exchanger

Vent Fan

Air Outlet

Insulation

Double Glazed Windows

Vapor Barrier on Inside Face of Framing

Oscillating Fan

Dehumidifier

Dryer Vent

Foundation Vent

4- or 6-mil polyethylene vapor barrier

78

moisture up through the floor of the structure. Use a heavy 4- or 6-mil sheeting and overlap the joints at least six inches and seal with duct tape. Adequate ventilation, generally 1 square foot of vent surface for every 1,500 square feet of floor area, should be provided in the foundation walls. Floor insulation should be installed to provide a thermal barrier between the crawl space and grow room.

Adequate ceiling insulation and attic venting are also a must for the indoor grow room, as warm, moist air will tend to rise through the structure. Double glazing or storm windows, while not required, will provide additional insulation between warm interior air and cool air outside, reducing heating costs and damaging condensation.

While they may add to the cost of your project, all of these measures represent a one-time investment with a guaranteed payback. All should be in place before more expensive solutions — air-to-air exchangers and dehumidifiers — are considered.

Certain gardening practices can also contribute to grow room humidity problems and should be avoided. Evaporation from uncovered nutrient reservoirs and starting trays can turn your room into a steam bath, as can some systems such as open ebb and flow tables. All of these factors should be considered in the design stage to head off future problems.

Air Circulation

Since heated air rises, air temperature stratification will be aggravated where there is insufficient circulation.

A well insulated and tightly sealed space does not tend to have any significant air temperature stratification because air is relatively easy to heat (due to its low density) if it is not constantly being replaced. Nonetheless, it is still important to run an oscillating fan or other internal air moving device to avoid CO_2 depletion zones around plants, to aid plants in transpiration of moisture and to keep mold spores from landing. During the lights-off portion of the daily cycle, leaf temperatures are lower and thus more likely to dew out moisture from the surrounding air making them more susceptible to mold. The oscillating fan can help evaporate water off the leaf surfaces. If CO_2 is being injected into the grow room, internal circulation is important so that the CO_2, which is heavier than air, doesn't just settle around the bottom of the room.

Since the exhaust fan needs to be able to draw in a sufficient quantity of outside air to flush the room in five minutes, the grow room will need an intake opening. One possible intake design using inexpensive, readily available materials consists of a hole cut through to the outside to accommodate the vents used for household dryers. On the outside of the building a metal vent acts as a rain shed. A plastic vent, a variation on the metal vent design, adds a flap inside the vent that opens when there is a sufficient air flow.

When used with a dryer it would be mounted on the outside and would flap open only when the dryer is running and pushing air out. In the case of the grow room the exhaust fan is able to create enough negative pressure (suction) to draw the flap open on the intake vent which, for a grow room, should face into the room. Window screening should be tacked across the opening on the outside of the cut just before mounting the metal vent so that critters of various sizes do not invite themselves in.

The exhaust fan should be located as high as possible on the wall to take advantage of the fact that hot air rises (convection). This, plus the placement of the intake vent near the floor across the room from the exhaust fan, will allow a quick flush of the room without needlessly mixing the stale grow room air with the fresh incoming air.

If you are constructing a grow room from scratch or even remodeling an existing room it would be helpful, not only for the protection of the structure and for the health of the plants, but also for savings in energy to investigate and employ energy efficient construction techniques and passive solar design strategies relevant to your situation, climate and budget.

This article was first published as a two-part series in Volume 1 Number 1, page 62 and Volume 1 Number 2, page 51.

The 50-Dollar Greenhouse

by Thomas H. Lavallee

When I was designing and building our greenhouses last year, I was struck by the number of options that kept jumping up. This type of "mind boggling" was not new to me. I design and build furniture and I've learned that there is always more than one way to attack a problem.

The result of that process is the structure described here. As you go through the procedures keep in mind that there are limitless variations on this basic design, some of which may be more suitable to your needs. The structure is not only user friendly, but open to all sorts of options for customizing.

A functional greenhouse is near the top of the wish list for most serious gardeners. But the expense and permanence of a traditional greenhouse structure is enough to scare off many. When you complete this project, you'll go to bed at night and enjoy sweet dreams of the bountiful harvest that will "soon" follow. You'll rest assured that you've provided the best possible home a plant could ever wish for. You will, of course, also have extended the growing season by 30 to 60 days and all for about $50 and a couple hours of creative effort.

The unit is a free-standing, expandable (vertically and horizontally), multi-function, moveable greenhouse. It is maintenance-free, except for the plastic covering, which will have to be replaced every few years. Other than that, it will be a life-long companion.

The frame is constructed of 3/4-inch polyvinyl chloride (PVC) pipe — strong, light weight and easy to move. The unit described here is 5 feet wide and 5 feet tall (fully extended), and 8 feet long, although it could be any length you wish to make it. (With some modification, the height could be reduced to 18 inches for use as a cold frame.) The total growing area is a whopping 40 square feet; plenty of room to get a head start on any garden.

Assembly is easy — downright simple if you follow the instructions. One person can do it, but it's more fun if you've got a friend to make it a social activity. The materials listed are for the basic unit. The numbers reflect the price I pay for living 150 miles from nowhere, which means I

LIST OF MATERIALS

Item	Quantity	Price
3/4" PVC pipe	100 linear feet	18.00
3/4" PVC crosses	4 pieces	4.80
3/4" PVC tees	20 pieces	5.00
3/4" 90° PVC ells	4 pieces	1.00
3/4" 45° PVC ells	6 pieces	1.00
3/4" PVC couplings	6 pieces	3.54
PVC cement	1 can	1.00
25 lb. test fishing line	1 roll	1.00
2" duct tape	1 roll	1.00
1X2 furring strips	2 @ 8', 1@ 10'	3.00
lath	26 linear feet	1.65
4 or 6mil. plastic	178 sq.ft.	9.50
	Total	**$50.99**

paid "gold plated" prices for everything. Yours will no doubt be lower. But higher or lower, you'll get your money's worth.

The tools required for the project include: a hacksaw or hand saw; a tape measure; a marking pen; a nail or super-sized sewing needle; and scissors or a utility knife. To get absolutely square ends on the cuts, a miter box is nice but not necessary.

Base and Side Wall Assembly

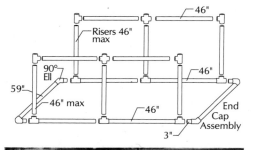

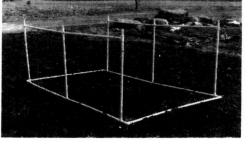

As with any construction process, we'll start with the bottom and work up. Refer to the illustrations provided for cutting and cementing the pieces together. If you go with a custom design, make a simple drawing of your own and follow it.

For the base assembly, cut the following pieces from the straight sections of PVC pipe: eight pieces at 46 inches; two pieces at 59 inches; and four pieces at 3 inches.

- Now grab six tees and four of the 90-degree ells (double check to be sure they are 90-degree). To get things square and flat, it is helpful to work on a flat surface such as a garage floor or driveway. Assemble the pieces according to the illustration at left and the following instructions:
- Cement the 90-degree ells to each end of the 59-inch lengths of pipe. Be sure that the ells on either end of the pipes face the same direction. PVC cement sets up quickly so you need to move fast and check the alignment as you work. Cement the 3-inch lengths of pipe to the 90-degree ells. These assembled sections make up the permanent end caps.
- Take two of the 46-inch sections of pipe and cement a tee to each end, again making sure that the tees face the same direction. Take the other two 46-inch sections and cement one tee to one end of each.
- Now friction fit the pieces together as illustrated. Do not cement the remaining joints. If in the future you wish to extend the greenhouse, simply remove the end cap assembly and add one 46-inch section of pipe and one tee fitting for each 4-foot extension, then reinstall the end cap. This will also permit you to break down the base unit completely for storage or transport.
- Now install the risers in the base frame. Cut six sections of pipe to whatever length you desire up to 46 inches and insert them into the tees on the base frame. The length of the risers will determine the height of the finished greenhouse. If you want to raise the structure as the plants grow, start with a shorter riser, then add a coupling and more pipe as needed.
- To complete the side wall assembly, simply friction fit a "cross" fitting to each center riser and a tee to each end riser as illustrated. The four remaining 46-inch pipe lengths are fitted between the tees and the center crosses.

Bow Assembly

The roof framing for our greenhouse consists of three bow assemblies (as in bow and arrow) — two identical end sections and one slightly modified center section. The following pieces need to be cut to construct one bow. (Remember, there are three bow assemblies for the basic 8-foot greenhouse. To expand the greenhouse, you will need an additional center assembly for each 4-foot extension.): one piece at 59 inches; two pieces at 30 inches; two pieces at 6 inches; and two pieces at 3 inches

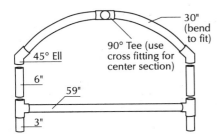

30" (bend to fit)

90° Tee (use cross fitting for center section)

45° Ell

6"

59"

3"

- Take the two 30-inch lengths of pipe and cement into each end of the tee as illustrated at left. Then cement the 45-degree ells to the other ends of the pipes. Again, make sure that the fittings are properly aligned. Finally, cement the two 6-inch pipes into the 45-degree ells and set this assembly aside.
- Take the 59-inch length of pipe and cement a tee to each end. Be sure that the long parts of the tees are parallel to each other. To complete this assembly, cement a 3-inch piece of pipe to the "bottom" of each tee.
- Now put the two sections together by inserting the 6-inch pipe into the tee on one side. Gently bend the bow assembly and slip the other 6-inch pipe into the tee on the opposite side. Do not cement this joint; tension will hold it in place.
- Repeat the above procedure for the other end section. For the center bow, the tee at the apex is replaced with a cross.

Frame Assembly/Sheeting

Install the end sections into the tees on top of the end risers. Install the center bow into the crosses on the center risers. Cut two more lengths of pipe to 46 inches and install these along the ridge.

Walk around the structure and press all parts firmly together and manipulate the frame into square. We now have a good looking skeleton ready for a plastic covering.

In a test I ran this winter, my 6-mil plastic held up to a typical snow load and gusting winds of 40 to 60 mph. That was in Salmon, Idaho, in the middle of the Rockies. If you live in a more hospitable climate, you might try 4-mil plastic. It is less expensive and also easier to take down and put up if you plan to store your greenhouse for part of the year.

The following sheeting method was done, as with the rest of the project, with cost and portability in mind. Again, feel free to use methods and materials that best suit your purposes.

- Take a 6-by-6-foot sheet of plastic and lay it up to the end section allowing a 6-inch overhang at the top and both sides. Temporarily tape the plastic in position at the apex and at the side struts. Using the knife or scissors, make a cut down from the top of the plastic to within two inches of the tee at ridge.
- Using the nylon line and the needle or nail, sew the plastic to the bow using a loop stitch or saddle stitch. Start at the ridge and sew down one side. Sew through the overhang, pulling the stitch around the pipe as you go. Run the stitches to the bottom of the tee at the side strut. Stop there and tie off the line leaving a loop about 4 inches long (you'll need it later).
- Repeat this procedure for the other side of the bow and trim the overhang to one inch.
- Staple the bottom edge of the plastic to a 5-foot length of 1-by-2 lumber. Now place a 5-foot piece of lath on top of the plastic and nail through into the 1-by-2. The wood is heavy enough to hold the flap shut when ventilation is not needed. To open the vents, roll up the plastic from the bottom and secure with the loops (remember the loops?) left over from sewing the sides.
- Repeat the procedure for the other end section.
- To form the roof covering, cut a piece of plastic 16 feet by 8 feet. This should cover the entire top and sides of the frame with a couple of inches overlap on the sides.
- Starting from one end at the apex, use 2-inch duct tape and secure

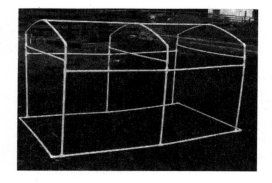

the roof to the bow of the end section, again ending at the first tee. Complete the other side of the bow and repeat the procedure on the other end. Be sure to press the tape firmly in place and to smooth out any wrinkles.

■ Secure the wood to the bottom of the plastic as discussed for the end sections.

We now have a completed greenhouse or coldframe, depending on the length of your risers. The design permits great flexibility in operation. Venting is adjustable from 2 to 4 feet, depending on how much plastic you roll up. You can vent from the ends or the side or any combination.

The frame can be anchored in place with light-duty hose anchors, or you can make heavy-duty anchors out of rebar, depending on the wind conditions in your area. For high wind areas, the structure could be anchored with guy wires from the corners of the ends.

Some readers may detect some compromises in the above design. The purpose here is to be "all things to all men." As mentioned earlier, the unit is user friendly and is amenable to endless modification and customizing. Whatever you do with it, good luck with your endeavors and keep talking to your plants.

First published in Volume 3 Number 4, page 49.

The Garden Hacker — Computer Control Techniques

by Jay Green

Wouldn't it be nice if you could control your hydroponic system with your home computer today? The technology has been there for years, but most people have enough trouble with computers without being inclined to learn computer interfacing (a term referring to physically connecting a computer to the environment) and all of the electronic engineering that involves.

As a long-time hacker, I live to wire my IBM PC to everything in the house for monitoring as well as for control. Of course, it is not necessary to carry things to that extreme, but for those gardeners who own a personal computer, the advantages of computer control systems are great and it is not nearly as complicated as you might think once the basic concepts and terminology are understood.

To get a computer to control something, it must have some sort of line of communication, so to speak. This is the interface. A monitor, printer or disk drive is controlled by the computer through a "computer card" and cables supplied by the manufacturer. All of the things mentioned so far are "hard wired" to the computer, meaning that there is a physical link such as a big wire running between the "outside" device and the computer itself.

Computer control can be done in this way and it has some advantages, but it also has some drawbacks. If, as is the case with the do-it-yourself interface, there is not a manufacturer supplied computer card, one must be designed by the owner/operator. Another drawback is the expense and mess of running huge cables all over the house. Fortunately, neither problem is insurmountable.

The first is solved by using a common, readily available interface that almost everyone who owns a computer has. RS-232 is the fancy name for it; if you own a computer printer then you probably already have one. (This applies to the IBM PC series of home computers as well as the Macintosh, Apple IIe/IIc, and Commodore 64/128.)

The second problem is solved almost as easily, but requires a bit of explaining. If you understand how cable television works, that's a good start. The idea is to have your computer use the existing wiring in your home in place of the cables. As complicated as that sounds, it is surprisingly easy to do with a device marketed by X-10, Inc. (185A LeGrand Ave., Northvale, NJ 07647, 1-800-526-0027).

This device hooks up the RS-232 that is probably already in your computer, and then into the nearest electrical outlet. It takes commands from your computer and transmits them over the household wiring. At the other end, any electrical outlet in your house, a small module translates the message sent by the interface and determines whether it should turn itself on, off, dim the lights a bit, or ignore the message altogether since it is for some other module. The device comes with a program to help you set up the system quickly and easily.

The price is about $50 for the interface and program and another $11 for each receiver module — more expensive than those archaic light timers, maybe, but so much more control. The receiver modules are readily available from X-10, Radio Shack, Sears, Stanley's Heath-Kit and others.

The nice thing about this system is that it is possible to store all of the settings for different seasons and cycles, giving you an incredible degree of control over your garden's environment. Cycles can be fine tuned since the system allows adjustments to be made in minutes. You can also have the computer change the settings according to the day of the week, like having the garden start up later on the weekends so that it won't wake you up. Once all of the information is logged into the interface, the computer does not even need to be turned on for the system to work.

The same company also offers a wide variety of related items to make your system customized and as complex as you would like. For example, you can connect a telephone interface so that you can operate your system via any touch-tone phone while you are away from home.

The Two-way Interface

The X-10 is a simple way to get commands out from the computer to the application. But this allows the computer to operate only on the "slave" level — simply acting as a sophisticated timer. While this may be adequate for some applications, it does not begin to use the full potential of the computer as a control device.

The next logical step toward automated gardening is to allow the computer to take in information from the outside world (the application) and act on that information. Instead of making decisions based on the predetermined timer schedule, the computer can change its output in response to changes in the real environment. Once this connection is established, the computer can turn things on and off via the X-10 interface. Not only can anticipated events be controlled, but adjustments can be made for unforeseen events as well.

The following is a simple input that would be applicable to most home computer systems. I call this a "simple weather report" because the interface is restricted to only yes/no, on/off type of information.

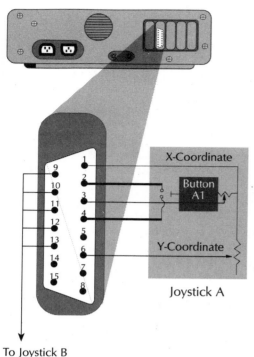

X-Coordinate

Button
A1

Y-Coordinate

Joystick A

To Joystick B

Whenever possible, it is best to use the mechanical interfaces that are already present in the computer. Of the numerous interfaces found on all home computers — printer, monitor, mouse, keyboard — what we need is an electronically simple interface that we can take over and use for our own purposes. We already have a method to output commands (via the X-10 interface) so we are looking for an input interface. One interface that fits the bill and can be found on almost all computers is the game port. This is the input used to receive information from the joy stick used in many computer games.

In order to provide a concrete example of how the hook-up works the following description will be based on the IBM-PC's game port (with apologies to all the Mac users out there), although it should be simple enough to translate to other computer systems.

The IBM game port allows for the attachment of two joy sticks. This allows four digital (on/off) inputs to be simultaneously monitored through the game port. For simplicity, I will refer to a single joy stick, designated joy stick A. On the joy stick there is a single two-directional stick and two buttons, A1 and A2. I will be using only button A1 for this example.

Of course, the computer doesn't know what a joy stick is, it doesn't know what a keyboard is for that matter. What it knows is that when you press the key marker "a" a specific switch has been closed (turned on) which is normally open (turned off). It is only the program running the computer that "tells" the computer that when switch number 999-what-ever is closed that the "a" key has been pressed.

If, for example, we mounted the keyboard itself in our hydroponic greenhouse and hooked up a stick that would press the "a" key when-ever the door was opened and at the same time ran a program that told the computer that whenever switch number 999-what-ever is closed that means that the greenhouse door has just been opened. So instead of being the "a" key it becomes the door-has-just-been-opened key.

Using the keyboard, or the joy stick for that matter, in this way is not really practical. But remember that joy sticks and keyboards are nothing more than a collection of simple on/off switches. What is practical is to run a pair of wires from the computer to the hydroponic system and attach our own switch to them.

Consider again the simple door-open monitor described above. A simple on/off switch such as those used for burglar alarm systems could be installed on the greenhouse door. On the computer end of the set-up the wires are connected to the terminals used by the joy stick button. There is no need to destroy a joy stick to get at the needed connections, only a recognition of the proper interface inputs.

The two wires need to be connected to pins 2 and 4 of the game port as illustrated at left. A 15-pin DIN female connector is used for the connection. (Your local electronics store should carry these parts.) Run the two wires that are now connected to the computer to the greenhouse door. Install the NO (normally open) door/window (magnetic reed) switch to the door and the connecting wires to the terminals on the switch. The hardware portion of this basic digital interface is now complete.

Of course, the computer still doesn't know what's going on, much less what to do about it. It still needs a program to tell it what it means when the door-has-just-been-opened switch is closed (turned on). Computer programming is beyond the scope of this article. But a skeleton program is needed to illustrate the workings of the example given above.

BASIC Program "Door Open"

Command entered	Result
10 STRIG ON	Allows computer to read joystick button
20 X = STRIG (0)	Computer inputs joystick button A1 and puts -1 in variable X if it was pressed
30 IF X = -1 THEN PRINT "DOOR HAS BEEN OPENED"	
40 GOTO 10	Repeat routine

Computers, and the people who program them, understand the BASIC language which I will use here. The program must be able to "see" that the joy stick button is closed (turned on) and then take some action based on that information. In this example the computer is connected to the door switch on the greenhouse; I want the computer to tell me when the door is opened. (The BASIC program is given at left with a simple translation.)

Obviously, the open-door interface and program is just a simple example. It is possible to monitor any condition in the greenhouse or grow room for which an on/off sensor is applicable. A water overflow condition might be monitored, for example, by taping the two bare wires to the floor of the greenhouse. Water on the floor would "close" the connection between the wires alerting the computer to shut down the pumps. (A float activated switch placed in a floor sump could also be used.)

Another example could be connecting the two wires to the output terminals of a thermostat (the part that would normally connect to a fan). When the temperature reaches a pre-set point, the thermostat would close. A program could be devised to "see" that the thermostat has closed and turn the fans on. (Be certain that only the computer, not the fan, is connected to the thermostat to prevent household current from reaching your sensor lines.)

Your imagination is the only limit to the possibilities. Remember, there are four of these digital inputs in the IBM game port, so four separate systems can be monitored at once.

Getting the Full Input

The simple digital input system described above allows the computer to respond to yes-no types of situations. Sometimes that is all the information the computer needs. For example, the digital input can tell the computer that it is time to turn on the exhaust fan if the temperature is above 90 degrees, just like a thermostat would.

But what if you want more from your control system? What if you want the computer to record exact temperatures for later evaluation, or if you want to have different things happen at different temperatures? What if you want all of these things to happen simultaneously? To take full advantage of the power of the computer as a control device, the simple on-off input is not enough.

What we need is a way to monitor not just a single event — temperature at 90 degrees — but several related events — temperature at 90 degrees, temperature at 91 degrees, temperature at 92 degrees and so on. This is called analog input. Since our computer only understands digital input, we need something called an analog-to-digital converter (AD converter).

Before you rush off to the parts store for an AD converter, you may want to look for one closer to home. You may be able to make a converter from parts that are already on hand. In fact, you may have an AD converter, literally, in hand.

AD converters are commonly used with joysticks to tell the computer where the stick is positioned at any time. A joystick is simply two variable resisters which change value as they move. The game port's AD converter takes the resistance readings from the joystick and assigns an arbitrary number to it. The computer program interprets this information as the X and Y coordinates of the joystick's position.

So the joystick is ready to accept a resistor value and tell the computer what it is. You can take any resistor within a specific range, stick the leads of the resistor into one of the two pairs of joystick inputs and a simple BASIC program can tell you what the value of the resistor is. It really is just that simple. Best of all, there are two AD inputs for each of the two joysticks, giving you four converter inputs in all.

Hardware

Now that we have an AD converter (one of the joystick inputs), all we need is a resistor that changes with temperature — a thermistor — available at just about any electronics store. Connect the thermistor to the joystick input and place it in any location. The resistance will change with the temperature and the AD converter will turn the resistance value into a number which the computer program can access.

For a concrete example of how this connection might be made, I will, again, use the IBM PC, although it should work with just about any computer. The IBM technical manual says that joystick inputs read resistance values of between 0 and 100 K ohms. So we need a thermistor that will read between these two values.

Radio Shack has a thermistor (catalog number 271-110) that converts temperatures to proportional resistance from -50 C to 110 C (10 K ohms at 25 C, room temperature). At $1.99, this should fill the bill nicely.

Your temperature probe will consist of the thermistor soldered to a couple of lead wires. Place the probe in the environment to be monitored. The two lead wires plug into pins 1 and 3 of game-port A1, X-coordinate (see illustration at left).

Software

The software consists of reading the joystick A1 X-coordinate, and assigning a temperature to the resistance reading. First, write the BASIC program to read the port and display the results (see Program 1 at left). You will need to do this first before you calibrate the probe.

The computer still doesn't know what resistance values go with what temperature values. You need to tell it. To do that, you need a good quality thermometer with easy to read graduations, a cup of hot water and a cup of ice water.

Run BASIC Program 1 to give you a read out of resistance values. Mix hot and cold water to obtain a steady temperature, say 50 degrees (10 C), according to the thermometer. Immerse the probe and record the resistance displayed on the computer. Adjust the water temperature to 60 degrees (16 C) for the example given here and repeat the process, again recording the resistance value and the corresponding temperature.

The number and range of temperatures you will want to test for will depend on the application. For simplicity, the program described here is calibrated in 10-degree increments. It is possible to derive a formula to convert the resistance number from the AD converter into a recognizable temperature, but at this point, that would only be confusing. For now we will stick with the straightforward approach described above — testing for each temperature to be used.

This approach has its limits, but it can be the basis of a sophisticated control system. If your program is going to be controlling multiple functions at different temperatures, you can calibrate your thermistor for those specific temperatures.

Be aware that individual thermistors vary in their output and that other factors, such as the length of the lead wires, can affect resistance. You

BASIC Program One

Command entered	Result
10 STICK (0)	Resistance read
20 DISPLAY R	Resistance displayed
30 GOTO 10	Repeat routine

BASIC Program Two

Command entered	Result
10 STICK (0) = R	Input resistance from probe
20 IF R > READING-AT -50°F THEN T = 50	Replace "reading at" with value obtained at 50°F
30 IF R > READING-AT -60°F THEN T = 60	Repeat test as needed
40 IF R > READING-AT -70°F THEN T = 70	
50 IF R > READING-AT -80°F THEN T = 80	
60 IF R > READING-AT -90°F THEN T = 90	
70 PRINT T	Print actual temperature
80 GOTO 10	Repeat routine

will need to calibrate each probe — resistor and lead wires — separately.

Once you have assembled a list of the needed resistor values and corresponding temperatures, you need to create your working program. BASIC Program 2 is, again, simplified. You can add as many gradations in temperature as you need. In the program illustrated the "PRINT T" command is the output, or action, initiated by the input information. Instead of telling the printer to print, your computer could tell some device in the greenhouse such as heating cables or an exhaust fan to turn on or off instead.

The Real World Connection

The final link between your computer and the outside world may be made through a device called a transducer.

The transducer transforms mechanical energy into electrical energy — something that your computer can understand. The thermistor described above is a type of transducer that changes resistance in response to changes in temperature. But there are a number of other types of transducers that can be used to set up a unique monitoring system designed for your situation. All of the probes described are variations on the same theme — they are all electrical resistors.

Since the IBM technical manual says that the joystick inputs will read resistance values of between 0 and 100K ohms, all of our resistors will need to read within this range.

In some cases it is easier to purchase ready-made resistors found at Radio Shack or in laboratory or electronics catalogs designed to change resistance in response to certain environmental changes. You may find just the type of probe you need ready to plug in and use.

If not, you may be able to build a probe at home out of materials at hand. All you need is a resistor that will register within the acceptable range. Anything that impedes the conduction of electricity through a wire is a resistor. A lamp cord with a nick in the insulation is a resistor, for example.

A simple but effective soil moisture meter can be constructed with two lengths of rigid copper wire and two lead wires. Solder one lead to each piece of rigid wire. Press the wires into the soil close to each other, but not touching. Connect the lead wires to one of the analog-to-digital joystick ports on the computer.

In this case, the soil acts as the resistor. Resistance falls as moisture increases, allowing more electricity to flow through the lead wires to the computer. As the soil dries, the flow of electricity slows. The various resistance values in between correspond with different soil moisture levels.

The distance between the wires will also affect resistance. You will have to experiment with the distance the wires are separated in the soil to get approximately 50K ohms (for the IBM) resistance measured with an ohm meter under "normal" soil moisture conditions.

Once you've worked out the correct distance, you can make your probe permanent and movable by placing a non-conductive material between the rigid wires above the soil line and wrapping the top with plastic electrical tape (see illustration at left).

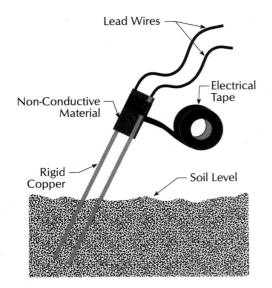

Lead Wires

Electrical Tape

Non-Conductive Material

Rigid Copper

Soil Level

Other Probes

The following is a list of other monitoring devices that you might find useful. Don't stop here, though. The real power of computer monitoring is that it permits the grower to design a system from the ground up:

- **Temperature** — The thermistor is a simple and inexpensive device that changes resistance in response to changes in temperature. It is the bread and butter of any serious computer control project and you'll want several of these babies around. They can be used to monitor temperature in nutrient reservoirs, nurseries, grow rooms or greenhouses.
- **Humidity** — A simple humidity meter can be constructed by connecting the outputs of a standard humidistat to one of the simple digital (on/off) inputs of the game port. The switch will turn on, initiating whatever action you've programmed into the computer, such as "exhaust fan on," at the level you've set on the humidistat.
- **pH Control** — pH probes are available individually from laboratory supply houses.
- **Electrical Conductivity** — Dissolved solids, such as the nutrients in a hydroponic solution, raise the conductivity of water. The more concentrated the solution, the higher the electrical conductivity. Electrical conductivity (EC) is often expressed in parts per million (ppm) of dissolved solids. A homemade EC probe can be constructed in a fashion similar to the moisture meter described above. You can calibrate your EC probe by mixing solutions of a known concentration of table salt and distilled water (see "PPM Explained," page 42).
- **Atmospheric Gasses** — Carbon dioxide (CO_2) and oxygen (O_2) can be monitored using specialized probes available from laboratory suppliers. Unfortunately, such probes are rather expensive.
- **Light** — Light levels are easily monitored with a simple cadmium diode, available from just about any electronics supplier.
- **Water Levels** — A simple device to detect the presence or absence of water — a flood sensor — can be made easily and quickly from scrap materials. Soak a piece of cardboard in salt water and allow to dry completely. Tape two lengths of copper wire close together on the board. Connect lead wires to each and run to the simple (on/off) inputs on the computer game port.

A true water level meter can be made by connecting ten 10K ohm resistors in a series (end to end) to make a single wire of resistors. Connect one end to the analog-to-digital game port, and lower the wire of resistors into the liquid to be monitored. To the other half of the game port, connect a single copper wire which is also placed in the liquid. As the water level falls, fewer resistors are shorted out and a higher resistance is "felt" by the computer.

This article was compiled from a series of four articles.

Carbon Dioxide Enrichment — Mass Through Gas

by Steven Carruthers

Carbon dioxide (CO_2) enrichment is one of the most interesting curiosities of modern horticulture and is yielding valuable primary data as research continues into the effects of increased CO_2 levels in the atmosphere. Unfortunately, the data collected is not generally published outside of scientific journals, and seldom reaches the agricultural industry where the effects can be better understood.

During the past century, the level of CO_2 in the atmosphere has risen steadily, largely from the combustion of fossil fuels. Atmospheric CO_2 has climbed from an average of about 0.028 percent (280 ppm) in 1860, to 0.034 (340 ppm) by 1981, an increase of more than 11 percent. Current estimates predict CO_2 levels will continue to rise, perhaps doubling in the next 70 years.

Pollutant or Plant Food? While CO_2 in this context is regarded as a pollutant by those concerned with the implications of the "greenhouse effect," elevated levels of CO_2 could to be of some benefit to agriculture. The genetic capacity of plants to absorb higher levels of CO_2 stems back to primordial times when plants adapted to CO_2 levels three to four times that which exists on earth today. In fact, horticulturists have for many years practiced CO_2 enrichment in controlled environments to increase crop yields.

An important focus of current research is the exchange of carbon dioxide between the biosphere and the atmosphere, and the effects of elevated CO_2 levels on plant species of economic value, to predict the likely outcome of future crop yields. Based on current projections, an increase in atmospheric CO_2 will induce higher global crop yields. Kanemasu (1980) estimates there will be an increase in wheat yields in the United States of about 59 percent with a doubling of CO_2 levels.

However, the implications for agriculture will depend strongly on weather-related factors, such as changes in rainfall patterns and the length of the growing season. Such predictions are also dependent on:

- The continued destruction of the great tropical and sub-tropical rainforests, since they act as the lungs of the planet, converting CO_2 into oxygen.
- The amount of CO_2 absorbed by the world's oceans, since they play a strong interactive role in both the global carbon cycle and the climate system.
- The continued burning of fossil fuels, given likely alternative technologies of the future.

Tucker (1981) suggests that a doubling of CO_2 could give an increase in photosynthesis of somewhere between 30 and 60 percent, but this may not result in increased crop yields. He reasons that increased yields are more likely to be attributed to increased precipitation, which is in turn caused by global warming as a result of increased CO_2.

Given a 30 percent increase in photosynthetic efficiency and a two-degree increase in average temperature, Baker and Lambert (1980) estimate a net increase in crop growth and development of 14 to 38 percent, depending on the availability of water. Pimentel (1980) further notes that a decrease in rainfall of between 10 and 30 percent over the United States, together with a temperature variation of plus or minus two degrees would reduce wheat and corn yields by 10 to 15 percent with no change in ambient CO_2 levels.

At present, such predictions are little more than conjecture, owing to our inability to make accurate climate forecasts. However, there are a small number of scientists now working to understand aspects of the biological consequences of elevated CO_2 in the future. Scientists can make much more progress in understanding the effects on existing genotypes and the ensuing phenotypes.

For example, yield responses can be studied for different crops, applying existing climate variations to estimate the future climate matrix, even if some of the more precise requirements concerning meteorological variables are the subject of conjecture. Much of this research is conducted using hydroponic techniques.

Water Use Efficiency

Carbon dioxide fixation and water use efficiency are only now being understood in detail. When considering CO_2 fixation, plants are grouped into three main classifications — C-3, C-4 and CAM (see article on page 106). These are abbreviated names for plants that share a preponderance of the same chemical bonding sites (receptor sites) for carbon dioxide. What they stand for is not as important as recognizing that different plants take up CO_2 in different ways and that these differences can affect such things as water use efficiency.

But what does it all mean to the grower who would like to put this knowledge to good use? In general, it is possible that the selection of crop species most suited to changing conditions may be one of the first elements in any planned contingency program to adapt to increased CO_2 levels of the future. However, the choice of future crops will depend as much on daily and seasonal patterns of temperature and rainfall as it will on CO_2 levels.

If some of the current climate projections hold true, we could see major shifts away from C-3 crops such as wheat, barley, potatoes and sugar beets, to more water efficient C-4 crops such as rice, cassava, sweet potato, maize, sorghum, pearl millet and sugarcane.

A side benefit of an enriched CO_2 atmosphere is increased water use efficiency in many plants. Under normal conditions, CO_2 diffuses into the leaf while water travels up the root system and transpires through the stomata. In the CO_2 enriched environment, the stomata shrink. As a result, plants transpire less water, becoming more water efficient.

Accelerated Growth

Over the past decade there have been many studies on the effect of CO_2 enrichment, but growth and yield rates have varied from model to model. For tomatoes, Slack (1986) showed a 30 percent increase in growth and yield, while Yelle (1987) reported a 36 percent increase. These results support earlier studies by Wittwer and Homma (1969) who reported accelerated growth rates, root growth promotion and earlier flowering and fruiting in tomato seedlings.

Other studies have shown a 31 percent weight increase in lettuce when exposed to 1600 ppm of CO_2, and a 23 percent increase in fruit weight for cucumbers exposed to 1000 ppm of CO_2.

Chrysanthemums, roses and carnations also respond well to elevated CO_2 levels. Experiments on roses have shown a 53 percent increase in flower weight when exposed to 1000 ppm of CO_2, with increased stem lengths, a greater number of petals and a shorter cropping time in winter. Carnation yields were increased by up to 38 percent, with increases in flower weight, stem thickness and reduced flowering times.

Results on asparagus and in-vitro cultured clones using CO_2 enrichment and supplemental lighting have been nothing short of spectacular. Desjardins, Gosselin and Lamarre (1990) reported increased root and fern dry weight for transplants of 196 and 336 percent, using 900 and 1500 ppm of CO_2 respectively. For clones, they reported increases of 335 and 229 percent respectively.

From these models, it can be seen that transplants respond better to

BLACKMAN'S LAW

The rate of any process which is governed by two or more factors is limited by the factor in least supply.

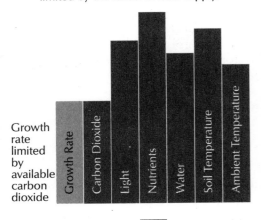

Growth rate limited by available carbon dioxide

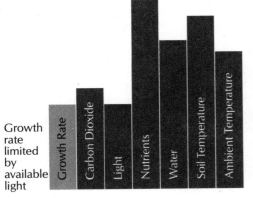

Growth rate limited by available light

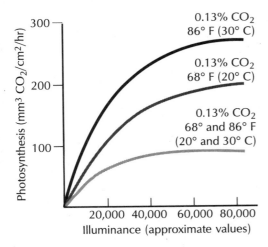

Effects of carbon dioxide, light intensity and leaf temperature on photosynthesis in cucumber. (Gastra, 1962)

higher levels of CO_2, while clones respond better to lower concentrations. A similar phenomenon was reported for tissue-cultured strawberries (Desjardins, 1987), and tomato transplants (Hurd, 1968).

For growers, this research has far reaching implications since transplants are becoming increasingly popular for the establishment of commercial plants. In the case of asparagus, the advantages of starts over conventional plantings of one-year-old crowns include the prevention of root diseases, superior stand establishment and reduced production costs associated with high seed prices and digging/replanting operations.

Desjardins, Gosselin and Lamarre concluded that CO_2 enrichment and supplementary lighting improved plant quality and reduced the nursery period. They further concluded that supplementary lighting contributed significantly to an improvement in plant survival. However, the effect did not contribute to improved yield components, such as number of shoots per plant or height of the plant. Nonetheless, they were able to demonstrate improved growth of plantlets in the field after two year's growth.

Carbon dioxide enrichment has resulted in a variety of useful effects on many other crops. White and Warrington (1984) reported significant growth increases in geraniums. Leaf area, shoot dry weight, specific leaf weight and plant height all increased, but enrichment improved growth only up to the visible bud stage. Similarly, while sunflowers gained increased stem thickness, enrichment was not helpful at the flowering stage, although the number of buds on each plant increased.

The physiological evidence strongly indicates that most plants have the potential for increased production, but the extent of plant response is also dependent on such factors as temperature, light and nutrition, as well as the CO_2 level.

Blackman's Law (see at left) states that the rate of any process which is governed by two or more factors is limited by the factor in least supply. The process of photosynthesis is a classic example. On an overcast day, it is pointless to raise the temperature more than 10 degrees above the night temperature in a controlled greenhouse because the low light level will limit the rate of photosynthesis. Any additional heat will be wasted. Conversely, if it is a bright sunny day and the temperature is not raised, then a lack of heat may become the limiting factor.

Carbon dioxide can also be a limiting factor in photosynthesis. Elevated levels of CO_2 will not be beneficial at low light intensities or temperatures. If light intensity or temperature is increased, higher CO_2 levels can stimulate growth. Elevated CO_2 levels can also increase fertilizer and water requirements.

The relationship between CO_2, light intensity and temperature are well illustrated in the curves developed by Gaastra (1962) for cucumbers (at left). In the lower curve, the rate of photosynthesis begins to plateau at a light intensity of about 40,000 lux (3800 footcandles), independent of the temperature being maintained at either 68 (20 C) or 86 degrees (30 C). The 300 ppm of CO_2 became the limiting factor at this point. When the CO_2 level was elevated to 1300 ppm at 68 degrees (20 C), the rate of photosynthesis increased. At this point, temperature became the limiting factor. With a temperature increase to 86 degrees (30 C), at the same 1300 ppm of CO_2, another increase in photosynthesis was recorded.

This does not mean that the rate of photosynthesis will continue to rise as the temperature rises. Generally, increases in temperature will affect other photosynthetic processes. Apart from faster growth, relatively high temperatures can cause a reduction in plant quality and yield, such as longer or thinner stems and smaller flowers.

While there is some variation in the results of different studies on the effects of increased CO_2 levels, the general conclusion must be that the effects are beneficial.

There are several types of horticultural CO_2 enrichment systems available today. The most sophisticated units rely on expensive infrared technology to measure CO_2, feeding this information to an electronically controlled injection unit or generator. There is now under development an automatic system which maintains a constant level of CO_2 in the growing environment, but also adapts data from the Gaastra curves to maintain the optimum photosynthetic response during the growth cycle of plants. Such a system will point the way to a future of maximal growth for chosen plant species.

References   **Desjardins, Y., Gosslin, A, and Lamarre, M.,** 1990, *Journal of the American Society for Horticultural Science*, 115(3): 364-368.

Desjardins, Y., Gosslin, A, and Yelle, S. 1987, Acclimatization of ex-vitro strawberry plantlets in CO_2 enriched environment and supplementary lighting. *Journal of the American Society for Horticultural Science*, 112:846-851.

92

THE CARBON CONNECTION

While it may lack the celebrity status of nitrogen or phosphorous, carbon is at the very heart of the energy producing capacity of plants. Carbon exchange is, in fact, the business of plants — taking in atmospheric carbon as CO_2 and producing carbon-containing (organic) substances as food for themselves and the animals that feed on them.

All green plants are equal in this regard, but some are more equal than others. There are three ways in which plants fix carbon dioxide depending on the presence of different chemical receptors that bind with the CO_2 molecule in the same way oxygen combines with hemoglobin in the blood.

The plant kingdom can be divided according to the chemical pathways involved in carbon dioxide fixation into three groups: C-3, C-4 and CAM plants. These differences are of more than mere academic interest. The method of carbon dioxide fixation can dramatically affect plant response to changes in temperature, light intensity and CO_2 concentrations. In a world of increased CO_2 levels and higher temperatures, the implications of these differences in response are more important than ever.

• **CAM** species (for crassulacean acid metabolism) are the slowest CO_2 fixers of the plant world. The CAM group is comprised mostly, although not entirely, of slow growing succulents. It is the smallest of the three groups and, except for the pineapple, contains no major crop species.

• **C-3** species make up by far the largest proportion of the earth's green plants. The group includes many important crop species such as wheat, oats, barley, sugar beets, soybeans, sunflowers, cotton and peanuts. In general, C-3 plants are more efficient at fixing atmospheric CO_2 than CAM plants. C-3 species, again in general terms, tend to reach maximum efficiency at lower temperatures and light intensities, and to lose relative efficiency as temperatures and light intensity increase. The optimum temperature range for photosynthesis for C-3 plants is between 60 and 77 degrees (15-25 C).

• **C-4** species such as corn, sorghum, rice and sugar cane are the champion CO_2 fixers of the plant world. At higher temperatures and higher light intensities, C-4 plants are more than twice as efficient at converting solar energy into dry matter as C-3 plants. The optimum temperature range for photosynthesis is between 85 and 105 degrees (30-40 C), and sometimes higher. The C-4 *Tidestromia oblongifolia*, a native of California's Death Valley, was found to have a photosynthetic optimum of 117 degrees (47 C). — *Don Parker*

Gaastra, P., 1962, Photosynthesis of leaves and field crops, *Netherlands Journal of Agricultural Science,* 10(5):311-324.

Kanemasu, E.T., 1980, Carbon Dioxide Effects Research and Assessment Program: *Australian Academy of Science.*

Tucker, G.B., 1980, Carbon Dioxide and Climate: *Australian Academy of Science.*

White, J.W., and Warrington, I.J., 1984, Growth and Development Response of Geranium to Temperature, Light Interval, CO_2 and Chlormequat, *Journal of the American Society for Horticultural Science,* 109(5):728-735.

First published in Volume 3 Number 2, page 23.

Photomorphogenesis

by Kathleen Yeomans

Plants are addicted to light. Just grow one plant in total darkness and another in light. You'll see a dramatic example of a plant's dependency on light. Typically, a plant grown in darkness will be tall, scrawny and pale; it looks like the proverbial "90 pound weakling" next to its light-grown cousin. Because light is the principal source of plant energy, a green plant deprived of it soon suffers.

Light controls plant growth and development, seed germination and root development. Plants know when to grow and when to sleep, when to bud, blossom and fruit, according to the quality and quantity of available light. *Photomorphogenesis* (*photo* — light, *morph* — form) refers to the pattern of plant growth and development in response to available light.

Plants differ in their need for light. Some grow best in bright sunlight, while others prefer shade. Light-demanding plants use carbon dioxide at faster rates than plants that prefer low-light conditions. These might be called the "high metabolizers" of the plant kingdom. But, as always, more is not necessarily better. Turning up the light on shade-loving plants, which transpire more slowly than sun-loving plants, can damage them. Very intense light can actually decompose chlorophyll and suppress photosynthesis. Subjecting low-light plants to over-bright light might be compared to requiring a marathon runner to sprint for 26 miles. Pacing is everything, even in the plant world.

A sun-loving plant in a low-light situation, on the other hand, responds in a different way. In reaching for stronger illumination, the light-starved plant may stretch and distort its stems and leaves, resulting in a tall, gangly, or bent plant. A deprived plant uses most of its energy to grow more light-capturing leaves (solar panels) at the expense of blossoms. This is why so many indoor plants refuse to bloom or set fruit. Depending on each plant's needs, the wrong amount of light can result in plants that grow either too fast (gangly), or too slow (stunted).

The various parts of a plant react differently to light. Leaf growth speeds up in bright light but plant stems react to strong light by slowing down. This helps to explain how light can both promote and inhibit growth. Generally, plants grown in bright light are short and bushy, while those grown in less light have long stems and weaker leaves. Aware of this fact, commercial growers often use supplemental light to inhibit

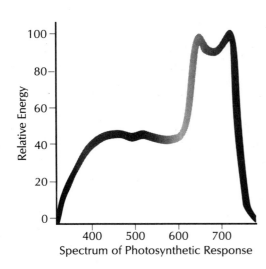

Spectrum of Photosynthetic Response

stem growth and keep transplants short and stocky.

Plant maturity, too, is affected by light. The length of days and nights, or light and darkness, controls the hormones that stimulate buds and blossoms. Blossoming time is dependent on the number of hours of uninterrupted darkness in a 24-hour cycle. This rhythmic cycle, called photoperiodism, also triggers tuber and bulb formation, leaf color and branching of stems. Some plants like long days and short nights, while others benefit from short days and long nights.

A plant's growing season is defined by these day and night periods and it can be fooled with artificially manipulated light cycles. Many growers use this trick to make sure that seasonal plants, such as Easter lilies, Thanksgiving chrysanthemums and Christmas poinsettias are in full bloom at the proper time.

How Plants Use Light

Pigments in plant leaves absorb and use various wavelengths, or colors, of light. Each plant pigment absorbs particular wavelengths of light energy and uses them for distinct purposes. This absorbed light causes photochemical reactions that stimulate certain plant hormones and biological responses. Green is the only wavelength in the visible spectrum that is not absorbed. It is, rather, reflected. That is why most plant leaves are green.

One of these pigments is *phytochrome*, which absorbs red light. Phytochrome is present in all green plants and could be called the primary pigment. It is responsible for regulating seed germination, root development, tuber and bulb formation, dormancy, flowering and fruit color. There are two forms of phytochrome, one absorbs red light and the other absorbs far-red. Each form of phytochrome can covert into the other form under certain conditions.

The red-light absorbing phytochrome is so important that even very low intensities and short exposures are enough to affect plant development. For example, only one minute of exposure to red light will start the leaves of a stunted, light-deprived plant growing.

Experiments with lettuce seeds showed that the quality of the red light is vital. Using the variety Grand Rapids, researchers found that when these seeds were exposed to a combination of red and far-red light, germination only occurred when the final exposure was to red light. Far-red in the final sequence inhibited germination completely. Red light evidently activates the pigment that stimulates germination, but that activity is canceled when far-red is absorbed.

Other pigments, such as the yellow-orange *carotenoids*, absorb blue light and control leaf fall and fruit ripening. *Riboflavin* pigment absorbs violet light and controls a plant's movement toward light. *Chlorophyll* absorbs both blue and red light. A plant without chlorophyll cannot convert sunlight into energy.

Effects of Color

Certain wavelengths, or colors, strongly affect plant growth. Most plants need some light in order to manufacture chlorophyll, the energy source for photosynthesis. Although all colors in the visible spectrum can activate chlorophyll formation, studies show that, in most cases, blue light accelerates chlorophyll production more than any other color.

Experiments with tomato plants show that green light makes them grow tall, while blue light produces short plants. In red light, tomato

SEEDS PROMOTED BY LIGHT

Adonis vernalis
Bellis perennis (English Daisy)
Chenopodium album (lamb's quarters)
Digitalis purpurea (foxglove)
Epilibium cicutarium
Fagus sylvatica (European beech)
Helianthum chamaecistus
Iris pseudaccorus
Juncus tenuis
Lythrum salicaria (loosestrife)
Oenothera biennis (primrose)
Ranunculus scleratus

plants grow to an average height, similar to the height achieved by plants grown in natural daylight.

To complicate matters, exposing tomato plants to a combination of colors results in other effects. Red light after blue and blue light after red brings about a short tomato plant. It seems that the blue light has a stronger effect than the red and keeps the plant short, just as if the tomato had been grown in blue light only. Other light-combinations produce plants either taller, more or less leafy, or bearing oddly shaped leaves.

Other plants have different responses to colored light. In experiments, four o'clocks (*Mirabilis jalapa*) exposed to red light grew extremely tall and gangly. It reacted similarly to green light, but grew short and sturdy under blue lights. Experiments with Petunias had just the opposite result. Blue light stimulated Petunias to grow tall, while red and green light encouraged short plants.

Flower and fruit color are also affected by wavelength. Experiments performed on apples show that only 48 hours of exposure to blue light caused the green apples to turn rosy, while red light produced hardly any change in fruit color. Researchers hope to learn the secrets of manipulating light and color exposure in sensitive plants to increase plant growth and crop yield.

Seed Germination

SEEDS INHIBITED BY LIGHT

Ailanthus glandulosa (tree of heaven)
Amaranthus caudatus (tassel flower)
Cucumis sativus
Euonymus japonica
Forsythia suspensa
Hedera Helix (English ivy)
Nemophila insignis (baby blue eyes)
Lamium amplexicaule
Lycopersicon esculentum
Phacelia tanacetifolia
Phlox drummondii (annual phlox)
Tamus communis

Even a plant's birth is dependent on light or the lack of it. Many plant seeds require light to germinate. One short exposure may be enough to get some seeds going, while others need several days of light. When seeds of light-sensitive plants are placed in water in the darkness, after an initial increase in respiration, (are they "gasping" for air?) metabolic processes slow and eventually cease. When light is admitted, absorption of oxygen begins again and continues until the seed germinates. Conversely, there are plants that need complete darkness for successful germination.

Experiments show, time and again, that the quality of light can be as important as its presence or absence. Some plants are exceptionally sensitive to red wavelengths and require red light in order to germinate, while far-red light inhibits many seeds from sprouting. Other seeds are inhibited by blue light, and then there are those that seem indifferent to light quality and quantity during germination. Profitable plant propagation depends on the knowledge and understanding of these requirements.

Leaf Development

Plants grown in darkness often have tiny, misshapen leaves. Light is essential to these "food factories" of the plant world and they are extremely sensitive to it. Plant leaf shape develops in response to the quality and quantity of available light. Most shade plants have relatively large leaves in order to efficiently absorb the little light that is available. Desert plants, in contrast, often sport tiny, thicker leaves. They don't need to work as hard to get adequate light, and in fact, have to protect themselves from the harsh rays of the desert sun.

Wavelength, or color, has an effect on leaf development too. Blue, violet and ultra-violet light cause thickening of leaves and leaves grown in red light may get a "bumpy" surface. Colored lights influence the leaf shape as well as thickness. Experiments with pea plants showed that their leaves grew larger when exposed to red light. Some other plants, when exposed to varied colored lights, responded by developing tiny, deformed or otherwise inadequate leaves.

Critical Light Periods

Plants can tell time. They flower and fruit only during the proper seasons. But how do they know when spring has sprung?

Most plants are sensitive to day length. There are plants that flower during the spring and summer, when days are longer than nights, and there are those that flower in the autumn, when nights are longer than days. Even the underground parts of a plant, the roots, tubers and bulbs are sensitive to day length. Experiments with long-day plants show that they will grow, but not blossom if nights are long.

It is the absence of light, rather than light itself, that regulates flowering. When the hours of darkness are artificially interrupted by as little as one hour of light, the plant senses a "short night" and starts producing flowers. This is how plants tell time. They get the message from their leaves which sense light, or the lack of it, and produce hormones that control the plant's growth, budding and blossoming.

This day length sensitivity can be a real problem for the city gardener who tries to grow lettuce, spinach, beets and radishes, which are short-day, long-night plants. Even the dim light of street lamps can sometimes stimulate these plants into "bolting" and producing flowers long before you've had a chance to harvest a decent crop. Once spinach plants have been exposed to just one twelve-hour day, there is nothing that can stop them from flowering. So if you garden under streetlights, cover your short-day plants at night to extend your harvest.

Growers in cold climates must often wait to start their gardens until the soil thaws. By this time, it may be late spring when the days are long and nights are short. Under these conditions, normally "easy" crops like spinach or lettuce can become difficult. To overcome this problem, plant earlier, under a protective cover, or later, at the end of summer when nights are growing shorter again.

If cultivation practices fail, modern agricultural science has come to the farmer's rescue. Varieties of plants have been developed with day-length characteristics that allow gardeners in "problem" areas to reap otherwise impossible harvests.

Effects on Yields

Crowding and shade are two factors that affect light intensity in the garden. Even in sunny situations, crowded plants shade each other, decreasing the amount of available light. Shaded plants grow tall and scrawny, and crop yields are poor because plant energy is diverted to leaf development rather than to blossoms and fruit. Plants subjected to inadequate lighting are under stress and therefore more susceptible to disease and insect attack.

High light intensity (full sun) inhibits elongation of stems and increases stem thickness, keeping plants shorter and stockier. The plant also responds to increased light by growing smaller, but denser and heavier leaves. The cuticle and cell walls are thicker and the stomata denser but smaller. These changes help make the plant more resistant to high temperatures, drought and infection.

Increased light intensity boosts vegetative growth, up to a point. Plants stimulated by increased light seem to respond positively at first and then "burn out." Overlong daily exposure to light can actually prevent chlorophyll formation in the leaf, causing chlorosis, decreased photosynthesis and poor health.

In tests with tomato seedlings, the quality of light had a great bearing on yields. Tomatoes exposed to red lamps for a test period of eight days grew faster than those grown under warm white, blue or green lamps. When plants were exposed to alternate colors, for example four days of blue light followed by four days of red light, the combination of colors seemed to promote a greater dry weight of plant material than each color used alone.

It was concluded that all parts of the visible spectrum are helpful, in some way, in promoting plant growth. In these experiments, it appeared that red light, alone and in combination with other colors, had a definite enhancing effect on plant growth and crop yield. Green light, on the other hand, was the only color that gave the lowest yields under all circumstances.

Other experimenters believe that blue light increases some plant growth. Studies done at Stanford University showed that blue light stimulates the opening of leaf stomata. It is thought that more open stomata allow more carbon dioxide to enter the leaves and thus increase photosynthesis. Orchids grown in conditions where the normal amount of blue light was doubled, showed growth increases of 50 percent or more.

In other research, USDA scientists in South Carolina have been working with colored mulch materials that reflect light to the plant. Red mulches used around tomato plants produced larger fruits and greater yields. White mulch improved yields of bell peppers and potatoes. Perhaps the white mulch reflects heat to the plant as well as light and growth increases are a response to a combination of factors.

So What?

Growers will certainly benefit from light research. Even now, many nurseries use light manipulation techniques to enhance growth.

Plants can be kept actively growing almost all year long. Supplemental light is used to increase carbon dioxide use, or transpiration, in young plants during winter, or non-growing months. This results in stronger plants, earlier crops and better resistance to plant diseases. Out-of-season fruits are possible too. Dormancy can be prevented in strawberries and they can be brought to fruit during the winter with extra light in the fall.

Light can also be used to stimulate vegetative growth and provide more material for cuttings. In addition, increased photosynthesis, brought about by the use of supplementary or varied colored light, can promote better growth of seedlings.

With light manipulation, blooms can be had practically "on demand." It's easy to prevent or temporarily delay the flowering of short-day plants. If light is switched on in the middle of the night, as little as three hours of illumination will bring about this result — the plants think the days are longer and budding does not take place.

Conversely, tarps or other covers can be used to black out light to induce short day effects during the summer or spring and plants can be brought to flower out of season, when there is a better market for them. Artificial lights can also extend the daylight hours for long-day effects. These techniques are commonly used with Begonias, Gesneria, Gloxinia,

FORCING FLOWERS

Keep plants in the dark from 6 a.m. to 6 p.m. for four to six weeks, blossoms will begin to form. A second crop can often be forced in the same way. Plants that can be forced to blossom early include:

- Chrysanthemum
- Euphorbia
- Kalanchoe
- Zygocactus
- Begonia

97

Kalanchoe, Saintpaulia and other commercially grown plants.

Research suggests that the use of colored mulches and reflected wavelengths could be a new low-cost, low-labor method to increase crop yields.

Plants may be addicted to light, but not just any light will do. The grower who can supply the optimal quantity, quality and color of light will be able to manipulate shape, size, maturity, color and crop yield as well as stimulate plant growth. It may not be long before photomorphogenesis becomes a household word.

First published in Volume 3 Number 1, page 56.

HID Lighting for the Home Grower

by Tom Alexander

There are four basic types of high intensity discharge (HID) lights. The oldest and the most used for general lighting up to the mid-70s was mercury vapor. Metallic (or metal) halide and high pressure sodium lamps are variations of mercury vapor bulb, using different metals in the vapor tube. Halides started to replace mercury vapor for general lighting, but because of their higher efficiency, sodiums now have 70 to 80 percent of the market. Low pressure sodium bulbs (LPS) are similar, but use no mercury in the arc.

All HIDs require ballasts, except for self-ballasted mercury lamps which are worthless for growing because of low light output, high lamp cost and relatively short life. The ballast limits the lamp current and gives it the proper running voltage. A ballast for a given wattage can operate lamps of only that wattage. Do not mix and match bulbs and ballasts. Use only a ballast designed for the type and wattage of your specific bulb.

Mercury vapor lamps are useful only in 400, 750, and 1000-watt sizes. The 1500-watt is the same as the 1000-watt but is over driven by using a special ballast. This raises light output by 20 percent but shortens lamp life by 80 percent. Mercury lamps put out 60 lumens per watt, about the same as VHO (very high output) fluorescent tubes, but are better because they are longer lasting and the light is concentrated in a 3-inch arc tube instead of 12 feet of fluorescent tube.

The 400-watt and 1000-watt mercury lamp is available in cool white, warm white, clear, color improved and natural. The different phosphor coatings on the bulb's glass case improve the spectrum, but certain wavelengths are missing with all coatings. A 400-watt unit hung 6 feet over the soil lights a 20- to 40-square foot growing area. A 1000-watt unit lights 50 to 100 square feet of growing area if hung 8 feet above the soil. These numbers are considered maximum and assume that a good reflector and reflective mulch and walls are used.

Mercury vapor lighting is the cheapest way to go; they can be purchased at state and school surplus sales as used units for a few dollars each. They are hardly used anymore except in very low wattages for yard lighting. Low wattage mercury lights are available in reflector lamp types, eliminating the need for a separate reflector.

METAL HALIDE LAMP

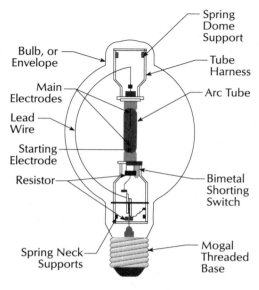

Bulb, or Envelope
Main Electrodes
Lead Wire
Starting Electrode
Resistor
Spring Neck Supports

Spring Dome Support
Tube Harness
Arc Tube
Bimetal Shorting Switch
Mogal Threaded Base

HIGH PRESSURE SODIUM LAMP

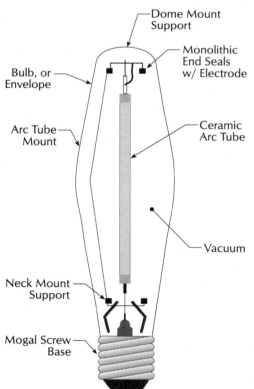

Bulb, or Envelope
Arc Tube Mount
Neck Mount Support
Mogal Screw Base

Dome Mount Support
Monolithic End Seals w/ Electrode
Ceramic Arc Tube
Vacuum

Metal halide lights, marketed under brand names such as Multivapor (General Electric), Metallic Halide (Westinghouse), and Metalarc (Sylvania), are mercury vapor lamps with sodium and scandium iodide added to the mercury in precise amounts and a thorium-coated electrode which fills the gap in the mercury spectrum. They put out 90 to 125 lumens per watt and are available in 175, 250, 400 and 1000-watt sizes.

There are 1500-watt halide lamps, but they put out hard ultraviolet (UV) radiation and are dangerous to be around when lit. Hard UV radiation causes blindness, cataracts, and skin cancer. Beware! Any metal halide burning more than 15 degrees off vertical center also puts out hard UV. It is advisable to wear UV blocking sunglasses whenever working around any HID light of any wattage. All HIDs create some hard UV light. Acceptable government levels don't meet my levels, so I wear protective eye goggles and clothing when working under HID lighting.

Metal halide lamps need special ballasts made specifically for halide systems. Growers have experimented with using mercury vapor or sodium ballasts with occasional success. It is recommended to use matched halide bulbs with halide ballasts. We are dealing with high voltages and electrical overload and fire danger should be kept to a minimum.

There are some metal halide lamps made that will fire up on mercury ballasts with some made to operate on one type of ballasts and others made to operate on another type. Experimenting can be dangerous because the wrong lamp and ballast combination can blow up the lamp.

The metal halide in the 1000-watt size is an inexpensive way to start an indoor garden. If hung 8 feet above the soil surface, it will light up to 100 square feet while a 400-watt hung 6 and 1/2 feet above the surface will light up to 40 square feet, assuming that there is good reflection on walls and floor. The halide is by far the best system for vegetative growth.

The one drawback to these lamps is the extremely long restrike time. If turned off after reaching full brightness, it can take 10 to 30 minutes for the lamp to cool down and fire up or light up again.

High pressure sodium (HPS) is the best single source for growing and flowering. It doesn't have as wide a spectrum as metal halide but is much more efficient, producing 110 to 140 lumens per watt. Lamp life is longer and light loss with age is low. In experiments with roses, production was 140 percent greater with HPS and sunlight than sunlight alone.

HPS lamps come in 250-watt, 360-watt self-starting, 400-watt and 1000-watt. The 250-watt is not as good for growing and more expensive than the 360-watt because of the special ballast required. The 250-watt will light an area of 20 square feet at a height of 6 feet; the 360-watt, 35 square feet at 6 and 1/2 feet high; the 400-watt, 40 square feet at 6 and 1/2 feet high; and the 1000-watt, 120 square feet at 9 feet high.

High pressure sodium lights can be mounted safely in any position, a real advantage in rooms with low ceilings.

Low pressure sodium (LPS) is the ugly duckling of the HID family and I mention it because it has been used for successful crops much to everyone's surprise. It is the most efficient commercially used light source, producing 180 lumens per watt in the 180-watt size. The lamp is three feet long, with a significant amount of sodium in it and takes a special socket and ballast.

Its 32,000 lumen output and large size make it a borderline solution because it must be hung too low over the soil. Its spectrum is mainly orange and nothing else. The cost is high and, if broken, the sodium inside can explode if it comes in contact with water.

In a scientific paper presented to the American Society of Agricultural Engineers in 1975, Dr. Cathy of the USDA labs in Maryland showed the effectiveness of LPS for growing. Even though the spectrum is mono-chromatic, if low levels of full-spectrum light (daylight or incandescent) were present, the plants grew very well. If the low level of full-spectrum light was missing, the plants still grew but abnormally. The LPS/incandescent combination was slightly better than any other light system used in the environmental chambers.

The experiments indicate that spectrum may be of less importance than it was once believed to be. If low-level light needs are met, high levels of excess wave lengths will be used by the plants.

Using HIDs

A timer is a must with any light system. Random day length hurts plant development as does continuous light. My recommendation is 15 hours maximum for starting, down to 11 hours for flowering for light hungry annuals. Plants will not flower with continuous HID light.

A combination of MH and HPS gives a full spectrum from ultraviolet to infrared. The two reinforce each other, one being strong where the other is weak. Either source of light is excellent alone, too. There is now a conversion sodium bulb that will light up in a halide ballast. The 360- and 940-watt sodium uses a 400- and 1000-watt (respectively) halide ballast. Iwasaki Electric Ltd. of Japan makes the bulbs. The regular halide bulb can be used during vegetative growth and switched to the Iwasaki for flowering periods.

Home growers should not try too large a setup. For most residential electric service, 4,000 to 5,000 watts is the most that should be used without some alterations to the wiring in and out of the house. That includes all of the electrical devices in the house, not just the plant lighting. The transformer feeding the house from the pole is usually good for 10,000 watts total load. Use common sense! Go to the library or local book store and find a book on household electricity and read it. Understand the power you are dealing with. If you are in doubt, consult a professional. It may be advisable to have a dedicated circuit installed for your greenhouse or grow room.

A dedicated 20-amp 120-volt circuit will run a 1000-watt and a 400- or 360-watt unit. The same circuit will run three 400- or 360-watt units, if each one is started 30 to 60 seconds after the other. Three small units started all at once can trip the circuit breaker because more power is drawn as they start up.

Ballasts are better remotely mounted from the light in indoor grow rooms. In greenhouses, ballasts can be mounted behind horizontal reflectors. The weight of a 1000-watt HPS ballast is 45 pounds. A 400-watt ballast could weigh as little as 10 pounds. Follow the manufacturer's recommendations for positioning and mounting.

Sometimes a lamp will burn even though the outer glass is broken. It should be turned off immediately. The bare arc tube could explode and emit a lot of hard UV radiation. Never change lamps or move them with the power on, or burn metal halide lamps tilted with open reflectors. Don't turn HID lights off and on at random. Use a 60-watt regular light bulb on a separate circuit for a walk light in the greenhouse.

Heat from the lights can be blown away by a fan in the summer. In the winter, if the lights are operated at night, the heat will keep the growing space — maybe even the whole house — at a comfortable temperature.

This article was first published in Volume 1 Number 1, page 48.

LEDS — LIGHTING THE FUTURE?

Providing adequate light for photosynthesis, whether in an orbiting space station or a lunar colony, presents a major challenge to NASA researchers. While High Intensity Discharge (HID) lights are used for some ground based research, the lights and the ballasts necessary to operate them are too delicate, too heavy and too power hungry to be practical for use in space.

For the time being, fluorescent lights are the best alternative, according to project manager David Bubenheim of NASA's Controlled Ecological Life Support Systems program at the Ames Research Center near Palo Alto, California. But a new technology based on the light-emitting diode (LED) shows promise for future development.

LEDs are known for their use in digital displays on calculators, VCRs and other electronic equipment. (LEDs have been replaced in a number of these applications by LCDs, Liquid Crystal Displays.)

Diodes are semiconducting devices based on the forward movement of electrons across the junction between the anode and cathode. In most diodes the energy produced by this action is given off in the form of waste heat. By using special semiconductive materials to form the junction, the otherwise wasted energy is released in the form of light.

Bubenheim said that LEDs offer several potential advantages over fluorescent lighting. The overall efficiency of LEDs is roughly comparable to fluorescent tubes, which is to say pretty good. Unlike fluorescent tubes, however, the light produced by LEDs moves in only one direction, eliminating the need for efficiency robbing reflectors; virtually all of the available light can be directed toward the plant. LEDs are lighter in weight than fluorescent lights and are extremely rugged and long lived.

LEDs are also more versatile, according to Bubenheim. Up to a point, light output can be increased by increasing the power available to the LED unit. LEDs could be used at lower power

levels, perhaps to power an on-board "kitchen garden" for a trip to Mars, and then be reinstalled for high-output use in the food production facility on the planet.

Individual LEDs are capable of producing light within a very narrow spectral band, similar to laser light. The color of the light is determined by the junction material used — gallium arsenide phosphide for red light; gallium phosphide for yellow or green light; and gallium nitride for blue light. For plant lighting purposes, LEDs could be grouped on panels with the different colors mixed and matched to meet the plant's needs.

This could prove to be one of the greatest advantages of LED plant lights, but there is a glitch. With current technology, blue emitting LEDs are inefficient to operate and expensive to produce.

Since thousands of individual LEDs would be needed for each plant, the cost of LED plant lighting is prohibitive for anything but the most specialized applications. Bubenheim said that the solution is likely to come from the private sector.

Electronics firms in the United States and Japan are pouring tremendous resources into the search for an inexpensive and efficient blue LED because it is the "missing link" in building a flat, tubeless television screen. With that kind of a prize at stake, Bubenheim is confident that an efficient blue LED should be on the market soon.

In the meantime, researchers at the Center for Space Automation and Robotics at the University of Wisconsin, Madison, have had some success using a combination of blue-light fluorescent lights and red LEDs. According to the study, leaf lettuce grown for 21 days from seed under the hybrid LED/fluorescent system performed as well as or better than previously reported growth rates under a combination of cool-white fluorescents and incandescent bulbs. — *Don Parker*

Chapter 5
Plant Varieties

Know Your 'Software' — Plant Selection for the Hydroponic/Greenhouse Gardener

by Don Parker

Picture your own hydroponic vegetable garden: ripe red tomatoes hanging on the vine; spinach, dark green and crunchy; sweet juicy strawberries just waiting for the shortcake to come out of the oven; tender shell peas grouped together in handful sized clusters.

If you think it sounds too good to be true, you're probably right. Despite the potential of controlled environment hydroponic gardening, there are limits imposed by the natural adaptation of various plants to different environmental conditions. The high light levels needed to ripen your hydroponic tomatoes would be more than enough to cause bolting (seed set) of your spinach. Likewise, the high temperatures necessary to ripen strawberries would almost certainly cause your shell peas to wither and die.

It's a hard lesson for most neophyte hydroponic growers that the selection of plants suited to the growing environment — and suited to each other — is probably the most important factor in determining success or failure. While there is plenty of information available on hydroponic hardware — systems, nutrients, lights — selecting the proper genetic "software," plants suited to the hydroponic environment, is the subject of much frustrating trial and error.

Successful outdoor gardeners actually plant several gardens each year. The "early" garden consists of cool weather crops such as peas, spinach and cabbage; the "late" garden of fruiting plants like tomatoes, eggplant and melons. Some species, such as beans and carrots, are able to bridge the gap between the two gardens, as can certain cultivars of typically early or late species. The production of heat tolerant lettuce, for example, can continue for some time after the first early tomatoes are harvested.

Outdoor growers use timing, cultivation techniques and plant selection to provide a variety of produce throughout the season with a minimum of waste. What outdoor growers cannot do is control the environment. It is that ability that provides indoor growers with their greatest opportunity and their greatest challenge. Outdoor growers talk a lot about the weather; indoor and greenhouse growers can do something about it.

The Live-In Plant

Within the broader category of controlled environment gardening there are several types of gardens, each with its own environmental conditions and each presenting a unique challenge to the grower: heated and/or humidity controlled greenhouses or grow rooms with supplemental lighting; unheated greenhouses with or without lighting; and heated spaces indoors.

■ Heated greenhouses and enclosed grow rooms offer the grower maximum control, permitting the cultivation of almost any plant imaginable. In practice, however, there are limits imposed mostly by economic factors. Raising a cool weather crop like spinach in the heat of a Georgia summer, for example, may not be economically feasible due to the high cost maintaining the necessary cool environment.

Cool Greenhouses (50-70 degrees)

Vegetables:	Herbs:
Beets	Chervil
Broccoli	Chives
Brussels Sprouts	Coriander
Cauliflower	Dill
Chard	Lavender
Kohlrabi	Leeks
Lettuce	Mint
(standard types)	Pennyroyal
Onions	Rosemary
Peas	Sage
Radishes	Savory
Spinach	Thyme

A Garden to Call Your Own

Warm Greenhouses (60-85 degrees)

Vegetables:	Melons
Beans	Peppers
Carrots	Strawberries
Chinese Cabbage	Tomatoes
Cucumbers	
Eggplant	Herbs:
Endive	Basil
Lettuce	Lemon Balm
(bolt resistant)	Marjoram
New Zealand	Sage
Spinach	Thyme

Within those limits, it is possible to custom design the environment to suit most plant varieties. In the home garden, where different species are likely to be grown in the same space, the compatibility of the varieties grown with the selected environment and with each other is crucial.

■ Unheated greenhouses impose many of the same seasonal constraints found in outdoor gardens. In cooler climates, the solar powered greenhouse is more of a season extender than a year-round gardening tool.

Depending on day length and winter temperatures, an unheated greenhouse can produce cool weather crops, brassica, lettuce, spinach, etc., from late fall to early spring and warm weather fruiting crops, tomatoes, peppers, etc., several months earlier than the outdoor garden. Unheated greenhouses are also great for starting plants to be transplanted outdoors and sheltering potted plants in the fall.

As with the outdoor garden, the timing of plantings to take advantage of changing environmental conditions is crucial.

■ The indoor environment, be it a pot of herbs in a sunny window sill or a full-sized hydro system in the corner of the living room, is generally maintained by way of central heating and air conditioning to maximize human comfort — not plant growth. For that reason the selection of plants is limited to those species and varieties able to thrive within the narrow set of conditions we define as "the comfort zone."

Fortunately, there are a number of vegetable species that make good live-in companions. Since environmental conditions indoors are generally given, the selection of appropriate species and varieties is crucial indoors.

In general, plant varieties can be divided into two groups: cool weather plants, those that are most comfortable between 50 and 70 degrees; and warm weather plants, those that prefer temperatures of 60 to 85 degrees (see chart at left). Such guidelines can be useful to the beginning grower. The chances of pulling a ripe cantaloupe out of an unheated Minnesota greenhouse in December are just about nil. But hard and fast rules should be treated with skepticism. Controlled environment hydroponic gardening is still a relatively new field; there is much yet to be discovered, even by beginners.

Remember, too, that the hobby gardener is not tied to the experts' notion of "ideal" growing conditions. In the home vegetable garden the "good enough" standard may be, well, good enough. Some plants will produce less than optimal yields under certain conditions, but still produce edible material. As a hobby gardener, the most important consideration has got to be the pleasure derived from growing and consuming your own produce, not the yield per foot.

Plant the kinds of things that *you* like, especially species that offer a great improvement over the store-bought alternatives. Tomatoes, lettuce, beans, peppers and herbs are good examples. On the other hand, your hydroponic garden could do little to improve on the quality or price of store-bought potatoes or turnips. It is also possible to grow more exotic varieties and species that may not be available at any price in your area.

Explore, innovate, enjoy. Try at least one or two things that aren't "supposed" to work, just for the experience. And remember to plant some flowers.

The following is a list of species suitable for indoor and/or hydroponic culture along with different cultivars recommended by individual growers, garden writers and seed producers for that purpose. Some were selected based on descriptions provided by the seller and are not necessarily "recommended" for hydroponic cultivation. (Cultivars listed here are based on those available when the article was written in the spring of 1990. Check with your seed supplier for current offerings.)

Beans (pole type)

Fortex	Northeaster
Kentucky Wonder	Romano

- While not as sensitive to cool nighttime temperatures as tomatoes and peppers, green beans require warmer conditions and relatively high light levels for maximum yields. Because of their versatility, beans can be grown through much of the year in unheated greenhouses in most areas, as well as indoors.
- Bush varieties are more compact, but pole varieties can produce several times the quantity from a given space, an important consideration in greenhouses and hydroponic systems. Train pole beans up strings, welded wire fencing or nylon netting, taking care that the fast growing plants do not shade their neighbors.
- Bean seeds may rot if planted too deeply. On the other hand, light exposure can reduce germination rates. When planting in starter cubes, place a small square of paper over the seed to protect from direct light until the seedling emerges. Sow the seed directly into loose media such as perlite. Optimum temperature for germination, 75 degrees (24 C).
- Beans are especially susceptible to overwatering. A well-drained medium is essential.
- Beans are light nitrogen feeders but can consume large quantities of phosphorous and potassium. Solutions high in nitrogen will produce lush vegetative growth at the expense of bean production.
- Harvest beans aggressively to extend production. The presence of overripe beans on the vines will stop flowering and the production of new beans.
- Compatible plants: radishes, summer savory, carrots and cucumbers.
- Incompatible plants: kohlrabi, shallots, onions, fennel and garlic.

Brassica (cabbage family)

Broccoli:	**Chinese cabbage:**
Green Comet	Lettucy Type
	Nerva
Cauliflower:	Michihli
Snow King	
Snowcrown	**Brussels sprouts:**
	Jade Cross

The members of the Brassica family are generally cool weather crops and difficult to grow in heated spaces. All prefer moderate light levels and a well-drained and aerated medium.

- Optimum temperature range for germination: 71 to 86 degrees (21-30 C), 66 to 81 degrees (19-27 C) for cauliflower.
- Brassica plants are heavy feeders, especially of nitrogen and phosphorous. Excessive nitrogen, on the other hand, can cause bitterness. Mix and monitor your solution carefully and replace regularly.
- High temperatures combined with high light levels can induce bolting (premature seed set), especially in broccoli. In warm environments, select slow-bolting varieties when possible.
- Compatible plants: All members of the Brassica family flourish when interplanted with aromatic herbs. In addition, herbs can repel insect pests that can plague cabbages. Brassica species are also fond of onions.
- Incompatible plants: beans, strawberries and tomatoes.

Carrots

Baby Spike	Parisien
Caramba	Parmex
Carrot Sucram	Planet
Little Finger	Short 'n' Sweet
Minicor	

- Carrots grow well in warmer (not hot) conditions, but can tolerate relatively cool nighttime temperatures, making them a good choice for both greenhouse and indoor gardens. They require only modest light levels and can be used to fill spaces beneath taller plants.
- Because they are a root crop, carrots can only be grown hydroponically in a loose medium such as perlite with a depth of 6 to 12 inches, depending on variety. For the same reason, it is best to grow only globe or half-long varieties.
- Carrots require a well aerated medium and a solution rich in potassium and phosphorous. Excessive nitrogen can cause bitterness and splitting.
- Plant carrots directly into the medium and thin as they emerge. Carrot seed can take up to several weeks to sprout. Optimum temperature for germination: 86 degrees (30 C).
- Compatible plants: onions, lettuce, radishes and most aromatic herbs. Carrots are a good choice for underplanting with pole beans.
- Incompatible plants: Avoid planting carrots with dill.

Cucumbers

Seedless	Toska-70
(all female):	
Aricia	**Seeded:**
Aurelia	Famosa
Corona	Fidelio
Farbio	Flamingo
Farbiola	Marillo
Farona	Salad Bush
Petita	Saria
Pioneer	Spacemaster
Sandra	

- Cucumbers thrive under conditions of moderate light and high humidity. The drying effect of central heating can make cucumbers difficult to grow in living spaces, although with proper care greenhouse crops can be impressive.
- The plants need plenty of water and will not tolerate even brief periods of dryness.
- Cucumbers are notorious space hogs and some kind of training and trellising will be needed to get the most out of limited spaces. Cage cucumbers like tomatoes or string like pole beans.
- Seeded varieties produce both male and female flowers. Don't be alarmed if early flowers (usually male) shrivel and fall; only the female flowers produce fruit. So-called "all female" (gynocious) plants are available. These varieties, called "forcing cucumbers," will set fruit without pollination and tend to produce fewer and smaller seeds.
- If your greenhouse is cool, provide root zone heat until your plants are well established. NFT tubes or rockwool slabs on concrete floors may need to be placed on foam boards for insulation. Optimum temperature for germination: 75 degrees (24 C).
- In greenhouses, plant seed in late summer for winter harvest.
- Compatible plants: beans, peas, lettuce and radishes.
- Incompatible plants: Some growers report stunted growth when planted near aromatic herbs.

Eggplant

Asian:	**Standard:**
Ichiban	Agora
Little Fingers	Moneymaker
Millionaire	Prelane
Orient Express	
Tycoon	

- Eggplant will grow well in any environment suitable to tomatoes or peppers as long as cool nighttime temperatures (below 60 degrees) are avoided. High light levels and long day lengths are essential to successful fruit production.
- The Asian varieties are more compact and suitable for small spaces. The small fruit ripen 10 to 15 days earlier than standard varieties.
- Seeds are slow to germinate and may require bottom heat. Optimum temperature for germination: 86 degrees (30 C).
- Eggplants are heavy feeders and prefer a concentrated nutrient solution (high ppm reading) with a pH of between 5.5 and 6.5. If possible, reduce nitrogen concentration after flowers begin to form.

- For larger fruits, pinch off some flowers leaving only a few per branch. If fruit development appears to stall, it may be necessary to remove smaller fruits. Eggplants keep very well on the vine and take some time to become overripe; pick fruits only as needed.
- Compatible plants: Eggplant appears comfortable in the company of most aromatic herbs. Some growers recommend underplanting with endive.
- Incompatible plants: With larger plantings, avoid placing tomatoes with other members of the nightshade family (peppers and tomatoes) to avoid the transfer of common diseases.

Lettuce and Salad Greens

Endive:	Baby Bib
Broadleaved	Tom Thumb
Bavarian #5	Watercress
Salad King	
	Cool spaces:
Warm spaces:	Anuenue
Black Seeded	Apollo
Simpson	Baby Oak
Buttercrunch	Buttercrunch
Capitane	Canasta
Curly Cress	Diamante
Green	Lollo Rosa
Mignonette	May Queen
Kegran Summer	Morgana
Mirena	Oakleaf
Oakleaf	Red Salad Bowl
Ostinata	Salad Bowl
Summer	Salina

- Generally a good plant for cool, humid conditions, although some varieties are more heat tolerant. Plants should be shaded from intense sunlight to prevent bolting. In bed type systems, low growing lettuce may be planted between and under tomato or cucumber plants to maximize the use of space. In heated spaces, look for "summer" or very slow bolting varieties or substitute with endive.
- Although they are light feeders, lettuce needs adequate nitrogen to reach its potential in hydroponic systems. The plants are especially sensitive to root problems caused by poor drainage.
- Lettuce seeds need both light and moisture to germinate. Some lettuce varieties germinate poorly at room temperature and must be kept in a cool place. Optimum temperature for germination: 60-75 degrees (16-24 C).
- Lettuce can be close cropped in hydroponic systems and the outer leaves harvested as they mature.
- In greenhouses, lettuce should be planted in mid-fall for winter harvest. Plant every couple of weeks through December for a continuous supply.
- Compatible plants: tomatoes, carrots and radishes.
- Incompatible plants: An amiable plant, lettuce appears to have no real enemies.

Melons

Cantaloupe:	**Charentais melons (French):**
Chaca	
Earlisweet	Flyer
Hybrid Alaska	Savor
Itsy Bitsy	
Sweetheart	**Watermelon:**
Minnesota	Early Canadian
Midget	Garden Baby
Sweet Granite	Sugar Baby
Sweet 'n' Early	You Sweet Thing

- Although notoriously troublesome, melons should grow in any environment suitable for tomatoes or peppers as long as cool nighttime temperatures (below 60 degrees) are avoided. High light levels and long day lengths are essential to successful fruit production.
- Bottom heating with cables, especially for young plants, may be required in some environments. Optimum temperature for germination: 95 degrees (35 C).
- Melons are susceptible to fungal attack, especially by fusarium. Plant seedlings in a sterilized medium and avoid conditions of high humidity. Provide adequate ventilation.
- Melons are heavy feeders and it is important to keep a close eye on nutrient concentrations. If possible, reduce nitrogen content after flowers begin to form.
- Melons, like their cousins cucumbers, are space hogs and some kind of training or trellising may be necessary. Because of their sprawling habit, watermelons may not be practical in any but the most spacious grow rooms. Select "midget" varieties where space is valuable.
- In enclosed spaces, melons must be hand pollinated. Gently brush the inside of open flowers with a small paint brush or cotton swab.

107

- Compatible plants: The presence of morning glory is said to stimulate the germination of melon seed.

Peppers

Ariane	Lipstick
Bell Boy	Locas
Cadice Bell	Luteus
Cubico	Plutona
Delgado	Ringer
Evident	Samanta
Gold Crest	Spartacus
Latino	

- Peppers, like most fruiting annuals, benefit from direct lighting and relatively warm temperatures, making them a good choice for indoor gardens. Bottom heat may be necessary in some greenhouses.
- Optimum temperature for germination: 86 degrees (30 C).
- Peppers tend to suffer more from overfertilization than a lack of nutrients. High nitrogen levels will, at best, result in reduced fruit set. At worst, excessive nitrogen will cause curling and browning of upper leaves. With chemical based nutrients, flush regularly to reduce salt build up.
- Peppers prefer a neutral to slightly acid solution (pH 5.5-6.4). Alkaline conditions will result in stunted plants and reduced fruit set. Extreme acid conditions, can contribute to blossom-end rot, especially in water stressed plants.
- Pepper plants, especially those grown indoors, are brittle and easily damaged by rough handling.
- Compatible plants: Okra is the traditional companion plant for peppers. The plants also do well in the company of most aromatic herbs.
- Incompatible plants: With larger plantings, avoid placing peppers with other members of the nightshade family (tomatoes and eggplant), to avoid the transfer of common diseases.

Tomatoes

Determinate varieties:	Caruso
Celebrity	Danny
Floramerica	Dombo
Gem State	Early Girl
Laura	Fireball
Pixie	Firebird
Starfire	First Lady
Sub-arctic Maxi	Perfecto
Sub-arctic Plenty	Sierra
Superb Super	Tuckcross
	Vendor
Indeterminate varieties:	Cherry tomatoes:
Beefmaster	Cheresita
Better Boy	Evita
Big Boy	Gold Nugget
Buffalo	Tiny Tim
Capello	Whippersnapper

- Even short season tomato varieties benefit from lots of direct sunlight or high-powered artificial lighting in enclosed spaces. Generally, the higher the light level, the better the yield.
- Plants prefer warmer daytime temperatures — 60 degrees is about the minimum — and about 50 percent humidity. Optimum temperature for germination: 75 degrees (24 C).
- Low growing determinate varieties are recommended for indoor cultivation. Determinate varieties set fruit on the terminal bud and generally produce more fruit without pruning. Indeterminate varieties are more suited to large greenhouses; some pruning may be necessary to train or contain the plants.
- Symptoms of iron and/or calcium deficiency are fairly common with hydroponically grown tomatoes, although the culprit is usually poor root action and not a lack of these minerals in the solution. A fast draining medium and proper aeration should help.
- Tomato plants often require hand pollination indoors. Gently brush the inside of open flowers with a small paint brush or cotton swab.
- If you use tobacco products, wash hands well before handling tomato plants to avoid infection with tobacco mosaic virus.
- In greenhouses, plant seed in late summer for winter harvest.
- Compatible plants: basil, chives, garlic, parsley, marigold, nasturtium, carrot and lettuce. Alkaloids found in the leaves of tomato plants repel some crop damaging insects. Interplanting with garlic can provide some protection against red spider mites, a common and serious problem with tomatoes indoors.
- Incompatible plants: Tomatoes have a decided antipathy for members of the brassica family (cabbage, broccoli, kale, turnip, etc.). Fennel can

also stunt the growth of tomato plants if planted too closely. With larger plantings, avoid placing tomatoes with other members of the nightshade family (peppers and eggplant), to avoid the transfer of common diseases.

Spinach

True spinach:	Nordic[S]
Broadleaved Summer[W]	Tyee[S]
Indian Summer[J]	**False spinach:**
Italian Summer [S]	New Zealand[B,N]
Longstanding Bloomsdale[D,G]	Malabar[N]
	Tetragonia
Medania[S]	Expansa[W]

- A natural in cool greenhouses, spinach is tricky to grow in heated spaces. New Zealand and Malabar could be good alternatives indoors. Otherwise, choose a summer or heat tolerant variety. True spinach is very sensitive to photoperiod; even a night light or distant street light can cause young plants to bolt.
- Spinach seed is a slow starter. Score spinach seeds with a file or sandpaper to speed germination. Optimum temperature for germination: 70 degrees (21 C).
- Spinach, like most leafy greens, is a heavy nitrogen feeder. Yellowing at the edges of older leaves may indicate a deficiency.
- For maximum production in hydroponic gardens, harvest outer leaves as they mature. Not only will this provide you with more greens over a longer period of time, but will reduce the plant's natural tendency to go to seed.
- Spinach may be interplanted with strawberries. Spinach roots produce saponin, a mild wetting agent that can improve the nutrient uptake of other plants in soils.

First published in Volume One Number Four, page 29.

Hydroponic Herbs at Home

by Don Parker

Few people who have smelled and tasted fresh herbs are likely to be satisfied with the dried product. While an increasing number of food stores across the country have begun to stock fresh herbs, high prices, limited selection and poor quality continue to make home cultivation an attractive alternative. Because of their high value and ease of handling, perhaps no group of plants is more suited to indoor cultivation than culinary herbs.

An indoor herb garden can be something as simple as a soil-filled planter placed in a sunny location, perhaps a kitchen window. But the true herb lover is likely to outgrow this arrangement and larger, indoor herb gardens are better suited to the use of hydroponic techniques.

Herbs can be divided into two groups: annuals and perennials. But for the indoor grower a more useful classification is by optimum growing temperatures. Some herbs grow poorly or set seed too quickly in heated spaces indoors, while others thrive under the warm and dry conditions found in most homes. Greenhouse conditions can be altered to suit a variety of plants, but for indoor growers it is best to stick with the heat-loving varieties, a group including some of the most popular herbs such as basil, marjoram, oregano, sage, thyme and lemon balm.

Dill, chives parsley, rosemary, tarragon and mint may also be grown indoors with a little more attention to environmental conditions. Beginners would be well advised to stick with more reliable herbs.

Getting Located

Finding a suitable location for your indoor herb garden is an essential first step as it can influence the choice of plants and the best system to use. An area near a sunny window (facing south to southwest) in or adjacent to the kitchen is considered ideal by most gardeners. If you have such a spot available, great. If not, don't despair. As long as you choose your location carefully and match the equipment to the space you have, your hydroponic herb garden can be an attractive and functional addition to your home.

Adequate lighting is a primary consideration in choosing a location for your garden. If there are no sunny windows in your kitchen area, a well-maintained hydroponic herb garden can be an attractive addition to the living room, dining room, or recreation area. Most hydroponic systems allow the movement of plants, even mature plants, into and out of the system. Plants can be started in a nursery, perhaps in a utility room, and transplanted into the living room system to fill in open spaces and replace diseased or overmature plants.

If direct, natural lighting is not an option, you will need to provide artificial light. Generally, herbs do not need the intense light necessary for many vegetable plants such as tomatoes; a 4-foot, two-tube fluorescent fixture fitted with full-spectrum tubes should be enough to provide supplemental lighting for a small garden. Place fluorescent lights 12 to 18 inches above the garden and run on a 14-hour cycle.

Selecting a System

Even in soils, herbs require only a minimum of care and attention from the grower. A self-regulating hydroponic system can simplify the process even further.

Of course, self-regulation does not necessarily mean a lot of expensive high-tech equipment. For a small herb garden a basic wick system, for example, can be very effective, easy to set up and operate, if a few rules are observed.

One of the most important considerations for hydroponic herb growing is water control. With a few notable exceptions, most herbs are intolerant of excessive moisture, which can result in root problems and stunted growth. Fortunately, most hydroponic systems permit some degree of control over the quantity of solution delivered to the roots. With drip systems and flood systems, it is a good idea to reduce the duration and/or frequency of watering cycles. With wick systems, it may be necessary to remove a portion of the wicking material to slow the flow of solution up to the plant roots.

The selection of a particular system will depend in part on the availability of materials and grower preference. If floor space is precious, vertical growing tubes suspended in a window can provide plenty of fresh herbs (see "An Orchard of Lettuce Trees," page 29). For a larger, freestanding garden, a drip irrigated bed of expanded clay or perlite would be a good choice. Rockwool based systems also work well as long as steps are taken to avoid excessive root zone moisture that can cause damping off and other problems.

Getting Started

Many herbs can be easily and inexpensively started from seed in flats filled with perlite or another aggregate or in individual plugs or cubes. Some herb seeds are quite small and can be sprinkled over the growing medium and gently pressed into the surface. Use caution when handling commercially prepared seed; many are treated with powerful fungicides. Wash hands after handling seeds and keep fingers away from eyes and mouth.

Some herbs require light for germination, such as basil, lemon balm and mint. Others prefer darkness. If you are starting a large number of different herbs at once, you may want to use two flats, one covered with clear plastic and another covered with a square of plywood or some other opaque material. Replace the plywood with clear plastic as soon as the seedlings begin to emerge.

Maintain ambient nursery temperatures of 65 to 75 degrees. Root zone temperatures of 70 to 72 degrees are ideal for germination. Use heating cables if necessary to avoid any "cold feet."

Use plain water on seeds for a few days before switching to a half-strength nutrient solution. Water applied to the surface of a seed flat can disturb delicate seedlings. If possible, it is best to water seed flats from the bottom. A flat with bottom drainage holes can be lowered into a larger pan or other container filled with water or solution. Allow growing medium to absorb the liquid for 20 to 30 minutes and then drain.

Place full-spectrum fluorescent tubes 12 to 16 inches above emerging plants on a minimum 12-hour cycle. Thin the seed bed as the plants begin to compete for the available light, generally after the third or fourth set of true leaves appear.

Most herbs can be planted closely in hydroponic units. Recommended soil planting distances should be reduced by half or more. Generally, it is better to start with a dense planting and remove plants as needed.

Inspect plants daily for signs of nutrient imbalance and insect damage. Cull or isolate plants at the first sign of disease. Extra caution is advised when using control chemicals, including botanical insecticides, indoors.

Cultivation

An "herb," of course, is not a type of plant. Herbs are a diverse group of plants used for flavoring food and/or for medicinal purposes. Different herbs require different cultivation techniques and yield different results indoors. The following is a list of some of the most commonly used culinary herbs with specific information on cultivation and uses:

Basil
(Ocimum basilicum)

A member of the mint family, this annual herb is one of the most popular for home cultivation. Basil prefers a bit more light than some other herbs. Outdoors, basil will grow to a height of 12 to 18 inches. In heated spaces indoors it is better to prune plants vigorously to maintain a compact shape and to head off premature flowering.

Basil can be started from seed; it is also remarkably easy to start from cuttings. Since it is an annual, it is best to rotate mature plants with new stock from seed. Use cuttings to fill in gaps left by spent plants.

Basil is said to repel houseflies, but seems to have just the opposite effect on whiteflies and aphids. Inspect plants regularly, especially the undersides of leaves. Use sticky traps to monitor whitefly populations and to slow possible infestations.

Because of its popularity, a number of varieties of basil have been developed with different flavors and colors. The flavored basils are quite good eaten raw in salads. Deep purple basil can add color to your indoor herb garden, but most cooks prefer the more robust flavor of the green varieties. Basil may be dried or frozen for later use.

Chives
(*Allium schoenoprasum*)

A member of the onion family, chives are one of the easiest of all herbs to grow indoors. The slender grass like shoots can grow up to a foot tall indoors, although few plants are likely to reach that height.

Chives can be grown from seed. Simply sprinkle the fine seeds on the starting medium and press gently into the surface. Mature chives can be lifted from the growing medium and the roots separated to form new plants. Because of its small root structure and blade like shape, chives can be planted densely in hydroponic systems.

Chives may be clipped for fresh use with a sharp knife or scissors. Although chives can be dried, the resulting product is nearly tasteless. Fortunately, chives are easy enough to grow that there is no reason not to keep a fresh supply on hand.

Dill
(*Anethum graveolens*)

This annual herb can reach a height of three feet outdoors. Even with vigorous pruning indoors one or two dill plants can easily get out of hand. In addition, mature dill plants tend to have a rather unkempt appearance that some growers will find objectionable indoors.

Still, for the true devotee of this pungent herb, the rewards can be worth the effort. If your experience with this herb is limited to pickles you would do well to try the fresh product in salads or on fish before dismissing it entirely.

Dill does not transplant well and should be started from seed in the main growing system. Dill germinates quickly and easily, so take care not to over plant. Unless your system is huge (or you are especially fond of dill) thin to one or two plants. Heavy pruning will be a must with most indoor systems. Dry the clippings and store in a moisture proof container for later use.

Marjoram
(*Origanum marjorana*)

Grown as an annual plant outdoors throughout much of the United States, marjoram may be grown as a perennial plant indoors. It can be started from root division indoors, but many growers report better results from seed.

Marjoram is closely related to oregano (sometimes called wild marjoram), although its flavor is more delicate

Mint
(*Mentha cordifolia*)

Mint is one of the most vigorous of all perennial herbs and does very well in hydroponic culture. In fact, it does so well that it will, in a very short time, strangle all the other herbs out of your garden and clog the system with a mass of tough and hard to remove roots. Mint propagates itself by underground runners that can spread to other parts of your system in a matter of weeks.

On the plus side, mint is wonderful as a garnish and herbal tea. It is also used as a spice in some Asian recipes. The growing plants impart an aroma to stale indoor air that is clean and refreshing. It makes a delicious and relaxing tea that is often mentioned as a home remedy for insomnia.

If you must have this herb, plant it in a separate system or in a soil filled pot to place near your main garden. It is best to use prestarted plants or borrow a rooted section of runner from a friend. Mint is fairly tolerant of low light levels, although it does tend to flower prematurely indoors. Pinch off flowers as they appear to maintain a low, bushy look.

Oregano
(*Origanum vulgare*)

No Herb garden would be complete without this popular perennial. "Italian" varieties tend to be more flavorful, although a low-growing "Greek" variety (*Origanum heracleoticum*) may be more suitable for indoor use.

Oregano may be started from seed, but the best results are obtained by dividing mature plants or stem cuttings from new growth. Oregano is generally carefree, but can suffer from excessive moisture. Use a light, well drained medium and reduce watering cycles if necessary.

For fresh use, simply clip leaves as needed. Oregano may be dried or frozen for later use.

Parsley
(*Petroselinum crispum*)

Because it thrives in cool, damp conditions, parsley can present some challenges to the indoor gardener. Grown as a biennial outdoors, parsley is better treated as an annual indoors as the plants tend to bolt easily in their second year.

Parsley seed is very slow to germinate — according to one old tale, the seeds must go to the devil and back nine times before they will sprout. Soaking the seeds for 24 hours or scoring the outer surface to facilitate water uptake before planting are recommended by some growers.

Parsley needs plenty of water, a condition that could cause problems if it is planted with other herbs. Under low humidity conditions, parsley should be misted periodically to prevent drying and wilting.

Rosemary
(*Rosemarinus officinalis*)

With its spine-like leaves and gray-green color, rosemary is one of the most attractive of the culinary herbs. In a warm climate outdoors this perennial can grow as high has 5 feet. Even when grown indoors with heavy pruning, rosemary can get quite large. If space is limited, you may want to forego this one for your indoor garden.

Propagation from seed is painfully slow and the seedlings lack vigor. Propagation from stem cuttings is the preferred method, although it can take some skill and patience.

Like many other herbs, rosemary is sensitive to overwatering. Use a well drained medium and adjust watering schedules as needed. It is also easily damaged by the excessive nitrogen found in some hydroponic formulas.

Rosemary is susceptible to attack from whiteflies, although the pest will probably appear first on basil if both plants are present. Inspect plants regularly for insects and damage.

Sage
(*Salvia officinalis*)

This perennial herb will grow up to 30 inches tall outdoors, but is easily maintained at 12 to 16 inches indoors with pruning. Germination is slow, up to two weeks, but the seedlings are sturdy and transplant well.

While many herbs do not tolerate excessive moisture, sage is especially sensitive. A poorly drained medium can result in arrested growth and the development of fungal diseases of the roots and stem. Sage, like basil, requires higher light levels for healthy growth.

Tarragon
(*Artemesia dracunculus*)

One taste of fresh tarragon and you will forget all of the time and effort spent putting together your indoor herb garden.

This perennial herb requires adequate light and a well-drained medium. Otherwise the plant requires little special care other than regular pruning.

True tarragon, "French tarragon," is never grown from seed and must be purchased as a prestarted plant, or obtained from a friend. The tarragon sold in seed packets is so-called "Russian tarragon" (*Artemesia dracunculoides*), a poor substitute for the real thing.

Thyme
(*Thymus vulgaris*)

Thyme is another perennial herb that should be handled much like sage — lots of light and very little water. Thyme is more sensitive than some herbs to high acid conditions.

There are numerous varieties of thyme available to the home gardener, although all are some form of either "French," or "English" thyme. French thyme is slightly larger and is easily propagated from seed. English thyme is usually propagated from cuttings. Because of its more compact habit, English thyme may be more suitable for indoor cultivation.

First published in Volume 2 Number 3.

A Rose is a Rose …
Understanding Plant Names

by Joelle Steele

If you work with plants, you probably already know how confusing all of those Latin plant names can be, particularly if you don't know what they mean. Many growers undoubtedly consider the use of Latin names unnecessary, perhaps even a little snobbish. If a rose is a rose, does it really matter that it is also a member of the genus *Rosa* of the family Rosaceae and the order Rosales?

Understanding botanical classifications, however, is more than an exercise in vocabulary building. Taxonomy is the science of the classification of organisms into categories based on common characteristics. To understand the taxonomy of plants is to gain insight into the relationships of plant species and groups to each other.

This taxonomic system is called the International Code of Botanical Nomenclature (ICBN) and was invented by Swedish botanist Carl von Linne. It was first published in 1753 and is revised periodically to eliminate errors or confusion that can arise from misunderstandings or misidentifications, and to ensure that new plants are properly classified. This system of using a generic name and a specific epithet is called binomial (two name) nomenclature.

The following is an explanation of the hierarchy of taxonomic ranks beginning with the largest and highest level of classification, the kingdom, and ending with individual species and their hybrids and cultivars:

■ **Kingdoms** are the highest level in taxonomy. Traditionally, all living organisms are placed in either the Plantae (plant) or Animalia (animal) kingdoms, though in recent years other kingdoms have been suggested for certain kinds of fungi and unicellular organisms.

■ **Phylum** or division is the category of highest magnitude within a kingdom. The Latin names of phyla begin with a capital letter and end in "phyta," such as Spermatophyta (seed-bearing plants) and Pteridophyta (non-seed-bearing vascular plants).

- **Class** or association is a category consisting of plant communities within a phylum. Each class consists of plants with similar vegetation that have certain other characteristics in common. The Latin names of classes begin with a capital letter and end in "etum."

- **Order** is a major category in the taxonomic hierarchy and is composed of groups of families. Groups of similar orders are placed in classes. Latin names of orders begin with a capital letter and end in either "ales" (Rosales or Geraniales) or in "ae" (Rosae or Tubiflorae).

- **Family** is a major category comprised of groups of similar genera. Families represent the highest natural grouping. Their Latin names are capitalized and end in "aceae," except for eight groupings that end in "ae" such as Leguminosae (legumes) and Palmae (palms). Some other common families include: Araceae (aroids), Bromelioideae (bromeliads) and Moraceae (figs).

- **Sub-family** is a classification consisting of similar tribes.

- **Tribe** is a term applied to groups of similar genera within a large family. Their Latin names are capitalized and end in "eae."

- **Sub-tribe** is a classification consisting of similar genera within a tribe. The names are capitalized and end in "inae."

- **Genus** is a group of homogeneous species. The generic name forms the first part of the Latin binomial name and is usually singular, capitalized and lacking a uniform ending. Collections of similar genera are usually grouped into families. Large genera such as *Rhododendron* may be further divided into sections, series, subgenera, subsection and subseries. The name of a genus is usually written in italics and may be followed by the name of a person, the author. If the author's name follows a species or subspecies, it indicates the person who proposed the name. If it is in parenthesis, it means that the species or subspecies was originally placed in some other genus.

- **Species** is the fundamental unit of taxonomy. It forms the second part of the binomial name and is always written in lower case. The ending always agrees with the gender of the generic name.

- **Subspecies** is a group consisting of several biotypes which are a form of a species, usually defined by geographical region or range. Subspecies may share a common origin and display only slight differences.

- **Variety** is a category which consists of variants that may or may not have a specific geographical distribution. For example, a variety may exhibit a difference in color but share other characteristics and the same range with other members of the species or subspecies.

- **Forma** or form is the lowest rank normally used. It distinguishes variants of a subspecies or varieties, usually by a single characteristic such as albino flowers within a population of colored flowers.

- **Sports** are atypical forms of an individual or part of an individual due to mutation or segregation.

- **Cultivars** are cultivated varieties (culti-var) produced by human manipulations that usually do not occur in nature. Cultivar names are capitalized and enclosed in single quotes, as in 'Warnecki,' 'Silver Queen,' or 'Mauna loa.'

- **Hybrids** are produced from genetically different parents of the same or different species. Hybrids bred from different species are usually sterile. Those produced from within the same species are usually vigorous but may pose problems for commercial growers because they do not always breed true. You can recognize a hybrid name because it consists of two species names linked by an "x," such as *Philodendron* x 'Wendimbe.'

- **Common names** are those usually written in English or some language other than Latin, such as the Chinese evergreen which is the common name for *Aglaonema*.

To understand how this system works, consider the popular indoor plant Marble Queen Pothos. It belongs to the family Araceae, a group of mostly tropical plants including philodendron with arrowlike leaves and inconspicuous flowers. It belongs to the genus *Scindapsus* and its species name in binomial nomenclature is *Scindapsus aureus* (aureus means golden). The cultivar name is 'Marble Queen,' hence, its entire botanical name is *Scindapsus aureus* 'Marble Queen.'

Rubber trees offer another example. They belong to the family Moraceae, including fig and mulberry, and the genus *Ficus*. The species name is *Ficus elastica* and the cultivar name 'Decora.' Thus, their full botanical name is *Ficus elastica* 'Decora.'

From these examples you can see that the taxonomy of different plants can tell you a lot about the appearance, habits and culture of individual species or cultivars, as well as providing hints to their origins that can add interest to your gardening. In addition, plant classifications can reduce the confusion that often results from the use of common names that may vary from one region to another or change over time.

First published in Volume Four Number One.

PRONUNCIATION

Pronouncing botanical names can be a challenge to those who have not studied Latin. Even those who have may find some difficulty, since scholars do not agree on which form of Latin to use. This guide is based on the most often used form, that of the 14th Century.

Vowels
In Latin, the vowels are pronounced as follows:

a as in f**a**ll   **e** as in s**e**t
i as in p**i**n   **o** as in v**o**te
u as in f**u**ll

Consonants
In 14th Century Latin, c is pronounced like a k when it precedes a, o, or u. It is pronounced like an s or z when it precedes ae, e, i, oe or y. The letter g is pronounced hard as in "go" when it precedes a, o or u, and becomes a soft j sound before e or i.

Diphthongs
Latin has diphthongs, two-letter combinations that make a slightly different sound:

ai sounds like ah-ee or like the word <u>eye</u>
au sounds like the ou in h<u>ou</u>se
ae sounds like ah-eh   **ei** sounds like the ei in <u>eight</u>
eo sounds like ee-oh   **eu** sounds like eh-oo
ie sounds like ee-eh   **oi** sounds like oh-ee
iu sounds like oo-ee   **oe** sounds like oh-eh

Accents
Proper pronunciation depends on placing the accent on the proper syllable. For two or three syllable names, the accent is usually on the first syllable as in *au´re•us*. Words with more than three syllables have the accent on the next to the last syllable as in *ag•la•o•ne´ma*. Many names are not pronounced this way owing to common usage, but this is, scientifically and scholastically, correct. — *Joelle Steele*

Hardy Kiwi for Every Climate

by Martin P. Waterman

If one could custom design a new fruit for North America, ideally one would want a fruit that could be grown in almost every area and survive with little maintenance. With all the concern there is over pesticide use, it should be disease and pest resistant and ultimately, this new fantasy fruit should produce bountiful harvests that are healthy, delicious and exotic.

Unbelievably, the Kiwi (*Actinidia*) seems to satisfy these and other important requirements which is probably responsible for its meteoric rise in popularity — first as supermarket fruit and then as a popular offering at nurseries and garden centers.

There may be as many as 50 varieties of *Actinidia,* depending on who you believe. There seems to be no argument that there are at least three dozen distinct varieties. And now that more fruit hybridizers are playing with kiwis, we are certain to see many more specially adapted varieties for commercial and home use.

Kiwi History

Actinidia are native to Asia and found from India to the island of Sakhalin. In the wild, they tend to be climbers often growing to over 100 feet long. In China, all parts of the vine are used. The leaves are rich in starch, protein and vitamin C which has made them an ideal food for pigs. The roots are used to make insecticide and the stalks are used to make glue. The plant is also used for herbal cures such as improving blood circulation and lactation, reducing fevers and as a treatment for sprains, contusions and boils.

From its wilderness roots in the wild, kiwi fruit made the journey first to New Zealand and then to the United States in the 1930s. The varieties from New Zealand that were brought to the United States were *A. deliciosa*, a name that replaced the previous *A. chinensis*. The common name, Chinese gooseberry, was also changed along the way to help assist in marketing and promotion.

As perfect as some claim the kiwi to be, it is not without some short-comings. Late spring and early fall frosts can be damaging to the vines. Cats are attracted to the vines which contain a substance similar to that found in catnip. Site selection can sometimes solve the frost problems and a plastic tree guard or similar protection will help to fend off the felines.

It is also important to know that every variety has a different winter chilling requirement. A certain amount of chilling, a given number of hours at below 45 degrees (7 C), is needed to bear a crop.

Cultivation Requirements

Because of their growth habits, some kind of support or trellis system must be used with kiwi. These can be a simple grape trellis, to very elaborate designs that feature the female vines on one overhead level and the male vines for pollination on an upper level (see illustration on page 133). For the home gardener the kiwi lends itself well to use as a landscape plant where it can be trained to climb archways, arbors or up the side of a building.

Kiwis need to be pruned to remain healthy and provide fruit on a regular basis. Pruning balances fruitfulness and vegetative growth, allowing the right amounts of air and sun penetration and directing the vine to grow in the required direction.

The kiwi is not too fussy about its soil requirements. However, soil pH should be maintained between 5.0 and 6.5 and the soil should be able to provide adequate nutrients because kiwis are heavy feeders. The soil will also need to be well drained.

One requirement of all kiwis, particularly in their first year, is a regular supply of water. Watering is also crucial to insure good fruit set. In California, kiwi plantings are among the heaviest water users of any crop due to their expansive leaf area and large root systems.

Varieties

A. Arguta

Probably the greatest determining factor for kiwi survival is choosing the correct variety for your site. The following are the most common and important varieties:

A. arguta is hardy from -10 to -30 degrees (-23 C to -34 C) depending on whether the vine is young or one of the several clones that are damaged at -10 degrees (-23 C). There is a great variation in habit of *A. Arguta* and many growers report different results. *A. Arguta* also goes under the name of "Hardy Kiwi." It is one of the most vigorous of the kiwis. Considerable pruning is necessary to keep it under control.

Argutas have smooth leaves, stems and fruit. The fruit is smaller than the supermarket "fuzzy" kiwi. Fuzzy kiwis also need a pollinator except for the Issai. Many varieties are proving to be popular. *A. arguta Ananasnaja* came from Belgium and features some of the largest fruits of the *argutas*. Ananasnaja translates from Russian to mean "pineapple-like." The Issai, which is self-fertile, is becoming more popular. Coming from Japan, the *A. arguta Issai* features compactness and the ability to produce fruit often the year after planting.

All these good features are not without a down side. The Issai is probably the least hardy of the *argutas*. Another variety developed by Professor Elwyn Meader is named, simply, Meader. The Meader kiwi was selected by him because of its productivity and its sweet, medium sized fruit..

A. deliciosa is really the king of kiwis. It is the kiwi first made popular in New Zealand and is now being grown commercially in many countries, from Chile to Israel. These are the largest fruited kiwis and are also known as fuzzy kiwi. *A. deliciosa* can need at least 220 frost free days and they are only hardy to about 0 degrees (-18 C), depending on the particular variety. Many varieties should have their trunks wrapped so that the bark at the base does not freeze and separate from the trunk.

The most popular variety from New Zealand is the Hayward kiwi. It is adapted to both commercial and backyard use and is noted for its large attractive fruit. Blake is another self-fertile variety but the fruit is smaller than the Hayward — about the size of a small egg. Vincent is a low-chill kiwi for warmer areas of California and Florida. Apparently, Vincent may only require as little as 150 hours of below 45-degree (7 C) temperatures to produce its heavy crops. Another variety worth mentioning is called Saanichton 12 from Canada. This variety, which has been grown on Vancouver Island for over 30 years, is large and sweet and does not suffer too much winter damage. It has proven itself as a good variety for the home grower.

A. kolomitka is the hardiest of the edible species. The kolomitkas have given hope to northern growers because of its ability to survive temperatures of -50 degrees (-65 C). With hardiness like that, it is no wonder that one nursery has named them "Arctic kiwi." The fruit of *A. kolomitka* is smooth skinned rather than fuzzy and can be eaten like a grape when fresh, or a raisin when dried. The green fruit is grape shaped and many people find the flavor better than *A. deliciosa*.

The vine is compact and seldom reaches more than 15 to 20 feet. *A. kolomitka* vines need a pollinator, thus a male vine must be purchased which should pollinate up to a dozen female plants. *Kolomitkas* only need 130 frost-free days for fruit to mature.

There are some unique features particular to the *kolomitkas*. They need shade, even into USDA. zone 4 and cooler climates. This is because they are native to Manchuria and Soviet Asia and are used to a shaded forest environment. Without shading, the leaves of the vines tend to get scorched by the sun. Some growers grow grapes on an overhead trellis system and then let the kiwis grow along lower trellis lines.

Another unique feature is the variegated leaves. These appear on both

SUPPORTING YOUR KIWIS

The kiwi plant is an avid climber and the growing vines need support for proper growth and fruit production. Listed below are a few of the most widely used methods of supporting kiwi.

Building Tips
If you make your trellis so that the top is at least 6 inches above your head, you won't get a sore back or neck from crouching under the trellis and the hanging fruit will be easier to pick.

All materials that will come in contact with the soil should be pressure treated with a copper-based preservative. Creosote and Penta-based materials are toxic to plant roots. Use a high-tensile wire to avoid stretching. — Courtesy Northwoods Nursery, 28696 South Cramer, Molalla, OR 97038 (503) 651-3737

T-Bar Trellis
One of the easiest ways to support the more vigorous species, the T-Bar Trellis is also easily expandable to add more plants. Although it is not particularly attractive, it is a sturdy system and widely used in commercial operations. Note the extra anchoring required.

Fence
Although generally not satisfactory for the more vigorous species (*deliciosa* and *arguta*) the modified fence works quite well for the smaller hardy varieties. In some cases it may be necessary to increase the height of the fence with vertical extensions 5 or 6 feet in length. Strong bracing is important.

Arbor
A more attractive method of support is the arbor. It is also more rigid and more expensive than the T-Bar system. The size is flexible and it also offers a nice shaded area on hot summer days. Since there is no anchoring, it is more compact than the T-Bar system.

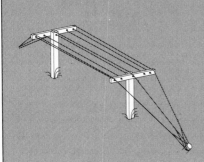

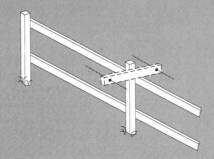

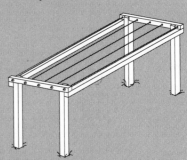

the male and female vines but the male vines are usually more spectacular. The male kolomitka has gone in and out of fashion in the nursery industry, especially in England, as an ornamental because of their beautiful variegated leaves with bands of green, pink and white. *A. kolomitka* is very high in vitamin C and a rich source of minerals and fiber, with a natural sugar content that can go as high as 30 percent.

A. Kolomitka fruit can be easily dislodged by the wind, particularly when it is ripe. However, with yields reported as high as 75 pounds for a mature vine, this may not be an insurmountable problem.

Fruit breeders are already working with the *kolomitka* to lend its hardiness to other *Actinidia* as well as improving existing *kolomitkas*. Of the many varieties available there have been some that have shown some superiority. These include Krupnopladnaya (means "large fruit" in Russian), Arnold Arboretum (a fine quality sweet early ripening variety), and Pautske, selected in Lithuania by plant breeder V. Pautske. Many find the taste of these varieties far superior supermarket kiwis which are not always ripe and have often been stored for an extended time.

A. polygama is hardy to -30 degrees (-34 C) or colder. The fruit tends to be orange in color and the round shaped leaves are often large and variegated. Some of the varieties are self fertile and do not need a male vine in order to set fruit.

The kiwi is as versatile and good tasting as it is fun to grow. About the only thing the kiwi grower is likely to tire of is the constant harping of backyard "experts" who'll tell you that "you can't grow them here." Just smile politely and nod your head; they'll find out soon enough. If you live just about anywhere below timberline and south of the Arctic Circle, chances are that there's a kiwi variety for you.

For More Information

- Actinidia Newsletter, published by The Friends of the Trees Society, PO Box 1466, Chelan, Washington, 98816.
- The North American Fruit Explorers' (NAFEX) Kiwi Fruit Testing Group, Rt. 1 Box 94, Chapin, Illinois, 62628.

Frst published in VolumeThree Number One, page 36

Growing Citrus Indoors

by Martin P. Waterman

When we think of growing of citrus indoors, we naturally think of oranges. This is unfortunate because there are many other types of citrus that will thrive as houseplants. These other citrus varieties deserve consideration for indoor culture.

Experienced indoor citrus growers prefer the limes and lemons because oranges and grapefruit will not achieve high sugar levels indoors. In addition, when you have a small crop you can do a lot more with a flavorful lemon than you can with a sweet orange.

Citrus is known for its shiny green foliage, fragrant white blossoms and attractive fruit throughout the year. Some trees are real attention grabbers. The fragrance can fill an entire home and is one of the foremost reasons why citrus are one of the most desirable of houseplants.

Cultivation

Citrus does not require the high levels of light that doom some other tropical plants to artificial lighting or southern latitudes. However, they do need a good sunny spot. Most growers find that bringing them outdoors in the summer and keeping them in a sunny location in the house in winter will suffice as long as they are not exposed to temperatures of less than 45 degrees (7 C) in winter. Some leaf drop is normal when plants are moved outdoors in the spring or indoors in the fall due to the sudden change in temperature and humidity. The leaves will grow back once the plant is accustomed to the change.

There are differing opinions on the humidity requirements for citrus. Some say that citrus dislikes really dry air. However, citrus has done well in desert conditions and in dry houses in the winter. Citrus will benefit by occasional misting, especially during flower bloom.

Probably the biggest mistake that is made, and it is made quite often, is to feed and water the citrus plant in the winter as if summer conditions still existed. In the winter the plant is semi-dormant and cannot use the excess food and water. Water moderately throughout the year making sure that the surface dries between waterings.

All types of soil mixes are used for citrus. Many growers start with a premixed soil such as Promix and then add ground clay, colloidal phosphate and greensand. However, I have had good luck with just plain potting mix.

Young plants do best in 1- or 2-gallon containers for several years. Root restriction is the key to successful indoor container grown plants. If citrus is placed in a container that is too large, there will be rapid outward root growth and the plant will respond with too much rapid growth. Every three years, preferably in the spring, consider repotting your citrus.

At the start of new growth when the leaves are half size, some growers will apply fertilizer in the form of a foliar spray with trace elements. If the tree is indoors during the bloom period, you should shake it to insure better pollination. You can also take a small artist's paint brush and pollinate by brushing from flower to flower.

A tomato type of fertilizer (rich in potash) is a good food for citrus during the growing season. Apply at two-week intervals. If the trees turn yellow, this could indicate an iron deficiency. This may be corrected by using a plant food that has iron. A special citrus fertilizer is also available from some mail-order nurseries and garden centers.

Pests are usually not a serious problem, but Wayne Chadwick, greenhouse manager at the Raintree Nursery, says that scale can be a problem with indoor citrus. He reports that a mixture of 50 percent alcohol and 50 percent Safers Soap works well. This mixture is sprayed or rubbed on the effected plants. Another control for scale is to simply take the plants outside and remove the scale with a jet of water. Jerry Black of Oregon Exotic Nursery says that his major problem is thrips but since the damage is minimal he does not take any control measures.

Acquiring Citrus

It is not unusual to see 3- or 4-foot citrus trees selling for up to $50 at the nursery. The alternatives are buying from a mail-order nursery, growing from seed or taking cuttings from a friend's tree.

Starting your plants from seed has both benefits and drawbacks. They are relatively inexpensive, especially compared to buying a plant. However, it can take a while for a seed to mature into an attractive tree.

In the spring, growers have had success growing citrus from the pips left over from oranges, tangerines, grapefruit, lemons, limes and other kinds of citrus. A temperature of about 70 degrees (21 C) is best for germination. Many of the seeds will probably be sterile. However, if you grow enough of them, you will have the law of averages on your side.

Unfortunately, these may not be dwarf trees but the seedlings of full-sized orchard trees. If you are patient and want to dig a massive hole in your sun room, you could have a citrus tree that would be the talk of the town. However, for most growers that would be impractical. It is difficult to find sources that will sell just a few citrus seeds. The price of commercially bought seeds can be prohibitive because of the minimum quantities required.

An alternative worth exploring is contacting the various organizations that have seed exchanges. The North American Fruit Explorers (NAFEX) does not have a formal seed exchange. However, it has a citrus group and members can join this or other groups of interest. Citrus group members exchange information, seeds and cuttings. Contributions are entirely up to the member. There has been some interesting and valuable information as well as seed data mentioned in *Pomona*, the quarterly journal of NAFEX, concerning unique hardy citrus from Asia and the Orient.

Propagating citrus from cuttings is not difficult, but there are some traps. The first step is to make certain that the cuttings you take are, in fact, a dwarf variety of citrus and not a regular citrus on a dwarf rootstock. Recently, there have been some great advances in the area of dwarfing rootstock for citrus. Many of these compatible rootstocks are not even citrus. It is easy to tell if a citrus tree has been grafted because the graft union will be visible as an enlarged part of the lower stem.

In the spring, when the citrus should be given a light pruning, cuttings can be taken. Place the cuttings in good soil after dipping them in rooting hormone. They should be provided with some warmth and they will usually root without difficulty. Place a plastic bag over the cutting to increase humidity and make certain that the soil does not dry out.

If your citrus cuttings are not of a dwarf variety or come from a grafted plant, you may want to start some rootstock cuttings. Pencil-sized cuttings are ideal, whether used for budding or grafting. When grafting citrus, make your graft about 2 inches above the soil line to limit the length of the trunk.

Varieties

- *Citrus mitis*, also known as the Calamondin orange, is one of the most common commercially available citrus. It originated in the Philippines and has become popular because of its ability to bear fruit when it is just a few inches high. It is a hybrid cross of a mandarin orange and a kumquat and the fruit is small, 1 1/2 inches in diameter, and sour. It is a true dwarf plant, rarely growing much taller than 3 to 4 feet.
- *Citrus limon* is another plant that often shows up at plant centers. It is a lemon tree with dark green and somewhat oval leathery leaves. The fruit takes several months to ripen from a dark green to yellow.
- *Citrus taitensis* is the Otaheite orange, a dwarf plant originating in China. The flowers are a beautiful pinkish white with a very strong pleasing aroma, but the fruit is too acidic to eat.
- *Owari Satsuma Mandarin* has become one of the most popular varieties grown. They are dependable bearers of excellent fruit and are

Thomasville Citrangequat

ideally suited to container growing indoors. If properly cared for, the plant will produce delicious seedless fruit that will peel easily.

- *Thomasville Citrangequat* is a hybrid of kumquat and citrange. Although this citrus is grown outdoors in Oregon, it could be a striking houseplant because it is more vigorous than kumquats and requires less heat to ripen the fruit. The fruit is high in acid and makes an excellent marmalade or juice. When the 2-inch fruits are ripe, usually in October or November, they are sweet enough to eat out of hand.
- Ichandarins are relatives of the Mandarins and are cultivated in China and Japan. Most are hardy and dwarfing which would make them ideal candidates for houseplants. The fruit is also described as quite good.
- Citranges are also available, but their habit of growing up to 12 feet high would make them unsuitable as houseplants except, perhaps, in a large solarium or sun room. The USDA developed citranges by crossing the common sweet orange with the Trifoliate orange to extend the range where citrus could be grown. The fruit of citranges is acidic and the best use is in baking, marmalades and juices.
- Ichang Papeda is a variety I would like to grow for no other reason than I like the sound of the name. It comes from China where it grows wild in the hills of the upper Yangtze Valley at altitudes as high as 6,000 feet. The lemon like fruit is round and 3 to 4 inches in size. In the wild it is dwarfing, often growing less than 3 feet tall; under cultivation it can range from 5 to 15 feet tall. This may be an interesting plant to play with. Ichang Papeda was used as the hardy parent for the Ichandarins listed above.
- Khasi Papeda is a plant from the Khasi Hills of northeast India and produces a fruit that resembles a 3- to 4-inch grapefruit. It tastes somewhat spicy, and has a peppery tang reminiscent of spiced tomato juice. When sweetened, it makes an exotic breakfast. Khasi Papeda can also grow large but, again, may provide many years of enjoyment before it outgrows its indoor environment.

There is a substantial amount of breeding work being done to improve citrus so the resulting varieties could become suitable houseplants. With so many new varieties and so much interest, there is no doubt that citrus will become even more popular as a houseplant in the years to come.

For More Information

- The North American Fruit Explorers (NAFEX), Route 1, Box 94, Chapin, IL 62628.
- California Rare Fruit Growers, California State University Arboretum, Fullerton, CA 92634.

Plant Sources

- The Northwoods Nursery, 28696 S. Cramer Road, Molalla, OR 97038)
- Edible Landscaping, PO Box 77, Afton, VA 22920, (804) 361-9134. (A care guide for citrus is available for 50 cents.)
- The Oregon Exotic Nursery 1065 Messinger Road, Grants Pass, OR 97527, (503) 846-7578.
- The Raintree Nursery, 391 Butts Road, Morton, WA 89356 (206) 496-6400.

First published in Volume 3 Number One, page 44.

Growing Bananas Indoors

by Martin P. Waterman

As a small child, I can remember seeing bananas growing in a large arboretum. I was spellbound by the large tropical leaves and the enormous bunches of fruit that appeared to be miles above my head. This must have made a lasting impression on me because I often get that same feeling when I see a banana plant today.

It may be one of the best kept secrets among houseplant enthusiasts that bananas will thrive and fruit regularly indoors with a minimum of bother. Many growers still believe that the banana is just too exotic and too difficult to grow.

In fact, all banana varieties will do well indoors with the proper care. William Lessard of the W.O. Lessard Nursery in Homestead, Florida, describes bananas as "being a wonderful, user-friendly indoor plant."

I know of one individual who built a two-story, south facing sun room just so he could grow a 25-foot-high banana plant. Although the plant has yet to break the 15-foot mark, it is already a striking specimen and the talk of the neighborhood.

The tropical looking foliage is attractive and when loaded with fruit, the banana is definitely a conversation piece and can be the focal point in any interior landscape.

Culture

Bananas are herbaceous perennials, not trees. Originally native to Southeast Asia, they are now found in most tropical and subtropical regions. They propagate themselves from underground rhizomes, or corms. New stalks grow from the rhizomes and will usually produce one large flower cluster that will result in fruit. The stalk usually takes from nine to 18 months to grow and after that another four to eight months for the fruit to mature.

The rhizomes become suckers and are continually being sent up from the base of the plant. When they reach about a foot in height, they can be removed and started as a new banana plant. After a stalk has fruited, it will die back. Allow one sucker to grow as a replacement. Bananas are self-fruitful and do not need a pollinator.

If you live in Florida or California, you should be able to select healthy potted plants. But due to the subtropical nature of the banana, most of us must acquire plants by mail. Bananas by mail usually come as a corm with the stalk and the roots trimmed off. When you receive the corm you should wash it in lukewarm water being careful to remove any fungal or bacterial growth that may have occurred during shipment.

One of the advantages of growing bananas indoors is that you do not have the same problems to contend with that most tropical growers have. For outdoor growers, site selection and pest management are important considerations. When grown outdoors, bananas have to be planted in an area that is sheltered from the wind. Winds will tear the leaves and often will blow over bananas because of their shallow root systems. In addition, bananas cannot take frost. However, if the frost is not too severe, they can grow back from the roots.

Finally, the insects that prey on bananas in their native tropics are not found in most of North America, let alone in an indoor environment. Because there are no insect problems with bananas, they can be grown organically which is important, especially indoors.

As for soil requirements, bananas prefer a pH of between 5.5 and 6.5. The soil should be deep and as well drained as possible.

Use a container that will allow at least three inches between the corm and the inside. Approximately the top 20 percent of the corm should remain above the soil level until your new plant has produced several new leaves. Allow enough room so additional soil can be added to cover the corm completely. This will promote additional roots that will improve growth and stability.

The large leaves of the banana can transpire tremendous amounts of water, especially in a dry indoor environment, so an ample supply of water is essential to success. It is just as important, however, not to overwater. Saturated soil will cause root rot. It may be wise to mulch your banana to retain moisture and to moderate the cycle that promotes drying or saturation.

Bananas are heavy feeders. Fertilization is usually done about once a month using a water soluble fertilizer. Feeding is especially important when the banana plant is producing fruit. Use a fertilizer that is rich in potassium once the fruits begin to form.

Bananas will thrive in bright indirect sun. An ideal location is near a window with a good southern exposure. Bananas will fruit indoors without artificial lighting, but supplemental lighting in some areas can speed the process. Do not keep bananas where temperatures are likely to drop below 60 degrees (16 C).

Flowering and Fruiting

The flower stalk produces rows of female flowers. The fruit begins to develop at the base of the stalk. Fruit clusters can weigh more than 100 pounds. The bunches of fruit are commonly known as "hands" and the fruit, actually a berry, as "fingers."

After the fruit has begun to grow, the male flowers develop. Commercial banana growers will remove the male flowers just below the last hand so that there will be more energy available for the fruit.

Although the amount of fruit produced by indoor bananas can be substantially less than their outdoor counterparts, harvests can still be very large. Banana plantations can produce between 10 and 25 tons of fruit per acre. Some indoor growers have grown bunches as large as 100 pounds, although smaller bunches are more typical, depending on the variety and conditions.

HYDROPONIC BANANAS

Bananas are heavy users of both nutrients and water. As a result, they are especially suited to hydroponic culture, as long as a few simple rules are observed.

Use a good quality nutrient mix, relatively high in nitrogen and potassium. Mix nutrients at full recommended strength during periods of rapid growth and fruit production; dilute the mix by approximately one-third when growth slows during winter.

Use a dilute solution and reduced watering schedule with newly planted corms to reduce the risk of fungal infection. Switch to full-strength once leaves emerge.

Because of their size, rapid growth and shallow root systems, banana plants may need additional support in some hydroponic systems. — *Don Parker*

Selection Some bananas are the best tasting when cooked, while others are better eaten raw. Most mail-order nurseries that sell bananas will describe the characteristics and suitability of the fruit for cooking or eating.

For indoor growing, there are several dwarf varieties all of which offer alternatives in taste and texture to the near-bland supermarket varieties.

There are banana plants that will never fruit or have inedible fruit. Some growers opt for the ornamental varieties in the mistaken belief that bananas will not fruit indoors, or that the fruiting varieties are troublesome. Fruiting bananas make wonderful foliage plants and the fruit, besides the good eating, provides even more beauty and interest.

When choosing a variety, height is your first consideration. You should know how high your ceiling is so that you can choose the ideal size banana for your purposes. Most mail-order retailers will list the height parameters and this data is usually reliable.

Banana varieties are known by many synonyms, so it is a good idea to read catalog descriptions carefully. Nothing could be more frustrating that having to dispose of a prized plant because it has outgrown its space. While visiting one nursery, I noticed several varieties of bananas in pots. Some had red leaves, others green. All the plants were labeled simply as "banana." Especially if you are growing bananas indoors, you should know exactly what you are getting.

There are many dwarfing varieties and these are the most common ones selected for indoor environments. Your own circumstances and tastes will dictate the varieties that you may want to try.

126

RIPENING BANANAS

To insure full enjoyment from your homegrown bananas, it is important to understand how to properly handle and ripen the fruits.

Bananas are extremely sensitive to bruising by the slightest blow, fall or scrape. This is true even when the bananas are green and seemingly impervious to injury, and increasingly so as the bananas ripen and soften. The key is to handle the fruit carefully and respectfully if you want to enjoy beautiful, unblemished fruit.

There are many things to know about ripening bananas if you are to obtain the best quality possible. When you buy a banana from a grocery store, it is generally already yellow, or turning yellow. This is the product of a sophisticated ripening process in which temperature, humidity, ethylene and carbon dioxide levels are carefully controlled. When you harvest your bananas, you will want to replicate these conditions at home, albeit in a simpler fashion.

Place unripe bananas in a paper bag with a ripening piece of fruit, such as an apple, avocado, or a banana that has begun to show some yellow color.

The purpose is to expose the bananas to the ethylene gas given off by the ripening (not ripe) fruit. Ethylene acts as a catalyst to trigger the ripening of the green fruit. Fully ripened fruit will not produce ethylene gas.

Open the bag daily to inspect the fruit and release the carbon dioxide that is also produced by the bananas and will retard ripening. Maintain the temperature at between 64 and 66 degrees (18-19 C) until the yellow color begins to develop. After that, remove the bananas from the bag and allow to ripen further at 68 to 80 degrees (20-27 C).

Under no circumstances should the unripe bananas be exposed to temperatures of less than 56 degrees (13 C); do not refrigerate bananas. Excessively warm temperatures and direct sunlight will also result in an inferior product. The best location for ripening is a cool cupboard, pantry or closet.

Finally, taste each variety at different stages of ripeness to learn how the flavor and sweetness can change and to determine the ideal stage for each.
— *Courtesy, Richarson's Seaside Banana Garden, La Conchita, California*

Varieties
- Dwarf Cavendish (Musa Cavendishii) is by far one of the most common bananas sold as an indoor variety . This variety is also known as Chinese, Dwarf Chinese and Canary Island. It is a regular fixture in many mail-order catalogs and is very reliable. Dwarf Cavendish grows from 6 to 9 feet tall and the fruit is 6 to 8 inches long. Expect the first harvest 18 to 24 months after planting, and then annually after that. Bunches in an outdoor environment average 40 to 90 pounds. Indoors, yields of about 4 to 12 pounds are common for a young plant. The fruit is sweet and similar to the popular supermarket varieties, to which it is closely related.
- Dwarf Brazilian grows from 10 to 15 feet in height. Fruit ranges from 5 to 6 inches in length. It has been described as one of the best tasting varieties around.
- Dwarf Jamaican is a form of Jamaican Red except that it will grow from 7 to 8 feet instead of the usual 25 feet. Jamaican Red is known for the coloring of both the fruit and the plant. The fruit pulp is a light orange color and has an aromatic and pleasing taste.
- The Rajapuri banana originated in India. Height is between 8 and 10 feet and bunches are on the small side, but the fruit is very good. Rajapuri is a sturdy variety and can withstand wind better than most bananas. This is especially important if you like to move your banana plants outside in the summer.

Sources
- Garden World, 2503 Garfield Street,Laredo, Texas 78043 (50 varieties, catalog: $1)
- W.O. Lessard Nursery, 19201 S.W. 248th Street, Homestead, Florida 33031 (40 varieties, catalog: $1)
- Thompson & Morgan Inc., P. O. Box 1308, Jackson, New Jersey 08527 (Banana seed, catalog: free)
- C.W. Hosking — Exotic Seed Importer, P. O. Box 500, Hayle, Cornwall, United Kingdom, TR27 4BE (Banana seed, catalog: $3)
- Richardson's Seaside Banana Garden, 6823 Santa Barbara Avenue , Ventura, California 93001 (50 varieties, catalog: $2)

First published in Volume Three Number Three, page 17.

Medicinal Plants — Nature's Pharmacy

by Michael Spillane

As far back as 5,000 years ago, early medical writings praised the health-giving, healing and rejuvenating properties of plants. Today, health food stores are booming. Herbal tonics and formulas are flooding the market. Naturopaths, homeopaths and herbal specialists are gaining increased popularity.

The powers of many herbs have now been studied and their claims substantiated — earning respect and approval, although in some cases grudging, from the medical and scientific communities. Many medical practitioners today are combining natural plant therapies with modern medicine and, in some cases, even referring patients to specialists in the "holistic" healing arts, naturopathy, acupuncture and homeopathy.

The so-called Chinese cucumber (*Trichosanthes kirilowil*) is now undergoing clinical testing due to its apparent ability to prevent the replication of HIV-infected blood cells. Taxol, a substance extracted from the bark of the Pacific yew tree (*Taxus breviofolia*), is already widely used in the treatment of ovarian cancer and may be useful in treating other forms of the deadly disease.

Even the most rigid skeptics now accept that certain plants have an often inexplicable power that can yield astonishing results when modern medical techniques have failed. Most medical professionals point out, correctly, that it is usually more a combination of factors that trigger such a recovery. Changes in lifestyle, stress management, nutrition, diet, exercise and expectations can all play a role in treatment and recovery.

Practitioners of naturopathy and herbalism do not claim that herbs "cure" illness in the same sense that antibiotics or allopathics do, by destroying toxic poisons or killing germs in the body. Herbal remedies generally assist the body by building and stimulating resistance to the attack. Symptoms are the result of an imbalance in the body. If they alone are treated, the disorder will manifest itself in some other way, perhaps in another part of the body.

Remember, many herbal remedies can be ineffective if not prepared and administered correctly. The potency of some plants can deteriorate with improper handling and long storage. Also, many plants can produce both beneficial and toxic effects. The castor oil plant (*Ricinus communis*), for example, produces raw seeds that are poisonous, yet the oil extracted from the seeds is commonly used as a laxative.

Other plants such as foxglove (*Digitalis sp.*), columbine (*Aquilegia vulgaris*) and aconite (*Aconitum napellus*), although they contain valuable medicinal substances, can be dangerous and should be taken only under medical supervision. Even relatively "safe" herbal treatments can cause adverse reactions in some people; when in doubt, consult a naturopath or a specialist in plant therapy. Always consult a medical practitioner about alternative therapies for serious problems.

The Magic of Herbs

With some study, the safe, tried and tested medicinal herbs can be grown in the home or garden for general use. A combination of herbal remedies, natural dietary supplements, seeds, teas, lotions and gels can be kept in the home for natural preventative care and for minor complains and injuries.

It is beyond the scope of this article to give an exhaustive list of medicinal plants. The following is a broad overview of different natural healing methods that rely on plants, together with examples of medicinal plants for home use, common wild flowers and herbs with health promoting qualities and exotic and legendary healing plants:

- **Chamomile** (*Chamaemaelum nobile*) flower heads prepared as a tea are renowned for their healing and soothing properties. Chamomile helps to promote sleep and relieves the excruciating pain of toothache and earache. Use the tea to cleanse the skin. Cooled chamomile tea sachets placed on the eyelids for 10 to 15 minutes is supposed to relax the entire body, inducing a calm and peaceful state.
- **Parsley** (*Petroselinium sp.*) is a well-known culinary herb that helps maintain general health. It is especially useful for its beneficial effects on the adrenal and thyroid glands.
- **Lemon Balm** (*Melissa officinalis*) is used as a tea to treat nausea,

abdominal pain, to soothe the nerves and stimulate the heart. The lemon-flavored leaves also add a delicate flavor to salads.

- **Thyme** (*Thymus sp.*) is the common name for several different species of aromatic herbs. English thyme (*Thymus vulgaris*), wild thyme (*Thymus serpyllum*) and creeping thyme (*Thymus praecox*) are among the best known. It is recommended for bronchitis, whooping cough and as a dressing for wounds.
- **Borage** (*Borago officinalis*), also known as the "herb of gladness" for its tonic effect, is highly recommended as a refreshing iced tea with honey and lemon juice.
- Other medicinal herbs include catnip (*Nepeta cataria*), clary (*Salvia sclarea*), comfrey (*Symphytum*), fennel (*Foeniculum sp.*) and mint (*Mentha sp.*).

Common Garden Weeds

A number of useful plants can be found growing just about anywhere. The following is a short list of common "weeds" with healing properties that rival the most pampered cultivated herb:

- **Dandelion** (*Taraxacum officinale*), despised by many as an unsightly presence in lawns and gardens, is blessed with a number of medicinal uses. The young tender leaves are excellent in fresh salads and a good source of health-promoting vitamins and enzymes. Roasted dandelion root makes a fine coffee substitute and can be taken as a vitamin-rich tonic. In ancient Egypt, the plant was used to treat kidney and stomach disorders and was said to relieve heart disease and rheumatism. Today, dandelion is also used to promote healthy liver function and to purify the blood.

- **Shepherd's purse** (*Capsella bursa-pastoris*) is recommended as a treatment for hemorrhage and to reduce excessive bleeding during menstruation.
- **Plantain** (*Plantago major*) is a small, rosetted herb that can be found growing almost anywhere. It thrives in poor soils, derelict sites and is often found growing out of cracks in old pavement. The leaves are used in a tea with mint, thyme and salt to counteract shock. It is good as a wash for eye inflammation and is widely used in Europe to treat wounds and sores.
- **Daisy** (*Bellis perennis*) can be used as a tea to treat minor stomach disorders and as a mild laxative.

Legendary Healing Plants

The curative power of some plants is well known, but a few stand out as worthy of further mention:

- **Aloe vera** (*Aloe barbadensis*) is a thick leafed succulent native to South Africa. It is one of the most popular healing, cosmetic and rejuvenating plants around and is now used as the base for a whole range of health and beauty products. It is also easy to grow at home.

  The plant itself is usually inexpensive to buy and is commonly found in florist shops and nurseries. A single leaf from a friend's plant can be rooted quickly and easily in regular potting soil, so there is no good reason not to have one of these incredible plants.

  The thick, mucus-like gel contained in the leaves acts both as an astringent and a stimulant to cellular growth. It can anesthetize and heal damaged skin and is therefore an excellent natural treatment for acne, scars, burns and wrinkles. It is also used to treat sunburn, eczema, athlete's foot and yeast infections. It may be taken internally for stomach disorders and ulcers.

The plants are easily grown in the home and the leaves may be sliced off and used as needed. Partially used leaves may be refrigerated for later use.

■ **Garlic** (*Allium sativum*) was used as a medicinal plant as far back as 3000 BC in ancient Mesopotamia. During the building of the pyramids in Egypt, slaves were fed garlic to keep up their endurance. The Vikings carried garlic with them on sea voyages and the British used garlic to treat the wounds of soldiers during World War II.

Garlic is used to clear skin blemishes and boils, lower blood pressure, ease intestinal distress, clear congested bronchial passages and to treat arteriosclerosis. Recent studies suggest that garlic may also increase the immune response and may have some applications in the treatment of AIDS.

■ **Feverfew** (*Chrysanthemum parthenium*) has generated much interest recently for

HOMEOPATHY

Homeopathy is a process of natural healing that has been in existence for nearly 200 years. Formulated in 1806 by German physician Samuel Hahnemann, homeopathy is becoming increasingly popular as an alternative to allopathic medicine.

The remedies used in homeopathy are derived from minerals and animals as well as from plants. Many of the same medicinal plants are used by both herbalists and homeopaths, although the treatment is different.

The word homeopath comes from the Greek, meaning "treating like with like." Similar to the way vaccines work, homeopathic remedies are used to restore balance and harmony by exciting similar symptoms in the patient, thus stimulating the body's healing powers. Whereas many of the drugs used in orthodox medicine suppress and counteract symptoms, homeopathy works in the opposite way.

Although many of the remedies used in homeopathy are poisonous in their crude form, the substances are diluted to such a degree, a process called potentization, that their effects become curative without unwanted side effects. The process is said to separate the healing power of the remedy and helps build resistance to the disease. Antidotes for many fatal snake bites, for example, are derived from similar diluted poisons. The proof of effective, in some cases miraculous, recovery confirms the validity of homeopathy as a safe and promising natural therapy.

Homeopathic home remedy kits are available at specialty stores and homeopathic centers. Homeopathic treatments rely on carefully measured doses and special handling and are not suited to the do-it-yourself approach. The following is a short list of plant species commonly used in homeopathic treatments:

Aconite (Aconitum napellus) is normally considered a poison. In homeopathy it is used in a greatly diluted form for the treatment of shock, croup, chills, distress, breathlessness, trembling and numbness.

Marigold (*Calendula officinalis*) is used locally as a tincture or ointment for treating open wounds.

Poison ivy (*Rhus taxicodendron*) is another plant with unpleasant associations. In homeopathy, it is used for flu, dry coughs, stiffness, itching blisters and shingles.

Windflower (*Pulsatilla sp.*) is used as a treatment for measles, to improve digestion and to relieve congestion.

Yellow jasmine (*Gelsemium sp.*) is used for nervous disorders and influenza.

Leopard's bane (*Arnica Montana*) is recommended for use after dental surgery. It is also useful for sprains, bruises, aching muscles and fatigue.

Stinging nettle (*Urtica urens*) is used as a cream or ointment for the treatment of burns, scalds and bee stings. — *Michael Spillane*

its use in the treatment of migraine headaches. Research in England has shown that a few leaves of the plant taken daily infused in tea or eaten raw in salads or sandwiches reduce the number and severity of migraine attacks.

It is also useful in treating other diseases caused by inflammation such as arthritis, as well as to relieve tension. The ancient Greeks and other civilizations used feverfew to treat aches, pains and to reduce fevers (hence the name).

Exotic Medicinal Plants

Many common tropical and oriental plants possess medicinal properties that have been recognized for centuries by indigenous people, yet remain a mystery in the developed world. The Brazilian jungles, for example, support an incredible number of medicinal plants, some of which have yet to be found and cataloged. Others have a long history of use:

- **The Ginseng Root** (*Acanthopanax sp., Panax sp.*), possibly the most well known of the rejuvenating and health promoting herbs, was dismissed by Western doctors as a mere panacea. Now, Russian researchers have confirmed its powerful tonic properties.
  It restores physical and mental well-being, stimulates the sex glands without harmful side effects, increases the rate of cell division and hormone production, strengthens the heart, and benefits the entire nervous system.
- **Fo-ti-Tieng** is a lesser known oriental plant with properties similar to ginseng. It was popularized by the renowned Chinese herbalist, professor Li Chung Yun. Yun, who regularly consumed a tea of ginseng and Fo-ti-Tieng is said to have survived to the age of 256, outlived 23 wives and died with his own natural teeth and hair. As fantastic as that story may seem, there may be some basis for the belief among the Chinese in the extraordinary powers of Fo-ti-Tieng. British and French researchers have isolated a substance in the plant that has since been identified as "Vitamin X," or the "Youth Vitamin."
- **Sarsaparilla** (*Smilax ornata*) is widely used as a flavoring, but a tea made from the roots of this tropical plant is used for the treatment of rheumatism, skin disorders, sexual impotency and fatigue. It is also known as a blood purifier.
- **Soursop** (*Annona muricata*) is a tropical fruit tree commonly found throughout the Caribbean and South America. The leaves are used in teas for coughs, colds and fevers.
- **Prickly pear** (*Opuntia sp.*) is native to much of the southwestern United States. The cut leaves of this cactus are used to treat wounds, swelling and headaches. Taken internally, prickly pear can reduce blood cholesterol and reduce blood sugar levels in diabetic patients.
- **Sea grape** (*Coccoloba uvifera*) may be found growing along coastal areas in most tropical regions. The bark of this low spreading tree is prepared in a tea and used to treat diarrhea.
- **Lime** (*Citrus aurantifolia*) is more than just a tasty fruit. The shiny leaves may be used as a tea to combat colds, influenza and stomach disorders.
- **Kalanchoe** (*Kalanchoe sp.*), commonly kept as a flowering houseplant, also has some little known medicinal qualities. The leaves and stems are used to treat sores, as a cooling tea and as a poultice.
- **Ginger** (*Zingibar officinale*) is one of the best home remedies for

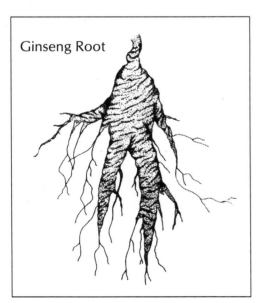

Ginseng Root

131

nausea, indigestion and dysentery. It is also an easy-to-grow and exotic houseplant. Simply plant the rhizome, the ginger root purchased at the grocery store, in a rich soil and place in a sunny location.

- **Toothache plant** (*Spilanthes acmella*) comes from Australia where it is used by aboriginal people to relieve, what else, toothache.
- **Verba mate** (*Ilex paraguarensis*) is a South American member of the holly family. The plant produces a beverage that is more stimulating than tea or coffee, but also rich in vitamins and minerals.
- **Passion flower** (*Passiflora sp.*) is a main ingredient in many non prescription sedatives and sleeping formulas, especially in Europe. It has been used to treat insomnia, nervous conditions and hysteria.
- **Caladium** (*Caladium bicolor*) is a striking foliage plant. The rhizomes are heated and used as a poultice for removing splinters.

Common Ornamental Plants

Many of these plants are indigenous, or easily obtained, and can be cultivated for their medicinal properties:

- **Coneflower** (*Echinacea purpurea*) is more than just another pretty flower. It is a blood purifier and is known to strengthen the body's immune system. Sometimes used as an infusion, most coneflower remedies are based on the extracted juice of the fresh plant.
- **Joe pye-weed** (*Eupatorium purpureum*) is a valuable remedy for kidney problems. The rose-pink flowers were used by native Americans to induce sweating and to break fevers.
- **Oak** (*Quercus robur*) is certainly a well-known species, although its medicinal qualities remain something of a secret. It is used as a tea to treat diarrhea, or the chopped bark may be infused to make a gargle for treating sore throats.
- **Birch** (*Betula pendula*) is another common tree with medicinal value. A tea made from the bark can be used to treat rheumatism, gout and infections of the urinary tract.
- **Juniper** (*Juniperus communis*) is also used for rheumatism. The juice from the berries is also effective in treating slow healing wounds.
- **Hawthorn** (*Crataegus oxycantha*) can be used as a tonic for sore throats and as a diuretic and astringent (the berries also make a nice jelly).
- **Goldenrod** (*Solidago sp.*) is used as a remedy for bladder and kidney ailments.

HERBAL TREATMENTS

Teas are the most commonly used method for administering herbs. Generally called "tisanes" in herbal practice, herbal teas are prescribed for headaches, insomnia, colds, chills, shock, fever and stomach disorders.

An infusion is made by pouring boiling water on the plants and letting it stand for 10 to 15 minutes. For decoction, place the herb in cold water and heat to a boil. Boil for 10 to 15 minutes and allow to stand for another 15 minutes. Both methods are suited to different herbs and for different uses.

Baths laced with aromatic herbs can relieve tension and induce relaxation. Some herbal baths may also be used for skin cleansing or to heal minor wounds.

Poultices and pulp from medicinal herbs can be applied directly to wounds, bruises, sprains and sore muscles. The leaves of some plants can be crushed, heated and used as a dressing. — *Michael Spillane*

- **White willow** (*Salix alba*) bark is a traditional remedy, dating back to the early Greeks, for arthritis, fever rheumatism and diarrhea.
- **Sumac** (*Rhus typhina*) Although they are not edible, juice from the berries of the sumac can be used topically to treat skin irritations.
- **Oregon grape** (*Mahonia sp.*) is an attractive evergreen shrub, the root of which contains Berberine, an excellent blood purifier.
- **Rosehips** (*Rosa sp.*) are an invaluable source of vitamin C, with a much higher content than the fruit of many citrus species. The hips can be frozen and eaten throughout the winter months. Dried rosehips can also be used to make tea, rosehip jam and rose oil, a popular cosmetic.
- **Blue flax** (*Linum perenne*) is a blue flowered perennial whose seeds contain linseed oil. It has been used to treat coughs, rheumatic pain and diarrhea.
- **Elderberry** (*Sambucus canadensis*) is a well-known medicinal plant. The flowers are commonly used in teas for colds and fevers.
- **Cardinal flower** (*Lobelia cardinalis*) is a wildflower native to the eastern United States that is said to contain an anti-spasmodic drug.

Seeds and Sprouts

Nature has endowed many of our common seeds with great nutritional value and curative powers. Seeds and freshly sprouted seedlings can promote health and combat many specific disorders:

- **Millet** is one of the oldest and most nutritious foods known. It is rich in vitamins, minerals and lecithin. Unlike some common grains, it does not ferment in the stomach. Ground meal or hulled seed is the best form to use.
- **Sesame seeds** contain calcium, phosphorus, iron and trace minerals. They are also a valuable source of B-complex vitamins.
- **Clary (sage) seed** used in a tea for the treatment of back problems.
- **Pumpkin seed** is revered by the Chinese for its powerful medicinal properties. It is rich in calcium, protein and B vitamins.
- **Sunflower seed** is a highly nutritious food source, containing protein, niacin and pantothenic acid. It is also rich in vitamin D, thiamin and iron. It is used to treat rheumatism, eyestrain, skin disorders, nervous conditions and to improve the complexion. It also contains a substance sometimes referred to as the "anti-gray-hair vitamin." A small handful of hulled seeds daily is said to be enough to induce major health benefits.

For spouted seeds, try the following:

- **Alfalfa** which is an excellent blood builder.
- **Red clover** to rejuvenate the liver and pancreas.
- **Radish** for cleansing the liver.

Most beneficial medicinal plants can be found in the form of tablets, roots, powders or teas at health food stores. But many of the remedies listed here can be found growing wild, or can be cultivated and grown quite easily indoors or out. Plants and seeds may be purchased at nurseries, florists, through specialty growers or herb farms. Some are available as seeds or starts from specialty mail-order houses.

However you obtain your plants, growing your own means guaranteed purity, greater freshness and superior quality. And that is bound to be healthier for both the mind and the body.

First published in Volume 3 Number 3, page 41.

133

Mushrooms — Grow Your Own Indoors

by Paul Przybylowicz

I t's an increasingly common problem — you want to raise mushrooms, but don't have a place where you can do it outdoors. Well, you're in luck. There are a number of mushrooms that can be grown entirely indoors with a little attention. Now this doesn't mean hauling truck loads of barnyard refuse up the elevator in plastic garbage bags. You can do it with a minimum of odor and mess in a relatively small space.

Mushrooms can be grown indoors on grain, wood or straw. These materials, as opposed to mixtures based on animal wastes, reduce the odor problems and the potential social stigma that you're "down there mucking about with...ahem, manure."

Growing mushrooms indoors means creating one or more controlled environments conducive to mushroom growth in your home. As mushrooms grow, their environmental requirements change, requiring you — as the grower — to provide the needed changes. This can be as simple as moving a tray from one part of the house to another or can be quite involved with controlling temperature and humidity in an enclosed, insulated space.

Indoor mushroom growing also means some cleaning — rather a lot, really. If you're the type of person who doesn't notice dirt particles until they're large enough to support commercial agriculture, your temperament may be better suited to worm farming. People who have a knack for growing plants are said to have a green thumb, while indoor mushroom growers are said to possess a "white thumb." While this is the color of mushroom mycelium, a "white thumb" is more likely due to water-logged skin.

Successful indoor mushroom growers invariably are those people who are good observers, get a kick out of assembling an unlikely conglomeration of items into "Useful Stuff" and have a working knowledge of electricity. The focus of this article is how to create the proper environments for mushrooms in your home with a minimum investment. Cultivation of the button mushrooms (*Agaricus brunnescens*) and the almond mushroom (*Agaricus subrufescens*) on grain are covered briefly. (Cultivation of oyster mushrooms (*Pleurotus* spp.) on pasteurized straw and shiitake (*Lentinula edodes*) on sterilized sawdust using the facilities described here are covered in Vol. 1 #2 and Vol. 2 #3, respectively.)

Fun Guys

Mushrooms are part of a larger group of organisms called fungi. They spend most of their lives as a white cottony growth called mycelium which is the vegetative portion of the mushroom. Mycelium is composed of millions of thread-like cells which grow into the food (or substrate) and produce enzymes that digest it. Mycelium begins as a germinating spore and continues to grow, eventually producing a large, interconnected web of cells. Spores, which are similar to seeds, are produced on gills, located on the underside of the mushroom cap. These spores are the mechanism the mushroom uses to get from one place to another.

Unlike plants, mushrooms (and all fungi) can not produce their own food. They digest organic matter outside of their cells and absorb the resulting simple compounds. There must be a film of water on the

134

substrate so that the digestive enzymes can diffuse from the mycelium and the simple compounds resulting from degradation can diffuse back to the mycelium.

Environment

Three different types of environments are needed for indoor mushroom cultivation. First, a relatively clean, almost sterile, work area where mycelium can be transferred from one growth medium to another with little risk of contamination by molds and bacteria. Second, a warm spot with relatively uniform temperatures where the mycelium can grow and digest the substrate, and third, a moist, humid, usually cooler environment for fruiting. While it may sound complex, you can easily create these environments in your home with a little ingenuity and a small amount of space.

The Clean Area

Ah, fresh clean air! From a mushroom grower's viewpoint, there is no such thing. Every cubic inch of air is laden with millions of spores just looking for an opportunity to cause trouble. Creating a clean space in your home will minimize problems with competing fungi and bacteria in the substrate. It also gives you more options in the types of mushrooms you choose to grow. You can produce your own spawn, begin with some spores, create and maintain pure cultures, and take a clone from a fresh mushroom, There are numerous advantages to having this type of control, most notably the ability to cultivate mushroom species native to your area.

The easiest and cheapest clean work area for the home cultivator is a simple glove box (see drawing on page 136). A glove box is an enclosed work area that can easily be cleaned and allows you to work inside while minimizing exposure of the substrate to the air. Prior to use, the inside

CULTIVATION FUNDAMENTALS

Mushroom cultivation is the process of managing a natural succession of events to maximize mushroom production. There are three basic steps:

- **Create a selective substrate for the mushroom.** All other things being equal, the more substrate consumed by the mycelium, the more mushrooms. However, the substrate must favor the growth of the mushroom over that of competing microorganisms to insure that the mycelium will colonize and digest as much substrate as is practically possible. Indoors, this selectivity usually is created by heating the food source to reduce populations of competitors. The substrate is then physically protected to prevent contamination.
- **Introduce the desired mushroom.** Under natural conditions, a mushroom arrives at a new spot by an air-borne spore. If conditions are right, a new colony will be started; however, this process is too uncertain and slow for practical cultivation. Actively growing mycelium and nutrients — in the form of spawn — are used which results in rapid colonization of the substrate by the mushroom.
- **Manage the environment to favor mushroom growth and development.** Once the first two objectives have been met, the substrate must be incubated under favorable conditions to promote growth and eventual mushroom formation (fruiting). Each mushroom species has its own optimum temperature for growth and fruiting. — *Paul Przybylowicz*

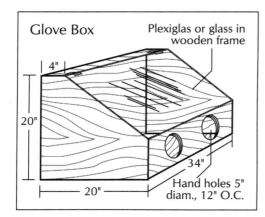

Glove Box

Plexiglas or glass in wooden frame

4"

20"

20"

34"

Hand holes 5" diam., 12" O.C.

of the box and the outside of all containers are sterilized with a 10 percent bleach solution to create a relatively sterile environment inside the box.

A satisfactory glove box can be constructed from 1/4-inch plywood or a plastic-coated particle board such as those used in kitchen cabinets (ask for hard density overlay [HDO] or Kortron), some 1- by 2-inch wood strips, a piece of Plexiglas and some hardware. The wood strips should be glued and screwed to the sides; make sure that you create a left and right side. Place the sides on the bottom with the wood strips on the outside. Screw the front, back, top and bottom into the strips on the sides. The front, which is hinged at the back, can be either glass in a frame or 1/4-inch Plexiglas. Place foam weatherstripping all around the top of the sides, front and back to provide a seal. The inside should be painted with a washable white enamel.

A relatively recent improvement in mushroom cultivation technology has been the use of High Efficiency Particulate Air (HEPA) filters. These filters — originally developed for electronic clean rooms — effectively sterilize the air by filtering out all fungal spores and bacteria. While more expensive than a glove box, HEPA filters are affordable for the serious home mushroom grower; plan on about $200 for a filter and blower.

HEPA filters can be used to pressurize a glove box or to create a "clean bench." A clean bench is work counter enclosed on three sides with a HEPA filter forming the back or top. Air flows from the filter face in a uniform stream, creating a clean working area because the outside, "dirty" air is continually flushed away.

Construction of a clean bench is straightforward (see drawing below). The cabinet can be made of plywood or HDO. The working surface should be covered with Formica or a similar product. The key points are

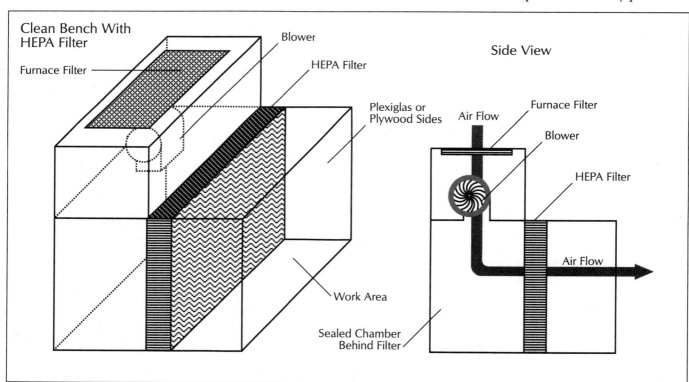

Clean Bench With HEPA Filter

Furnace Filter

Blower

HEPA Filter

Plexiglas or Plywood Sides

Work Area

Sealed Chamber Behind Filter

Side View

Air Flow

Furnace Filter

Blower

HEPA Filter

Air Flow

assuring a good seal between the filter and the cabinet to assure that no air slips around the filter and getting the right blower/filter combination.

The blower capacity must be matched to the filter size. HEPA filters (5 7/8 inches deep) are commonly available in the following sizes: 1 foot square, 2 foot square, 2 by 3 foot, and 2 by 4 foot. The resistance to air flow created by the filter (known as inches of static pressure) is about 0.8 inches for a HEPA filter rated at 99.99 percent efficient at removing particles 0.3 microns in diameter (the standard for clean benches). The air velocity out of the filter face must be at least 100 feet per minute to maintain sterile conditions. For example, a 2-foot-square filter (4 square feet of surface area) will require 400 cubic feet per minute (cfm) coming out of the filter (4 square feet times 100 feet per minute equals 400). When sizing the blower, add 25 percent more capacity to ensure minimum air speed as the filter ages and becomes partially clogged. Thus, the blower for a 2-foot-square HEPA filter must deliver about 500 cfm at 0.8 inches static pressure.

Warm and Cozy

Mushroom mycelium will grow fastest when the temperature remains relatively constant near its optimum temperature for vegetative growth. The common button mushroom, the oyster mushroom, and shiitake prefer temperatures of around 78 degrees (26 C). There may be areas in your home that will make satisfactory incubators with little or no modifications. Likely spots are: cupboards, above refrigerators or freezers, and in closets near the hot water heater. Check these areas using a maximum/minimum thermometer. Ideally, temperatures should stay between 70 and 78 degrees (21-26 C).

If you don't have a suitable cupboard or closet, a temperature-controlled incubator can be easily and inexpensively built. The necessary items are: an insulated "box," a heat source, a thermostat and, if the box is large, a small fan to circulate the air.

Insulated boxes come in a wide variety of sizes and shapes. One of the most convenient (and cheapest) for mushroom cultivation is a "dead" refrigerator. They can be obtained for free at a local appliance shop, have an interior that is easily cleaned, already have shelves and come in a wide variety of sizes and shapes.

If a refrigerator is too big, a large picnic cooler will work well. Slightly smaller Styrofoam boxes used to ship tropical fish can often be had at the local pet shop for free. They work quite well as small incubators and fruiting chambers.

Although a variety of heat sources can be used, the cheapest and most widely available is the lowly incandescent light bulb. Mounted in a porcelain socket on a waterproof junction box, 60 to 100 watts will heat even the largest refrigerator. A piece of aluminum flashing or similar material should be placed on the shelf directly above the light bulb to diffuse the heat. For picnic coolers, lower wattage bulbs (15 or 25 watt appliance bulbs) should be used. In a cooler, the bulb should be surrounded with a metal chimney constructed out of a #10 metal can to prevent overheating near the bulb and to promote air circulation.

Just about everybody is familiar with the household thermostats that control furnaces and air conditioners. Thermostats contain a temperature-sensing element — usually a bimetallic spring — which operates a switch. Thermostats which control heating devices complete the circuit

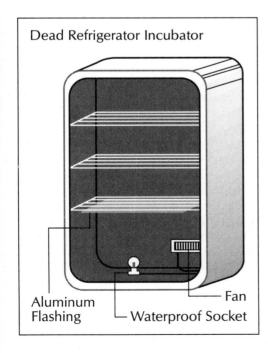

Dead Refrigerator Incubator

Aluminum Flashing

Waterproof Socket

Fan

(switching on the heater) when the temperature drops and the contacts open (turning off the heater) on a temperature rise. Those that are used for cooling devices are just the reverse. Most household thermostats are not suitable for use in small incubators because they are designed for 24 volts of direct current. In simple incubators, the thermostat must switch line voltage (110 to 120 volts AC). Commercial thermostats by companies such as Penn, Dayton and Honeywell are available for this job, but they are expensive.

Fortunately, a solution can be found down at the local farm and garden store in the form of a chicken incubator thermostat. This switching device is inexpensive, reliable and quite accurate. Furthermore, they are easy to wire. The temperature-sensing portion looks like two tin can lids soldered together. As they warm up, they bow outwards, pushing on a switch. The desired temperature is adjusted by a screw which varies the distance between the "can lids" and the switch.

Getting Wired

Wiring the heating unit is straightforward. Use 16-gauge appliance wire, similar to that used for vacuum cleaners or refrigerators. The thermostat must be wired in between the plug and the light bulb. All connections should occur in the junction box under the light bulb. Attach one lead from the plug to the light socket and, using a wire nut, attach the other lead from the plug to one lead going to the thermostat. Attach the other lead from the thermostat to the light socket (see drawing number 5). Trace the current flow through the system, in one lead from the plug, up through the thermostat, through the light bulb and back out the plug.

Fruiting Chamber

During fruiting, most mushrooms like it a little cooler, moist and humid. Most cultivated mushrooms will fruit at ambient household temperatures, 60 to 70 degrees (16-21 C); however, unless you live in a damp cave, you need to provide an enclosed space (fruiting chamber) where the relative humidity can be maintained above 90 percent.

A fruiting chamber can be as simple as a picnic cooler with a sheet of plastic over the top to admit light (for those mushrooms that require light), some water in the bottom and a rack to keep the mushrooms out of the water. Several mistings per day with a plant sprayer will keep the humidity high enough. If you want to get more complicated, you can add a humidification system to your incubator to create a fruiting chamber. Household steam and cool mist vaporizers are inexpensive humidifiers which can be connected to a timer that will switch on or off every 15 minutes. By adjusting the amount of time per hour the humidifier is on, the relative humidity can be maintained above 90 percent.

With the facilities described above, you can grow a variety of mushrooms in your home. You have created a small mycological laboratory where you can isolate pure cultures, make spawn and experiment with a variety of mushrooms — which will be topics for future articles.

To begin with, methods for producing button mushrooms using grain spawn available from commercial suppliers are briefly outlined below. The button mushroom (*Agaricus brunnescens*), the almond mushroom (*Agaricus subrufescens*) and related species are normally grown on compost. However, the production of compost is a science of its own and is too complicated for all but the most dedicated mycophiles. Fortunately, most of the compost-inhabiting *Agaricus* species will fruit nicely on a layer of grain spawn that has been covered with a layer of peat moss/lime mixture.

You will need some spawn of either one of the *Agaricus* species listed above. You can prepare your own spawn if you have the cultures or you can purchase spawn from a spawn supplier (see resource section). Once the spawn is finished or has arrived, it should be refrigerated immediately until several days before use. In addition to spawn, you will need some trays that are 2 to 4 inches deep (casserole dishes, baking pans, kitty litter trays etc.), a spray mist bottle, liquid bleach, a large metal spoon, some plastic wrap to cover the trays and some casing soil.

Cleaning Up

The first step is cleaning and sterilizing (you were warned). Begin by making up a 10 percent solution of bleach (one part bleach to nine parts water). Wearing rubber gloves (unless you enjoy smelling like Mr. Clean), moisten a rag or sponge with bleach and wipe down the inside of the glove box or flow hood. Wipe the trays carefully and place them in the glove box. This effectively sterilizes the surfaces, killing spores of competing fungi.

Shake the spawn jar or bag to break the spawn into small clumps or individual grains. Wipe off the outside of the spawn container with the bleach solution and place it inside the glove box as well. Cut enough pieces of plastic wrap to cover the trays and place inside the glove box.

Now the trays are ready to receive an even layer of grain spawn. Wipe off the rubber gloves (with your hands inside them) and reach into the glove box. Bring a rag soaked with bleach into the box with you and wipe your hands on it from time to time. Wipe the spoon off thoroughly to sterilize it. Open the spawn bag (or jar) and with slow deliberate movements that minimize stirring up the air inside the box, transfer enough grain into a tray to form a layer about 1 inch thick. Pat the grain with the spoon to make a nice even layer, then place a piece of plastic wrap directly on top of the grain. Wipe your hands and the spoon down with 10 percent bleach between trays and continue until the spawn is gone or the trays have been filled, which ever comes first. If you have spawn left over, close the spawn container and incubate it for several days until it turns white again. It can then be stored in the refrigerator for future use.

When you shook the grain spawn up and transferred it to the trays the white mycelium on the surface of the grains mostly disappeared. The next step is to incubate the trays to allow the mycelium inside the grains to grow out and knit the grain together again. This will make the mushroom less susceptible to competition from other fungi. Carefully place the trays in your incubator. Make sure that they are well sealed to prevent the grain from drying, use tape if needed. Incubate the trays at 75 degrees (24 C) for one to three days, or until the grain is knit together with mycelium once again. While this is happening, you can prepare the casing mixture.

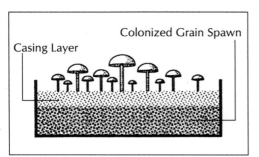

Casing

Commonly, casing "soil" is a mixture of peat moss and lime which is applied to the surface of the substrate to promote mushroom formation. Some mushrooms — button mushrooms, Wine-red Stropharia, and the paddy straw mushroom — require a casing layer to fruit, while others — shiitake, oyster mushrooms, enoki — do not. The exact influence of the casing layer on the mushroom is not totally understood, but there are some generally accepted theories regarding its function.

Casing soil is almost devoid of nutrients for the growing mycelium. The change in nutrition experienced by the mycelium as it grows into the casing stimulates mushroom formation. Casing soil also acts as a water reservoir for mushroom development and provides a humid micro-environment for the initiation and development of mushrooms. In addition, it functions to keep the substrate from drying out and supports the growth of other beneficial microorganisms. In order for the casing soil to perform properly, it must be open, porous and capable of absorbing and releasing water throughout the fruiting period without becoming water-logged and compacted.

Prepare the casing soil using four parts coarse sphagnum peat moss to one part ground limestone by volume. Dolomitic limestone should not be used due to its high magnesium content which inhibits mycelial growth. Thoroughly mix the ingredients dry, then add about 1 to 1.5 parts water and allow to stand overnight. This allows the peat moss to fully hydrate. The optimum moisture content of the casing soil is just below saturation.

A simple test for the proper moisture content is to grab a handful of casing soil, but don't squeeze it, yet. Transfer the soil to your other hand and look at your palm. It should have a thin film of water on it from the casing soil, but no big drops. Lightly squeezing the casing should produce a few drops and a firm squeeze should yield about a tablespoon of water. Another test is to place some casing soil in a clear glass. Allow it to stand for an hour and then examine the glass/soil interface at the bottom. It should not be any wetter looking than the soil above it. If the soil is too wet, add more peat moss. It is better to have the casing soil a little dry, than a little wet because water can be always be added. If the casing is too wet, water will seep down to the substrate surface, saturating the casing soil there and preventing any oxygen from reaching the substrate. This will inhibit or kill the mycelium and promote growth of undesirable microorganisms.

Applying the casing layer to the grain in a glove box or clean bench will reduce the chances for contamination, but isn't absolutely necessary. Remove the plastic wrap and cover the grain layer with 3/4 to 1 inch of casing soil. Keep the casing layer as even as possible to promote uniform fruiting. After casing each tray, place the plastic covering on top of the casing layer and put the trays back into the incubator.

Fruiting

After three to six days, mycelium will begin to appear at the surface of the casing soil, usually at the edges first, then the middle. This means that the casing layer is fully colonized and it's time to move the trays into cooler fruiting conditions. Remove the trays from the incubator before dense mycelial growth occurs on the surface of the casing layer because it will inhibit mushroom formation.

Fruiting is triggered by several events: applying the casing soil, moving the substrate into a cooler, humid environment and removing the plastic covering. Mushroom formation is inhibited by high carbon dioxide levels. The plastic covering on the surface of the casing soil prevents drying and also keeps the carbon dioxide produced by the mycelium from escaping. Removing this plastic allows the mycelium to get a breath of fresh air, stimulating mushroom formation.

The optimum temperature for fruiting of the button mushroom is about 60 degrees (16 C), while the almond mushroom prefers slightly warmer temperatures, 65 to 70 degrees (18-21 C). Once the trays have been placed in the fruiting chamber, you should lightly mist the casing soil surface and the interior of the fruiting chamber several times per day to maintain high humidity and to keep the casing soil moist. Several light waterings per day are better than one heavy one. In addition, the casing soil must be watered as needed to provide adequate water for mushroom growth and development.

Knowing how much water to apply is an art which distinguishes a good grower from a mediocre one. Look carefully at the surface of the casing before watering. It will appear lighter in color as it dries. As you water, notice how quickly the water is absorbed by the casing soil. Initially, the water will rapidly disappear, slowing down as the soil approaches saturation. Avoid creating puddles or saturated areas in the casing soil.

After seven to 14 days, you will notice small white buttons appearing on the casing soil surface. These "primordia" or "pins" are the baby mushrooms. As the pins develop and expand, more water will be needed. However, do not water directly on the pins, but rather the casing soil around them. The primordia should not have water on them for more than several hours per days. If they have water standing on them continually, they may abort and die.

The mushrooms will continue to grow and expand for up to a week. They should be harvested once the veil covering the gills has ruptured. Pick them by gently twisting them out of the casing soil. Usually a clump of casing will come out as well; this can be trimmed off. Fill in the hole in the casing layer with fresh casing soil. Generally, all the mushrooms in a tray will mature within several days — this is called a "flush." After the first flush, any aborted mushrooms or primordia should be removed. Cover any exposed mycelium with a light sprinkling of casing soil and level the casing layer. With proper water management, up to three or four flushes can be harvested from a single tray.

Although this mushroom is grown in an indoor setting, there is the slight possibility that other mushrooms will fruit from the trays along with *Agaricus*. Therefore, it is very important to positively identify the mushrooms you harvest. *Agaricus* species are very distinct and are easily recognized; nevertheless, if there is any doubt in your mind, you should consult one or more of the field guides listed under resources or someone with experience identifying mushrooms.

Button mushrooms are currently enjoying a resurgence in popularity — brown, off-white and mature mushrooms are being sold as portobello and crimini in trendy markets. Using the methods outlined above, you can produce organically grown *Agaricus* for your table, in your home or apartment. *Agaricus* mushrooms are one of the most popular in the world and when you try some very fresh ones, you'll understand why.

First published in Volume 1, Number 4, page 54.

141

Chapter 6
Plant Propagation

Plant Propagation for Beginners

by Michael Spillane

For many growers, propagation is a strange and mystical word, vaguely connected with the multiplication of plant stock. Although the term is widely used in gardening circles, the process itself is rarely understood. There is nothing too difficult or mysterious about plant propagation, as long as you understand the basic techniques and which is more suited to a particular plant species.

Plants are increased in two basic ways: by seed (sexual reproduction) and by vegetative means (asexual reproduction). Sexual reproduction involves the male and female parts of the plant and culminates in the production of a seed — an embryonic plant.

Plants grown from seed can be unpredictable in form and habit and may differ from the parent stock. Vegetative or asexual reproduction produces genetic replicas of the parent plant, providing uniformity and consistency.

Sowing plants from seed is a process familiar to most gardeners. But other methods, raising ferns from spores, leaf, stem and root cuttings, division, offsets and stolons, layering and air layering greatly enhance your ability to produce healthy stock and preserve rare or hard to reproduce plants.

Stem Cuttings

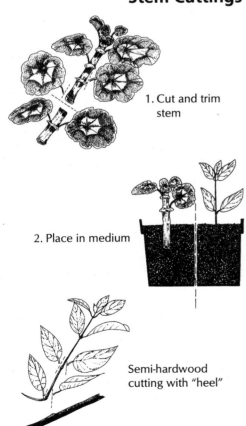

1. Cut and trim stem

2. Place in medium

Semi-hardwood cutting with "heel"

Stem cutting is by far the most popular method of asexual propagation. Fleshy softwood cuttings such as those from geraniums or impatiens are easy to root and establish quickly. (Softwood refers to the current year's growth. Softwood cuttings are usually taken in the spring through mid-season. Hardwood, old growth, cuttings are usually taken at the end of the growing season.) Most softwood tip cuttings can be rooted in soil in 3-inch pots, or in water. For best results use healthy, non-flowering side shoots and provide shade, moisture and bottom heat where possible.

Pots trays and flats are all suitable for stem cuttings. Plastic containers retain moisture better than clay pots. A medium for rooting cuttings should have good water retention capacity and allow for efficient air circulation. An ideal medium contains a mix of sand and peat, vermiculite or perlite.

Hormone rooting powders are often used to speed the rooting process. Semi-hardwood cuttings such as fuchsia are more difficult to root than softwood material and rely more on the use of rooting powders.

To make stem cuttings, prepare the soil medium and water with a fine mist spray. Choose disease-free side shoots 4 to 6 inches (10-15 cm) in length, or tip cuttings 3 to 4 inches (7.5-10 cm) long. With a sharp, clean knife, cut just below a node (leaf joint). Remove all buds, flowers and lower leaves, leaving at least three sets of leaves. Dip the end of the cutting in hormone powder and shake off the excess before planting.

Insert cuttings into the medium and cover with plastic or poly sheeting. Place in a bright, not sunny, location and keep warm. Mist with a fine spray twice daily. Remove the cover once roots are established, 10 to 14 days after planting. Transplant into 3 1/2-inch pots as soon as possible to avoid root or stem rot and nutrient deficiency.

Semi-hardwood cuttings are usually taken with a "heel," a sliver of bark or stem, and inserted to about half their length in soil.

Leaf Cuttings

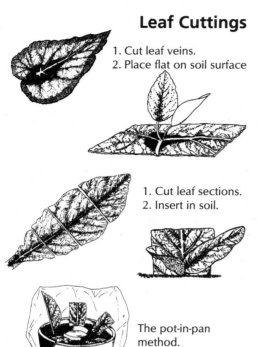

1. Cut leaf veins.
2. Place flat on soil surface

1. Cut leaf sections.
2. Insert in soil.

The pot-in-pan method.

Many plants can be propagated quite easily from leaf cuttings, including African violet, *Begonia rex*, peperomias and a variety of succulents. There are a number of different techniques. With African violets and peperomias, simply insert a leaf with a portion of the stem attached into the cutting medium or water.

The large decorative leaves of the *Begonia rex* will produce plantlets not only from the leaf stem, but from the actual leaf surface as well. Cut off a mature healthy leaf with an inch or so of stem. Make cuts along the main veins at the back of the leaf. Place the leaf flat on the soil and weigh it down with small stones or pebbles. Press the cut stem firmly into the soil.

Plantlets will form at the cut veins and can be potted individually once the roots are well established. You can also cut the leaf into small squares, each with a piece of the main or lateral vein, and place them flat on the soil.

Whole leaves or leaf sections of *streptocarpus* (cape primrose) or *sansevieria* (mother-in-law's tongue) can be inserted vertically into the soil. New plantlets will grow from the base.

The pot-in-pan method (see illustration at left) is ideally suited to leaf cuttings. Fill a small clay pot with water and place in the center of a larger pot or bowl. Water will seep through the clay into the growing medium and provide humidity and moisture to the leaf cuttings. Cover the bowl or pot with plastic to retain moisture. Leaf cuttings can also be rooted in covered pots or trays.

Division

Divide roots, then pot individually.

Division is the simplest method of vegetative propagation. Most plants that form multiple crowns, such as ferns, spider plants and African violets, are suited to this technique.

Simply knock the plant out of its pot, shake off the excess soil, and divide the plant into two to five pieces, each with an ample portion of root and foliage. Split the parent plant with your hands or cut cleanly with a knife if the plant is pot bound and difficult to separate. With a large pot bound plant, it may be helpful to rinse the soil from the roots before dividing.

Plant all divisions immediately and water thoroughly to prevent drying of the roots. Water frequently and keep the plants in diffused light until they recover and begin to show new growth. Foliage plants are best divided in the spring, flowering plants during their dormant, non-flowering period.

Offsets

Offsets on spider plant.

Offsets are miniature plantlets that arise from the parent plant on long stems or creeping stolons. The spider plant (*Chlorophytum*) with its pre-formed offspring reaching out in all directions for new soil to colonize, is the best known example of a plant that produces offsets. Spider plants will develop more offsets if kept slightly pot bound.

Offsets can be severed from the parent as soon as they develop aerial roots, then planted, or they may be removed at an earlier stage and rooted in water. You can also root offsets by pegging them down into small pots filled with rooting medium placed next to the parent plant. Sever the offsets from the stock plant once the plantlet is established (new growth appears or the plant seems to be well anchored in the medium).

144

Air Layering

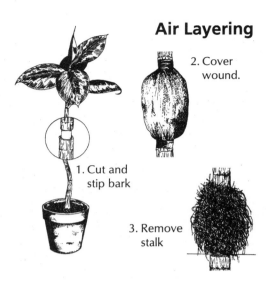

2. Cover wound.

1. Cut and stip bark

3. Remove stalk

Many exotic plants, including dracaenas, ficus and dieffenbachias, have a tendency to become tall and leggy, discarding their lower leaves as they grow. Air layering is useful to reproportion the plant and rejuvenate its growth habit. The top portion of the plant is rooted to produce a new compact plant, and the bottom part is either cut back to encourage new growth or discarded.

Choose a point 10 to 12 inches (25-30.5 cm) below the top of an actively growing plant. With a sharp knife circle the stem removing a 1 1/2-inch strip of outer bark and exposing the underlying wood. Cover the wound with damp sphagnum moss, dust with rooting powder, then pack the area above and below the cut with damp moss. Wrap with plastic sheeting and secure both ends to retain moisture and encourage root formation.

Within a few months, roots will be visible through the plastic. Once they are full and well established, cut the stem below the roots, remove the plastic and pot the new plant.

Layering

Anchor stem to soil.

Similar in principle to air layering, this method of propagation is well suited to trailing philodendrons, pothos (*Scindapsis sp*) and syngoniums. Repot the plant into a larger container with clear areas of new soil. Make shallow cuts in the stem between nodes. Gently bend the stems over the new soil and anchor with bent or U-shaped wire pins.

Press firmly making sure that the wounds come into contact with the soil. Once the plantlets become established, sever from the parent plant with a clean, sharp knife and pot each separately.

Spores

Ferns can be increased from the dust like spores found on the underside of the leaves. Shake the ripe spore cases onto newspaper and then store in a paper bag to dry for a few weeks before sowing.

For successful germination, provide high humidity and sterile growing conditions. Thoroughly moisten a sterile medium such as perlite or screened peatmoss before sowing the spores. Sow into trays or boxes and cover the container with glass or plastic sheeting to retain moisture. Place the container in a warm, dimly lit place and keep moist, not soaking wet, at all times.

On germination, a green moss like growth will appear on the surface of the soil. This is the fern's sexual reproduction stage. When true fronds start to appear, transplant the clumps individually into 3-inch pots filled with potting soil.

Root Cuttings

Many plants with thick, fleshy roots, such as begonias or sansevierias, or plants that have a tendency to produce suckering shoots, can be propagated from root cuttings. Cut portions of the root into sections and insert vertically in pots filled with a moist rooting medium, or lay them flat on the surface of the soil in trays and cover lightly with sand.

For tuberous or bulbous plants such as gloxinias or tuberous begonias, cut the bulb or tuber into segments, each with a bud. Dust each root segment with a fungicide and plant separately in a moist rooting medium.

First published in Volume 4, Number 2, page 56.

Soft Wood Cloning

by Walt Wilson

Whether or not a clone roots and develops into a mature plant depends on the type of plant material selected, the way the material was taken or "cut," the rooting hormones used, the media used for propagation, the anti-fungus, anti-bacterial and growth inducing agents used.

Many parts of the plant will root — leaves, stems and growing tips or buds. Selection of plant parts depends on the time allowed for rooting and the sophistication of the grower and his or her equipment. Leaves can root, but generally take twice as long as growing tips and require another degree of sophistication.

For our purposes, we will concentrate on the fastest methods available for simple propagation, with the least required equipment. We should, however, understand that the fastest methods are not the least expensive. In particular, the medium selected and the required hormones may or may not be feasible for propagation of non-valuable production plants. On the other hand, the method described here has been used to propagate production cuttings with a better than 90 percent success rate, with roots in three weeks or less.

The Mother Plant

The plant that produces the cuttings or clones is the mother plant. Clones from the mother plant will replicate the mother plant in every general way: size, color, taste, smell and so on. Remember that each clone will still possess some individual characteristics that relate more to vigor; some cuttings, for whatever reason (usually environmental), may take longer to root and grow vegetatively than others. However, most clones will follow the exact same course as the mother plant. Therefore, the mother plant should be outstanding in every desirable characteristic.

The mother plant should be maintained on a low- to medium-nitrogen diet for the most part. Low nitrogen content of the stem speeds rooting. This presents our first trade off: Nitrogen in soft wood cuttings gives stiffness to the stem. Stiffness of the stem is crucial in placing the stem into the medium without bending. Mother plants should be maintained on a minimum of 150 parts per million (ppm) of nitrogen to maintain growth and continued life.

Phosphorus should vary between 75 and 150 ppm to restrict root growth in proportion to vertical height. To increase root growth, as in the case of a young mother plant that has not achieved her ideal size, 300 ppm phosphorus in proportion to 100 ppm nitrogen (3 to 1), is recommended. Mother plants that produce large numbers of clones should be periodically dosed with 300 ppm nitrogen to encourage new and replacement growth.

Potassium should follow nitrogen in the same proportion (1 to 1) for sustained growth unless seed production is indicated. Typically, a mother plant is kept in perpetual vegetative growth, without pollination. Should seeds be necessary, elevate potassium levels to twice the nitrogen dose one week following pollination. Depending on the variety, a mother plant grown with this method will produce approximately 50 clones every two weeks.

After a plant has been grown and certified to be a mother plant because of its outstanding characteristics, use no growth regulating hormones (auxins, cytokenins, etc.) The mother plant is not a production plant. We wish her to remain as nature intended. Production plants are pushed to their limits in order to produce better fruits, bigger yields. Mother plants are grown to produce clones.

The Three-node Consideration

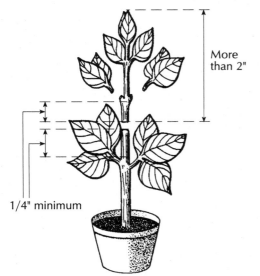

More than 2"

1/4" minimum

The growing tips we desire may come from the sides or top of the mother. This is what we are looking for: an active growing tip with a pair (or one) of sun (or sucker) leaves beginning to unfold from the tip.

Looking at the mother plant, select an active growing tip. Follow the tip down toward the plant one branch or internode. At the intersection of the leaf branch and stem you should find another active growing node; the sun leaf (or leaves) that emerge from the stem should be more developed than the leaf found at the growing tip. Moving down one more internode, find the third growing node with an even more developed sun leaf (see illustration at left).

An active growing tip with three active growing nodes and two to three sets of sun leaves and 2 to 4 inches in total length is what you are looking for with most plant varieties. The exact size of the clone is determined by internode spacing. If your internode spacing (the distance between growing nodes) is 1 inch, then your clone should be 3 inches long. Whether or not to keep the third set of sun leaves is dependent on the total length of the clone at the third internode: If the clone is 2 inches or shorter, keep the third set of sun leaves. If the clone is longer than 2 inches at the third internode, remove the third set of leaves.

How to Cut

Use a sharp blade or surgical scissors to take soft wood clones (Hospital Grade, Operating Suture, 5 1/2 inch, straight, Sharp/Sharp, stainless). Surgical scissors produce a clean cut by slicing plant tissues, rather than tearing. A razor may be used in a pinch, but scissors are safer.

When cutting plant tissues, do not cut exactly at the intersection of growing nodes or cut leaf branches close to the stem. Cut above or below intersections leaving a "tail" of at least 1/4 inch. This is done to allow the mother plant to repair herself. Remember that removal of any plant tissue causes some injury to the mother plant.

Where to Cut

Locate a growing tip and apply the three-node consideration. It is important that any trimming (removal of leaves) be done while the clone is still attached to the mother plant. After trimming, prepare to take the clone by cutting from the mother at the midway point between the third and fourth internode. The cut and transfer of the clone to the rooting compound should be accomplished as quickly as possible.

Rooting Compounds

Use of a rooting compound is necessary to the propagation of soft wood cuttings. When used in conjunction with a combination fungicide (Maneb, Thiram or Captan) and anti-bacterial agent (streptomycin sulfate), it will induce callous formation (an undifferentiated mass of cells) in the presence of competing organisms.

Rooting compounds may be powders, thin liquids or thick liquids. Liquid formulations are preferred to powders; not only do they coat the stem better, liquids help prevent embolisms. Embolisms occur as air becomes trapped in the junction where the clone is severed from the mother or the stem close to the cut has been bent or bruised. Embolisms spell death for the clone.

Embolisms may be avoided by the quick transfer of the clone to the liquid rooting compound and into the rooting medium. Literally, no more than a couple of seconds should pass from the cutting of the clone to its placement in the rooting compound. Growers who insist on using a rooting powder should make a slurry with distilled water.

The Rooting Medium

The rooting medium must be sterilized, drain well and be able to hold air (oxygen), water and nutrients. Soil and organic amendments (peat moss and compost) are not indicated for clone rooting. Even with proper preparation, organics attract and promote the growth of living organisms, good and bad. In cloning we must create a temporary environment for the promotion of rooting. After the clone has rooted, it has certain protection from diseases and can coexist with them.

A fifty-fifty mix of virgin vermiculite and perlite make a basic rooting medium that is inexpensive and adequate. Wear gloves or use cups or spoons to mix or handle the mix. Do not wet the mix, but avoid breathing any dust. Distribute the mix into small containers of a minimum of one cubic inch (9 cubic inches is about the maximum). Each container is a cell, usually made of plastic with drainage holes. A number of cells may be made into a sheet so that each cell may be cut or snapped away from the sheet. The sheet should be placed into a flat without drainage holes. An example of this system is the Kord™ #812, a sheet of 96 cells designed to fit into a standard 21- by 11-inch flat (Kord #1020NNH, without drain holes).

An alternative to the vermiculite/perlite mix is rockwool. Rockwool is the spun thread of molten rock. It can be compressed into layers and formed into cubes of many sizes. The advantage of rockwool for cloning is that it is far less labor intensive than the vermiculite/perlite mix.

An example is Grodan™ #AM 36/40, a sheet of 98 1 1/2-inch rockwool cubes that fit into a standard 21- by 11-inch flat. These cubes are pre-formed with angled sides and holes on the top. The grower needs only to cut clones, dip into rooting compound and place the clones into the pre-punched holes.

The disadvantage to using rockwool for cloning is cost. Each rockwool cube (as described) will cost approximately 10 to 12 cents. For most clones this cost is insignificant. However, the cost of the same amount of vermiculite/perlite mix with a container would be less than 1 cent.

Nutrient Solution

The rule in feeding clones for their first three weeks of rooting is complete nutrition. A balanced NPK of at least 20-20-20 is indicated. Since very little vertical growth is desired during the rooting process, nitrogen should not exceed 75 ppm. What is more important during this process is micronutrients. Clones that are beginning to root require all the available micronutrients to knit the mineral salts into vegetative root structures. Only after roots have formed is there a need for increased nitrogen and phosphorus.

Production of good clone nutrient concentrates is a complicated affair. Extracts of White Willow (*Salix alba*) encourage callous formation (stage 2 rooting) when used with the proper hormones. The solution should also include a fungicide (whether organic or synthetic) and protection from bacteria. Advanced formulations also include automatic pH correction for various water types. Growers who are not inclined to produce their own concentrates and suffer the failures that so often result would be better off purchasing a commercial preparation.

Preparing the Cubes

The grower is the source of most infections. Before preparing the trays, wash hands thoroughly. Gloves are not optional for beginners unless the grower is familiar with sterile procedure.

Wash every tray before use (even new trays) in the following manner: Apply a jet of water to the inside and back of the tray and pour off the standing water. With the tray horizontal, shake a generous amount of dry scouring powder that contains chlorine (sodium hypochlorite). Wet a clean rag and scrub the inside of the flat or tray. These trays are ribbed inside and the cleanser must contact all surfaces of the inside of the tray. Scrubbing the outside of the tray and the bottom is optional.

Allow the cleanser to stand in the tray for five minutes and then forcibly remove the cleanser with water. No trace of cleanser should remain in the tray! From this step on, do not touch the inside of the tray without clean gloves.

For the production of 49 clones (enough to fill a standard 21- by 11 inch nursery tray), place 64 ounces of nutrient solution into a cleaned, empty tray. If rockwool is used, divide a 98-cube pad in half with scissors; do not break off individual cubes. Wearing gloves or using sterilized tongs, place the half pad into the center of the tray containing the rooting solution. If using vermiculite/perlite, place a filled, half-sheet of

AERO-HYDROPONIC PLANT PROPAGATION

In controlled experiments with Chrysanthemum and Ficus at the University of California at Davis, researchers have demonstrated dramatically improved performance of cuttings in a hybrid hydroponic/aeroponic (aero-hydroponic) system over those propagated in solid media.

The Ein Gedi System (EGS) propagation unit, developed at U. C. Davis by Hillel Soffer and David Burger, employs an integral reservoir with aeroponic action provided by a rotating impeller. It is said to combine the stability of hydroponics with the superior oxygenation capacity of aeroponics.

In the February '89 issue of *HortScience*, they reported a higher rooting percentage and number of roots for both plants in the EGS than in the two solid media tested: a one-to-one mix of perlite and vermiculite and a mixture of equal parts sand, peat and redwood bark. All three systems were tested with and without overhead misting.

Ficus cuttings in the sand/peat/bark mix failed to root in both tests while cuttings in the perlite/vermiculite mix did better with the overhead misting, 17.3 roots per cutting compared with 10.7 without misting. Rooting in the EGS system was actually greater without misting — 30.3 compared with 21.1 roots per cutting — and substantially better overall. The findings were much the same for the more easily rooted Chrysanthemum, except that the overhead misting had no significant effect on the EGS propagated cuttings.

The authors say that the system has also proven effective with difficult-to-root species such as *Arctostaphylos uva-ursi* (Bearberry), *Eucalyptus sideroxylon* (Red Ironbark) and *Salix scoulerana*.

SWEETER CUTTINGS

Geranium starts soaked in a dilute sugar water after cutting showed improved survival rates when compared with their unsweetened siblings in a test at Wye College in England.

According to a report in the January '89 issue of *Greenhouse Grower*, cuttings soaked for 24 hours in a 5 percent sucrose solution were better able to survive several weeks of storage, especially at higher temperatures. Survival of the sugar soaked cuttings, stored for nine weeks under continuous low intensity light at a temperature of 35 to 40 degrees was about 50 percent.

The researchers found that high concentrations of sucrose, 15 percent or more, can damage cuttings.

cubes into the tray in the same manner.

Remember that clones in this process are watered from the bottom up, as opposed to the standard feeding from the top down. Top-down watering removes the rooting hormones that are placed on the stem. Top-down watering also promotes fungi and bacterial intervention with the formation of algae and the possibility of fungus gnats.

Disperse the nutrient solution through the cubes in the following manner (this method also applies to watering the clones): Slightly lift the left side of the tray allowing the solution to travel through the cubes to the right. Repeat the procedure from the right to the left and front to back. The idea is to evenly move the nutrient through all the cubes without wetting the tops. In large production facilities the wetting of trays may be automated with a shaker table.

Do not remove excess nutrient from the tray at this stage. Allow the tray to stand at least 15 minutes before placing clones. If using vermiculite/perlite, punch a small hole to a depth of 3/4 of the depth of the medium for clone placement.

If you are using rockwool with pre-punched holes, it still may be necessary to punch a smaller hole at the bottom if clones cannot be placed without bending the stem. Use a 1/8-inch dowel or ice-pick that has been dipped in rubbing alcohol.

If using vermiculite/perlite, place the clone into the hole and tap the sides of the medium to hold the clone in place. Regardless of the medium the base of the clone stem should rest in the medium 1/4 to 1/2 inch above the bottom of the container or tray.

Humidity

Clones require high humidity during the rooting stage. Clones lack roots and thus can only take nutrients through the cut stem and leaves. Most moisture is lost through the leaves. An artificial environment of at least 90 percent humidity can be created mechanically with a spinning-disk, cool-mist humidifier. Do not use ultrasonic or conventional steam type humidifiers as they may produce oxides of heavy metals. Water used to supply the humidifier must be disinfected with 1 teaspoon of household bleach per gallon of water to prevent the formation of algae and bacteria.

For the smaller grower, a humidity dome may be used. Domes merely restrict the moisture contained in the medium to the growing tray or flat. Clones kept in a humidity dome must be misted with distilled water every two days. Regardless of the method used, failure to maintain humidity for 24 hours during the first two weeks of rooting will probably cause the clones to wither and die.

An alternative for humidity control is cloning wax. Cloning wax is a liquid suspension of transparent, flexible wax, with nutrients and hormones. Clones sprayed with wax do not require a humidity dome.

Temperature and CO_2

Clones need a root-zone temperature of approximately 75 degrees (24 C) to promote rooting. Clones will root in lower temperatures but it will take more than three weeks. Root mats — heated pads that the trays sit on — are excellent but expensive. Sometimes a small heater with a thermostat is all that is required. In this case, raise the ambient temperature to 80 degrees (27 C) to insure adequate root-zone warming.

Remember that warm air rises and that the air temperature on the floor is lower than at the ceiling. Increasing CO_2 from atmospheric 300 ppm to 600 ppm is useful with large scale production but is not really necessary for the small grower.

Lighting

Most growers use fluorescent lighting to root clones. Fluorescents may be placed within an inch of the clones, as they produce little heat. High intensity lights may be used (with cloning wax) at a distance of 3 feet for growers who wish to root clones within a mother room or greenhouse.

A 4-foot lighting fixture with two 40-watt cool-white bulbs will support two trays of up to 100 clones each. Improvements on this system would be to increase the blue output of the bulbs by selecting lights with a higher Kelvin temperature. Bulbs with more than a 5,000 Kelvin output are easy to find in garden stores. Bulbs of more than 10,000 Kelvin are harder to locate and are often found only through scientific supply houses. Most manufacturers list the Kelvin temperature on the tube.

Clones root faster with 24 hours of light. However, this may not be desirable. A growing tip taken from a mother plant is accustomed to a certain amount of light for a certain period of time daily. The mother plant through internal mechanisms of hormones and auxins has predestined the fate of this tip based on her environmental influences.

The genotype of the mother plant are those factors that are inherent to the plant as a result of genes. The phenotype is the outcome of the plant surviving in the real world. Potential and reality can be very different. If it is desired that the clone be like the mother in every general way, then the clone should receive the same length of light as the mother plant. If, on the other hand, the mother was a good genotype, but a poor phenotype, the clone could be influenced to be a better phenotype by receiving more light.

Feeding

The clones must be fed every two days. For 50 clones feed 8 ounces of clone nutrient. If this is the first feeding following creation of the clones, pour any standing nutrient out of the tray (the grower may have to hold the pad or sheet in place while pouring). For every other feeding, apply nutrient to the tray, move the tray left to right and back and forth as was described earlier, and pour off any excess nutrient.

If at any time in the feeding the nutrient is fully absorbed, apply another measure of nutrient (8 ounces for 50 clones or 16 ounces for 100 clones) to the tray, shake and pour off the excess. The procedure may be repeated as often as necessary, but never is nutrient allowed to stand in the tray following a feeding.

Weeks One Through Three

The clone will live or die in the first 72 hours. The first day following cloning it is not unusual to see most of the clones knocked down. They should still be lush and green. Any clone that has wilted within 24 hours has developed a serious problem (probably an embolism) and should be pulled, recut, dipped and replaced into the medium (its survival rate is now less than 50 percent).

Mass wilting, more than 25 percent of the clones taken, indicates a fundamental problem that usually relates to environment. The second day, many of the clones should be looking toward the light. They may not be standing erect, but there should be some movement in the tip. On the third day most of the clones should have indicated movement toward the light; some may be standing erect. At this time, clones that have wilted or refused to stand, should be discarded as dead.

Little happens in the first week. The most that can be expected is that the clones will stand and look toward the light. Very little nutrient will be absorbed. Expect to pour 80 percent of the nutrient off the tray following a feeding. The plants are establishing a nutrient flow between the cut stem and the medium.

By the fifth day, the rooting hormones have initiated basal swelling (Stage l, the rapid division of cells) in the end of the cut stem. It is very important to leave the trays alone, except when feeding. Clones that have not stood at the end of the first week should be pulled, examined and then discarded. If it is a valuable clone and if it has shown some indication of life, then it may be kept with the understanding that it will be two to three weeks behind the other plants. Many valuable and endangered plants are kept this way to preserve genetic material until tissue cultures can be made.

Week two brings many changes. The lower leaves may begin to yellow. Unless a disease is evident, remove no leaves during the entire three-week cycle. Some bottom leaves may brown and wither. Withering bottom leaves when the tops are green and vibrant is an excellent sign that rooting is underway. The plant, in its economy, continues to live but now realizes that something has happened to its connection to the mother plant. It therefore consumes its own tissue (the bottom leaves) for nutrients and water. The problem to watch for in the second week is the overconsumption of tissue.

Should a clone start to "burn," the edges of the leaf turn bright yellow and the process begins to rapidly consume the leaf, the clone has not made a good connection to the medium. This may be solved by gently pressing the clone into the medium. If 50 percent of the original tissue is gone, then discard the clone. In week two the first spots of callous tissue form (Stage 2). These tissues are masses of undifferentiated cells capable of becoming roots. Expect as much as 50 percent of the nutrient to be consumed at each feeding.

Clones that make week three will more than likely become production plants. Color change, as in week two, will continue. Some lower leaf drop may occur. The upper leaves of the clones will begin to rise and may show some signs of burn. Burn in respect to week three looks the same as that described in week two with an important exception, the burn does not consume the leaf. This burn is the result of pH imbalances as the first roots appear and try to absorb nutrients from the medium. These nodes (Stage 3) are incapable of extending themselves deeper into the medium.

Adventurous roots must occur (Stage 4). These first true roots are water seeking roots that allow the plant to determine the extent of its growing area. New growth will begin from the top of the clones. Some stretching may be seen between internodes.

Week Four   Up till now we have treated our clones with great care providing an ideal environment for root development. After three weeks, rooting is done, and the time has come for the clone to become a production plant. A clone will not become a production plant until it has developed adventurous roots (rooting - stage 4). Adventurous roots are the familiar white roots that come out of the bottom of the medium.

Some clones are sluggish in putting out adventurous roots because the medium is too wet. Let the medium dry out on a day-by-day basis until these root appear. The amount of water in the medium is directly related to the weight of the medium. It is usually quite easy to feel the weight of the medium by lifting the tray. If the medium has dried out, do not use clone nutrient to water the tray. Use a 150 ppm nitrogen solution with 75 ppm phosphorus content (a 20-10-20 NPK is an example). Do not use more than 150 ppm nitrogen, the pressure on the embryonic root system would burn the clone up.

Most growers would consider using a high phosphorus to low nitrogen solution to build a better root system at this point. In cloning, after rooting, we need to push the clone to grow. High phosphorus is not indicated until a medium change has occurred. Nitrogen at this point will revitalize the plant giving it the encouragement to take off.

After the initial drying of the medium and the first application of nitrogen solution, feed the clones as little as possible with nitrogen solution until the roots show. As soon as the roots have shown, move the clone to the next step — a larger container — and water thoroughly with a 300 ppm phosphorus solution containing 100-150 ppm nitrogen (10-30-20 NPK is an example). Within two weeks, change to a 300 ppm nitrogen solution for maximum vegetative growth.

First published in Volume 1, Number 3, page 62

The Sip of Life — Water Control for Cuttings

by Stephen Jones

As a rule I have found that many homemade propagation units are not only less expensive, but will outperform some of the manufactured systems on the market today. Once certain requirements are met, it is the technique and skill of the grower that most often determines success or failure, not the equipment used. The following is a technique for the home grower called the "Sip of Life" that has proven effective in greatly improving the survival of softwood cuttings:

Materials
- Fluorescent light
- Liquid rooting hormone
- Superthrive™
- Plastic tub
- Sharp knife
- pH tester and adjuster

Select Cuttings

- Take cuttings from clean, disease-free stock. Cuttings taken from plants that have been deprived of nutrients, especially water, will respond poorly. Cuttings of equal length foliage and color should be selected and must not contain deformities in leaf growth pattern for optimum uniformity of the plants after rooting.
- Take cuttings from the most vigorously growing portion of the plant; this is where the highest concentration of auxins (growth hormones) are found. Cuttings selected should be green barked and should not contain any of the woodier type bark which indicates age.
- The finished cutting should be as short as possible; 4 to 5 inches is preferred. Remember, auxins are more concentrated at the growing tip. Three to four small, well-formed leaves should be left intact.

Take Cuttings

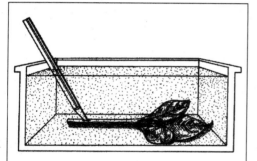

- The propagation area and all containers should be carefully cleaned to reduce the danger of infection.
- Fill the plastic tub or other suitable container with clean water. It should not contain fertilizer, but it is advisable to adjust the pH to 6.4 (6.2 to 6.6 is acceptable). Also, add Superthrive™ at a ratio of 10 drops per U.S. gallon. Maintain the water temperature at 78 degrees (26 C).
- The cuttings taken should be at least 1 inch longer than you are going to use. Make the cut with a sharp knife and *immediately* place the *entire* cutting into the pH adjusted water.
- While the cutting is underwater, cut it to the final length. Make the cut in a single, smooth motion at a 45-degree angle to the stem. If there is an internode at the cut point, make your cut directly below the node. With the cutting still submerged, remove any excess leaves.
- If there are no internodes at the cut, make three of four shallow vertical slits (no deeper than the outer bark) upward from the cut along the stem about 1/2 inch. These cuts must be made with the cutting submerged or air will be sucked into the stem causing what is known as an air embolism in which air bubbles block the movement of water up the stem. An air embolism can cause death or slow the

MICROWAVE SEEDS

We don't know how many of you have microwaves or who would want to try this experiment, but life after all is risky. And it just might work. It did with popcorn, wheat, pinto bean, alfalfa, castor beans, some clovers, crown vetch, ipomoea, millet, oats, okra, peas, peppers, annual rye grass, spinach and mung bean seeds as well as some grass, corn and tomato seeds — they grew 30 percent faster than unexposed seeds, and in some cases had a higher germination rate.

Exposed to what? Microwaves. Here is something to do with the microwave other than drying out the poodle. (Just joking about the poodle — don't try that. The poodle met an unpleasant end.)

Four 15-second bursts at a low intensity, around 30 watts, seemed to yield the best results. Typical microwaves designed for home use have higher wattages (200 to 700 watts) however, most of the newer models have setting controls that can "throttle down" to around 10 percent of their maximum output. If you are attempting experiments with a microwave that you cannot throttle down, use the lowest setting available.

One researcher, Stuart D. Nelson of the U.S. Department of Agriculture at the Russell Agricultural Research Center in Athens, Georgia, got the best results with seeds having a low moisture content — 6 to 7 percent. — *Erik Ackerson* rooting process by weeks. This is known as the Sip of Life technique. By making all secondary cuts underwater, you eliminate air bubbles, reduce unnecessary strain on the clone and allow the cutting to stabilize in a fluid environment.

■ After making your second cut and removing any excess leaves under water, remove the cutting and submerge the cut end in a liquid rooting hormone. Make sure that at least 1 inch of the cutting is placed in the hormone.

Reduce Cutting Stress

By controlling light levels, humidity and temperature, your job is to keep the cutting in a complete state of dormancy. Cuttings without roots are very sensitive to stress. Every effort should be made to minimize evaporation from the cuttings and to avoid extreme light and temperature levels.

Keep the humidity as close to 100 percent as possible and maintain water and substrate temperatures at between 70 and 84 degrees (21-29 C). Cooler water will slow root formation; warmer water will encourage disease. The lower the humidity level, the more water the plant will transpire, causing the cutting to use up stored food for things other than root production. It is important to hold the leaves as dormant as possible and permit the cutting to expend its energy on root development.

First published in Volume 2, Number 1, page 50.

Propagation in Rockwool

155

by Roger H. Thayer

Cloning, starting plants from cuttings, is one of the most popular uses of rockwool products. The following is a general step-by-step method for successful cloning. As any experienced gardener knows, the specific method used will vary some from one plant variety to another.

■ Rockwool cubes and bulk rockwool have an initial pH of about 8 (high alkaline). The pH should be lowered to 5.5 to 6.5 before the cuttings are inserted using one of the following methods: Soak the rockwool in a phosphoric acid solution with a pH of 3 to 4 for one hour prior to use. Or, soak cubes or bulk wool in a dilute nutrient solution for 24 hours.
Following either method, flush with fresh water and let drain freely. Be sure to keep the rockwool moist after this initial conditioning.

■ Take cuttings from healthy plants. Leave four or five leaf sets per cutting. Use a razor blade to trim off the lowest set of leaves next to the severed stem. This will reduce the exposed surface area and transpiration (water uptake), giving the cutting more chance to root. Do not rinse the cuttings.

■ As soon as possible after the cuttings are taken, dip them in Rootone "F" or "Dip & Grow" covering the depth of the cut and trimmed off lower leaves. Knock off any excess. Make a hole in the rockwool cube with a pencil. (Bulk rockwool may be packed into a Styrofoam cup for cuttings. Be sure to punch drainage holes in the bottom.)

Gently insert the cutting into the moistened rockwool.

■ Place the starter cubes (or cups) in a shallow plastic tray and place under Gro-Lux or Cool-White fluorescent lights. Set the lights about one foot above the cuttings (200 to 500 foot-candles at plant tops). Keep them shaded from direct sunlight or nearby high intensity discharge (HID) lighting.

Cover the tray with a clear or white plastic covering to create a moisture holding tent. A temperature range of 65 to 85 degrees is ideal for rooting, with a humidity of 40 to 70 percent. Keep 1/8 to 1/4 inch of half-strength nutrient solution in the bottom of the tray.

■ After four to seven days, or when roots start to emerge from under the starter cubes, place the small cubes inside of the larger cubes with holes in them, such as the Grodan DM-4 or DM-6.5. Flush with fresh water, drain and return to tray.

■ After about three weeks, the plants should be ready to transfer to your hydroponic system. Rockwool cubes can be placed directly into gravel or perlite beds or on rockwool slabs in the greenhouse or under lights. If bulk rockwool is used, remove the cup before transplanting.

Transplantone can be used at this stage to minimize root shock. Liquinox (Vitamin B-1) can also be used for cuttings or transplants to reduce shock and promote healthy root growth.

Starting Seed in Rockwool

Most seeds should be planted as deep as they are long. If the seed hole is too deep in the starter block, fill with perlite, vermiculite or rockwool to the proper depth. Lightly cover the seeds with perlite to shade them from bright light. If starter cubes are not used, space seeds 1 to 2 inches apart.

Seeds contain enough internal nutrient to sustain them after germination for three to seven days. Use only plain water at first until the first true leaves start to open. Seeds can be treated with vitamin B-1 before and during germination. Vitamin B-1 containing alpha napthalene acetic

THE STARTER BOX

Starter boxes are a great way of starting from seed. The drawing at right shows how a typical starter box might be arranged. A shopping list for the box pictured would include:
• An outer starter flat and clear lid.
• A 32-cup inner tray with pre-punched holes.
• A heating cable of the appropriate size with an adjustable thermostat.
• 32 rockwool starter cubes.
• Two pounds of pea gravel.
• Eight ounces of perlite.
• Rootone for cuttings.
• Rockwool nutrient mix.
A system like this will start seeds or cuttings rapidly and efficiently for later transplanting into pots,

flower beds, gardens or hydroponic systems. This gives you an extra jump on springtime! — *Roger H. Thayer*

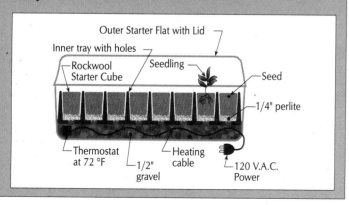

156

acid is a hormone-like substance and growth regulator promoting root formation.

The temperature at the roots should be 72 degrees. Air temperature should be about the same or slightly lower. No light is needed until the first (petiole) leaves appear. Feed with a half-strength nutrient solution and place under Gro-Lux or Cool-White tubes about 1 foot away. Keep the starter cubes moist at all times. A clear or white plastic tent helps.

Rockwool starter cubes are especially good for starting seeds. They are sterile, drain well, absorbent, nutrient retentive and light weight. The vertical fibers help the roots grow down and out of the cubes instead of sideways.

After plants are 3 to 4 inches high, or when six to eight roots can be seen growing out of the bottom of the cube, it is time to transplant cube and all to your hydroponic system. Make sure the cubes are buried with at least 1/4 inch of the growing medium. Water as soon as possible with a half-strength nutrient solution.

Plants can be exposed to HID lights and started on a full-strength solution after they have been established for a week or two. HID lights should be kept 12 to 18 inches from the tops of well established growing plants.

Wick systems using perlite, vermiculite or rockwool and a plastic tent germinate and grow healthy seedlings quickly. Bottom heat can be added with 6 feet of heating cable for every square foot of growing area.

First Published in Volume 1, Number 2, page 25

157

Tissue Culture — The Fine Art of Micropropagation

by Paul Olsen

The problems encountered with cloning start with the soil. Soil used for propagation may contain fungi and bacteria harmful to plant tissue. Damping-off commonly encountered in seed beds is caused by fungi such as species of *Pythium, Phytophthora, Rhizoctonia* and *Fusarium*. Fungus gnats, thrips, spider mites and others can sometimes be devastating, especially under warm, humid conditions.

Tissue culture avoids these problems by using and maintaining sterile conditions. Systemic pathogens, viruses and some bacteria, are not automatically eliminated by tissue culture unless this is a goal built into the system. The primary use of tissue culture techniques is the rapid mass propagation of disease-free clones.

The tissue for culture can be selected from almost any part of the plant, leaves, stems, stem tips, roots, anthers, petals, tubers, bulbs and seeds. Although the basic techniques of tissue culture are not sophisticated or difficult to learn, they have not been a part of the training for most professional horticulturists and others who are now becoming interested in the process.

The Process

Stage 1: In stage 1, also called the explant or establishment phase, a suitable plant part (an explant) is disinfected and cultured aseptically in a culture medium that will confirm decontamination from micro-organisms and allow growth. This is the stage where contamination is most likely to occur. Contaminated cultures can be identified at this stage and discarded.

The cultures are incubated in racks on lighted shelves in a controlled environment. Temperature is held at 80 degrees and fluorescent lighting provided at 100 foot candles. Photoperiods of 16 hours are common, but I prefer a 24-hour period.

Stage 2: Once established, stage 1 material is ready for stage 2 — multiplication. Here is the real power of tissue culture propagation. The objective is to rapidly increase the number of propagules (potential clones) as a result of either auxiliary branching (branching of lateral buds) or of adventive (new) bud formation. Cultures can be subcultured over and over until the required number of propagules have been produced.

Stage 3: In stage 3, the conditioning or pretransplant phase, allows the propagules to further shoot maturation and rooting. Stage 3 propagules are relatively tender and are next transplanted into a potting medium. They are gradually exposed to the higher light levels and lower humidity of the greenhouse or grow room until a normal, independent plant is obtained.

The Lab

The laboratory has the following functions: media preparation, aseptic procedures, incubation of cultures and general operations. The equipment needed to set up a tissue culture lab is minimal. If you are just beginning and don't want to invest a lot of money, you could purchase a ready-to-use culture medium and skip the first nine items on the list below:

- Hot plate or stove.
- Pressure cooker or autoclave.
- pH meter or test paper.
- Centigram balance scale.
- Glass or stainless steel container for heating the media.
- Culture tubes or bottles with suitable closures and a rack to hold them upright.
- Dispensing device or burette, a finely graduated glass tube.
- Dish washing and draining area.
- Glove box or laminar air-flow cabinet (see below).
- Disinfectants.
- Scalpels and forceps.

Media Preparation

For most commercial growers only a general understanding of the processes and pitfalls of the process are needed, due to the availability of prepackaged culture media.

All plants require 16 elements. Those that are required in large quantities are called macronutrients (macroelements) and those that are required in relatively small quantities are called micronutrients (trace or microelements). The macroelements include carbon (C), hydrogen (H), oxygen (O), nitrogen (N), phosphorous (P), potassium (K), calcium (Ca), magnesium (Mg) and sulfur (S). Microelements include: iron (Fe),

MURASHIGE AND SKOOG SALT BASE

Formula		mg/l
Ammonium nitrate	NH_4NO_3	1650.000
Potassium nitrate	KNO_3	1900.000
Calcium chloride dihydrate	$CaCl_2 \cdot 2H_2O$	440.000
Magnesium sulfate 7 hydrate	$MgSO_4 \cdot 7H_2O$	370.000
Potasium dihydrogen phosphate	KH_2PO4	170.000
Ferrous sulfate 7 hydrate	$FeSO_4 \cdot 7H_2O$	27.800
Disodium EDTA	Na_2-EDTA	37.300
Boric Acid	H_3BO_3	6.200
Manganese sulfate 4 hydrate	$MnSO_4 \cdot 4H_2O$	22.300
Zinc sulfate 4 hydrate	$ZnSO_4 \cdot 4H2O$	8.600
Potassium iodine	KI	0.830
Sodium molybdate dihydrate	$Na2MoO_4 \cdot 2H_2O$	0.250
Cupric sulfate 5 hydrate	$CuSO_4 \cdot 5H_2O$	0.025
Cobalt chloride 6 hydrate	$CoCl_2 \cdot 6H_2O$	0.025

HORMONE ADDITION STAGES

Plant	Stage	Auxin	Cytokinin
Strawberry	1,2	IBA 1.0	BA 1.0
	3	IBA 1.0	0
Lettuce	1,2	IAA 5.0	Kinetine 0.5
	3	IBA 1.0	0
African Violet	1,2,3	IAA 2.0	BA 0.08
		Concentration milligrams per liter	

chlorine (Cl), manganese (Mn), zinc (Zn), boron (B), copper (Cu) and molybdenum (Mo).

The first three macroelements, carbon, hydrogen and oxygen, come from air and water in the forms of CO_2, O_2 and H_2O. All of the other elements must be supplied in the nutrient.

In tissue culture, as in hydroponics, these other elements are supplied to the plant by adding dissolved mineral salts in water to make a nutrient solution. The most widely used mineral salt formulation for tissue culture was developed by Toshio Murashige and published by Murashige and Skoog in 1962. The formulation works well for a wide range of species and for all three stages of in vitro propagation. For chemistry buffs the formula is given at left.

Several companies now sell the basic Murashige and Skoog Salt Base conveniently packaged for 1-liter of culture media. It would not make much sense for anyone just starting out to mix their own. The difficulty of keeping a large inventory of chemicals on hand, not to mention the time and effort of weighing and mixing them, make purchasing a complete mix a logical alternative.

Sucrose is added to the medium as an energy source, usually 30 grams per liter. Vitamins such as i-Inositol and Thiamine are added to stimulate growth, usually at a rate of 100 and .4 milligrams per liter respectively. Agar, a gelatinous product made from seaweed, is added for tissue support, usually at 8 grams per liter.

Other possible additives include protein hydroslates from casein or other proteins primarily to provide organic nitrogen and amino acids. Citric or ascorbic acids are used to reducing browning of the medium. Activated charcoal is sometimes added to absorb certain inhibiting factors released by some tissues. Coconut milk, malt, yeast extracts, tomato juice and orange juice have also been used.

Two classes of plant hormones, auxins and cytokinins, are now widely used in tissue culture propagation to stimulate cell growth and division. The hormones control root, shoot and callus formation. Auxins, such as IAA, IBA, and NAA are for root growth. Cytokinins, such as Adenine Sulfate, BA, 2iP and Kinetin stimulate shoot growth.

In stages 1 and 2 low concentrations of auxins (less than .3 milligrams per liter) and higher concentrations of cytokinins (more than 1 milligram per liter) are typically used. In stage 3 the relative concentrations are reversed (see table at left).

159

BIOPROCESSING

Tissue culturing, the process of reproducing an entire plant from a small mass of undifferentiated cells, may seem pretty fantastic to some home growers. But a new technology, bioprocessing, sounds like something from science fiction.

By manipulating the hormone content of the growth medium, researchers at Texas Tech University in Lubbock have managed to skip the plant production phase of tissue culturing and produce the desired plant part, in this case cotton fibers, directly from undifferentiated cotton plant cells. The fibers are not only uniform in length and thickness, but they are cleaner than field grown fibers.

Other products can be produced in the same way. Federal researchers in California have already succeeded in "growing" orange juice and cherry pulp in test tube cultures. And the USDA is researching ways to apply the technology to large scale "food factories."

If you have no information on the proper hormone types and concentrations for the species you are propagating, you may have to conduct a little of your own research.

Start by holding the cytokinin level low and constant, .1 milligrams per liter, and vary the auxin concentration in amounts of .0, .1, .5, 1, and 5 milligrams per liter. Each group should have a minimum of 10 samples for your evaluation to have any meaning. Do this for each auxin. Then hold the auxin level constant at .1 milligrams per liter and do the same test for different concentrations of cytokinin.

The results are based on careful observation of tissue samples and careful recording of those observations. Remember to hold other variables—temperature, light levels and nutrient concentrations—constant. This type of testing can also be used to fine tune macronutrient levels.

The Sterile Environment

The importance of maintaining a sterile environment during the culture of plant tissue cannot be overemphasized. The air contains millions of spores just waiting to set up housekeeping in your medium. Just walking through a room creates enough of a draft to lift these spores into the air.

High Efficiency Particulate Air (HEPA) filters are very effective at removing these spores from the air, but they are also very expensive. The laminar air-flow cabinet mentioned above has such a filter and is designed to direct a gentle flow of ultrafiltered sterile air across a working area, virtually eliminating the risk of airborne contamination.

A relatively dust free space can be obtained with a so-called glove or transfer box. A small tabletop box with a transparent top and access for the hands on the front can be purchased or constructed inexpensively. A fish tank turned on its side (the top becoming the front) and fitted with a cover that will permit access by the hands could work for this purpose.

Once airborne contaminants are eliminated, the most likely cause of contamination is dirty hands. It is essential that hands and forearms be scrubbed with plenty of soap and hot water. Extra attention should be paid to the fingernails.

The outer surfaces of plants are normally infested with spores and other microbial cells and must also be sterilized. This is most easily accomplished by submerging the plant part in a strong disinfectant solution for a short time (usually five to 20 minutes), and then rinsing with sterile water.

A solution of sodium hypochlorite (bleach), one part to 10 parts water, works well. Because of the plants' waxy outer surface, it is necessary to add a small amount of detergent to the disinfectant to allow better penetration of the tissue surface.

All tools to be used in the operation and working surfaces should be sterilized with ethyl or isopropyl alcohol.

Virus Eradication

Virus infection can severely limit the yield of a wide range of plants. If vegetatively propagated plants are once systemically infected with a viral disease, the pathogen readily passes from one generation to the next. Viral infections can also be spread by infected seed.

"Virus-tested" means that a plant is no longer infected with any viruses that can be detected by one or more virus indexing techniques. Unknown viruses, however, may still be present within the plant tissue, so we do not use the term "virus-free" since it may not be literally true.

To free a plant of viral infection, the smallest shoot meristem explant (the growing root tip) is used in tissue culture. Normally the apical dome (the area of actively dividing cells at the root tip) is used as it is most likely to be free of viral organisms.

Apical meristem culture may be coupled with a thermotherapy treatment. This technique involves growing the plants for six to 12 weeks at 86 to 104 degrees prior to a excision of the apical meristem for culture. At this elevated temperature viruses are heat inactivated, though the plant tissues will continue to grow.

It should be emphasized that virus eradication by apical meristem culture is not always successful and its effectiveness must be confirmed by a testing program.

First published in Volume 1, Number 2, page 41.

Chapter 7
Production Methods

Commercial Basil Production for the Small-time Operator

by Michael Christian

Using the technologies of HID lighting and hydroponics, small producers of off-season produce will become an essential part of the community in the coming years. Pesticide-free produce and high-quality herbs are becoming the choice of the conscientious consumer. In order to test this hypothesis, we at Sun Circle conducted a sweet basil project to gather information on the profit potential.

The Market

Restaurants are a prime market for fresh, off-season sweet basil. They will pay a little extra for high-quality, clean produce. We visited local restaurants in our area with a proposition and samples. The enthusiasm was overwhelming; many of those we contacted submitted orders on the spot. Our selling price: one dollar for one ounce. We now have buyers for roughly 15 to 20 pounds per week, more than double our current production.

Some markets could realistically support a higher price and a more densely populated area could warrant a much larger project, possibly introducing some economies of scale. Such an operation might be able break into the retail grocery market, but because of the promotional effort involved — packaging, advertising and sales — this would be beyond the scope of our test. For the small-time operator, the restaurant market offers stability and a good return with a minimum of effort.

The Project

We planted a broad leaf version of sweet basil on January 10 (1989). The seeds were scattered over expanded shale in a 3-foot-square ebb and flow propagation tray. Lighting for the tray was provided by a single 250-watt metal halide lamp. The system was flushed and drained once a day with a solution at 700 parts per million (ppm) and a pH of 6.

Sweet basil grows slowly in the seedling stage, especially if root zone temperatures are low. So we installed a reservoir heater set at 70 degrees (21 C). A second propagation tray was planted on January 25. Transplanting from the propagation trays into the 9-by 9-foot ebb and flow system began on February 22 when the plants were 2 to 3 inches tall. The excess seedlings were transplanted into potting soil and sold for 89 cents per six-pack.

With the plants spaced 3 inches apart, 144 per tray, we detected little or no transplant shock. To supplement the four to six hours of natural light coming through the vertical windows of our grow room, we installed a 1000-watt metal halide and a 1000-watt high pressure sodium on a Sun Circle light mover to provide even distribution. Supplemental lighting was provided for 12 hours a day at 1800 foot-candles.

We began harvesting marketable **plant** tops by the first of April when the plants were 12 to 14 inches tall. By the end of the month we had harvested seven pounds from nine trays. From that time on, with very little labor, we've harvested 3/4 to 1 1/4 pounds per tray per week.

Sweet basil responds well to a continuous harvest whereby growing tops are harvested. Production has remained steady and the plants

continue to thrive. The nutrient solution in the 195-gallon reservoir is kept at 70 degrees (21 C), 1500 ppm and pH 6. It is changed once a month. The single reservoir was used to reduce the cost of pumps, plumbing and timers.

Aphids moved in by the end of May, but a couple thousand ladybugs every two weeks kept them in check with no interruption in the harvest. Using ladybugs as the primary means of insect control does have its problems. Since the growing area is in a larger room, the predators were free to roam. And roam they did. To keep our aphid eaters on task, we built a 2-foot high aluminum tube frame covered with a fine net to confine the insects to the basil plants. The netting should be fine enough to keep the ladybugs in, but light enough to allow the passage of light.

The Bottom Line

Expenses:	
Electricity	218.30
Nutrient	12.00
Ladybugs	21.00
Total Expenses:	251.30
Income:	
68 lbs. basil at	
$1 per ounce	1088.00
Less Expenses	251.30
	$836.70

By July 15 our records showed a total harvest of 86 pounds of superior quality fresh basil, an average of 3.75 pounds per tray per month. The income/expense breakdown for the period from April 1 to July 15 is given below. Since I wanted to evaluate a functioning continuous harvest system, I have excluded the start-up period from January through March. I have also excluded the initial equipment outlay, although depreciation and replacement costs should be figured into a more detailed analysis. Still it is possible to get a feel for the potential from the figures at left.

The sale of excess seedlings earned $89, less $16 for potting soil and containers. In fact, the sale of starts appears to have a good profit potential as a sideline and we plan to expand production next year.

With $836.70 remaining as profit, the yield per square foot per month was $5.10. The system was still in the trial-and-error stage during that period and we are confident that that figure could be increased to $6 or more next year. By expanding from nine to 20 trays next year we hope to top $1,200 a month with very little additional labor.

These figures are, of course, based on only one system in a unique market. Local conditions, especially the lack of potential buyers, could make such a venture impossible. Although some variables could work in your favor. Greenhouse space, for example, could dramatically reduce the largest variable cost, electrical power for lighting.

We will certainly be doing several things differently next time, but on the whole we feel encouraged and enthusiastic. Yes, there is money to be made in off-season produce, and you don't have to have several acres under glass to get your hands on some of it.

First Published in Volume 1, Number 2, page 20

Commercial Basil Production — One Year Later

by Michael Christian

Since the above article was published, we have instituted a number of changes in the project that should be of interest to both commercial and hobby growers.

As expected, the advent of the off-season (winter 1989-1990) brought on increased interest in our fresh basil. Production from our nine 3-foot-square growing trays continued to lag well behind the potential demand,

164

especially as the quality of locally imported basil continued to decline.

To further test the market, we placed some of our hydroponic basil in several grocery stores, usually right next to the lower priced imported basil. Despite the higher price, the visible difference in quality and freshness was sufficient to fuel consumer demand; we couldn't keep the product on the shelves. Even in our own sparsely populated area we could easily support an operation several times the size of the one we began with. Unfortunately, our production space was limited and we decided to stick with the more predictable and higher profit restaurant market.

Still, it appears that in any operation where economies of scale can be achieved by expanded production, the grocery store market should not be overlooked. Given our brief experience, higher prices at the market don't appear to be an insurmountable barrier to sales as long as the product is fresh, clean and attractively displayed.

Asexual Reproduction

We began our project with a broad leaf basil variety. However, early on we had noticed a particular strain from the original seed stock that grew exceedingly well and produced an exceptional aroma. We decided to isolate the strain — dubbed "Licorice" for its spicy aroma — and reproduce it asexually by way of cuttings. Our intention was to eventually fill the grow tables with this strain at the exclusion of the other plants. the "mother" plants were segregated from the growing area and kept scrupulously clean and insect free.

Since it takes 324 cuttings to fill our growing tables, the Licorice mothers needed to be kept vigorous and healthy. To our surprise, all of the 6-inch cuttings from the mother plants rooted in five to seven days and were ready for transplant in nine. Our propagation program was so much of a success, in fact, that we eventually dropped the rooting process and began placing fresh cuttings directly into the system. The plants grew vigorously and produced harvestable material in three weeks.

All in all, the mother/clone system worked out very well for us. However, after a few months we noticed a marked decline in cutting vigor. We now recommend that the mother plants be regenerated every three of four months from their own progeny. If plants are grown from seed, we suggest a nine-month growth cycle. The next generation of plants should be started from seed during the seventh month to ensure uninterrupted production. Cuttings should be culled from the growing trays at two to two and a half months.

This kind of preplanning is essential to profitable production. Healthy replacements must be readily available to fill empty spaces left by older or unproductive plants.

Ebb and Flow to NFT

Part of the reason for our success with cuttings was a switch from a gravel-medium ebb and flow culture to a nutrient film technique (NFT). Our previous method with 144 plants per three-foot-square tray proved to have its drawbacks. Too many plants failed to develop fully and rapidly. The change not only improved our success with cuttings, but increased total yields and reduced labor time.

Gravel is an excellent growing medium but we still had to wash it periodically to maintain a reasonably sterile environment. We designed an insert for the trays in which 36 1-inch PVC tubes were held above the nutrient solution. Into these tubes would go cuttings from our Licorice strain. With the nutrient at 68 degrees (20 C) and profuse aeration at the reservoir the plants thrived. Insulating the reservoir with a rigid foam material helped immensely, especially on cold nights. The plants quickly developed a healthy, white root mat in the trays.

The change from gravel to NFT had a noticeable effect on plant performance. Although we were raising fewer plants, our yield per tray continued to average between 3/4 and 1 pound of marketable material each week. In addition, maintenance was dramatically reduced and water/nutrient use was cut by one-third. The entire nine-tray system (81 square feet of growing area) was able to run off of a single 100-gallon reservoir. As a result, we were able to maintain an average profit per foot of $5.20 per month (slightly higher than that reported last time).

First published in Volume 1, Number 4, page 48.

Integrated Food Production

by Paul Przybylowicz

Food production systems in the future will, of necessity, produce more food per unit of energy. Many current methods of food production are possible only through the subsidies provided by "cheap" oil and will disappear or be drastically modified. The recent integration of aquaculture and hydroponics in many different places throughout the world has produced systems that give us a glimpse of what future food production may look like. The marriage of aquaculture and hydroponics appears to be "made in heaven." Waste products from one system provide energy for the other which greatly increases the overall efficiency.

Aquaculture and hydroponics have long histories and share some common principles and goals. They are adaptations of natural processes that are managed intensively to produce more food in less space than is required in natural systems. Each uses a water reservoir which carries the nutrients to the organisms being grown and also removes metabolic wastes. In non-integrated systems, the contaminated or depleted solution is discarded and replaced with fresh water or nutrient solution. This waste water often requires additional treatment prior disposal and represents a loss of energy from the system.

Plant growth in hydroponic systems slows when the nutrient concentration in solution drops and metabolic byproducts accumulate. Similarly, fish growth in aquaculture systems becomes limited as ammonia (a metabolic byproduct) concentrations increase. The advantage of integrating the two systems is several fold: the plants purify the water for the fish, the fish wastes provide a steady supply of nutrients for the plants (organic hydroponics?), and energy inputs into the system (for example, heat) produce two crops instead of one. An additional benefit for commercial growers is the plants provide a much needed cash flow before the fish are harvested.

The primary energy flow through these systems is outlined on page 167. The following is an overview of several types of integrated systems.

Finally, three actual operating systems — from large commercial operations to a backyard hobby system — are presented and discussed.

Energy and Nutrient Flow

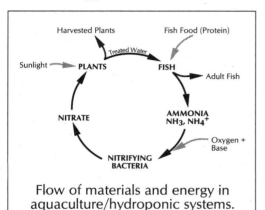

Flow of materials and energy in aquaculture/hydroponic systems.

The main energy inputs in integrated aquaculture/hydroponic systems are fish food, sunlight and electricity. Fish food provides most of the nutrients for the system; but in some systems, supplemental phosphorous, potassium, sulfur and iron may be added. Fish excrete ammonia which is toxic to them at very low levels. However, most plants can't use ammonia directly as a nitrogen source; it must first be converted to nitrate. This oxidation is performed by nitrifying bacteria (*Nitrobacter, Nitrosomonas*) in an aerobic process, usually on a biofilter of some sort.

Nitrate and other nutrients are taken up by the plants which also absorb sunlight, converting these inputs to plant material. Thus, the ammonia is removed from the water, making it suitable, once again, for fish culture. The treated water is then recycled to the fish tanks. Electricity may be used for heating, pumping and aerating the water, although different systems have varying requirements. The heat stored in the water is used by both the fish and the plants.

Fish are the primary product of these systems which also produce plants and a small amount of waste water (used to remove sediment). In contrast to conventional fish culture systems, the volume of waste water is greatly reduced and salable plant material is produced from a resource that was formerly a disposal problem.

The Organisms

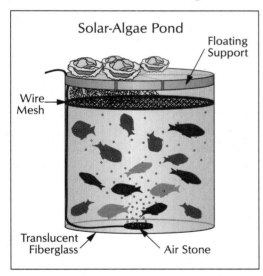

The fish most commonly grown in these integrated systems are species of *Oreochromis*, commonly known as tilapia. Tilapia have a number of characteristics that make them ideal for aquaculture. They tolerate poor water conditions and crowding, breed well in captivity and grow rapidly. In addition, tilapia don't require high protein fish feeds which are expensive and unavailable in many developing countries.

As adults, their favorite food is "bacterial/detrital aggregates" — suspended particles of organic matter. As a result, they keep their tanks very clean (unless they're overfed), grazing the algae off the walls and the sludge from the bottom. This is a big plus for small scale fish culturists. And last, but not least, tilapia are excellent eating — light, white, flaky fillets, similar in flavor and texture to flounder.

Initially, tilapia are carnivorous and, if given the chance, will cannibalize smaller fry. Their diet changes as they mature and adults are exclusively herbivores/detritivores. At one month, they weigh about a gram and can grow to a pound in as little as six months at an optimum temperature of 82 degrees (28 C). They don't do well at temperatures above 95 degrees (35 C) or below 68 degrees (20 C).

A wide variety of plants have been grown using water containing fish wastes, including tomatoes, basil, lettuce, spinach, cucumbers, watercress and other greens.

The Solar-Algae Pond

The most basic integrated system is closely modeled after the natural fish pond, consisting of a translucent fiberglass tank stocked with fish (usually tilapia) with floating supports on the surface for plants. The plant roots grow directly into water and are protected by a mesh basket from grazing by the fish. Nitrifying bacteria form a film on the plant

167

roots, converting ammonia to a usable form for the plants. The roots also function as a filter, collecting suspended organic matter which helps maintain water clarity. An entire ecosystem of zoo plankton, nematodes and insect larvae develops around the root mass, providing additional food for the fish.

In addition to providing oxygen for the fish and the nitrifying bacteria, continual aeration provides mixing of the water, moving ammonia-laden water up to the plants and "clean" water down to the fish. The energy inputs in a solar-algae pond are limited to sunlight, fish food and electricity for aeration.

Solar-algae ponds are a good example of a simple integrated system. Given proper design and minimum attention, they are fairly resistant to fluctuations. Algae, plant and fish growth tend to balance one another.

From a commercial perspective, these systems have a number of limitations. Fish stocking densities must be kept low because the rate of waste removal by the plants is limiting. Moreover, the tanks are covered with plants which makes harvesting and monitoring the fish more difficult. Thus, these systems are best suited for small-scale, home production.

Recirculating Systems

Recirculating systems usually separate the hydroponic and the aquaculture operations. This allows greater control over each module resulting in higher yields of fish and plant biomass. More energy and expertise are required for efficient operation, but this is offset by higher yields.

Fish food, heat and aeration are provided to the fish tank which is stocked with a higher density of fish than is possible in the solar-algae pond. Water is pumped from this tank into a settling (sedimentation) tank and/or through a particulate filter. Periodically, the sludge is drained or the filter is washed to remove sediment from the system. In most integrated recirculating systems, this step accounts for most of the water loss from the system.

The water then goes to some type of biofilter where nitrification occurs. Prior removal of the large particles of fish food and wastes is necessary to prevent clogging of the biofilter. Nitrification is an aerobic process which may be limited by oxygen and pH levels. Biofilters in recirculating aquaculture systems improve the rate and degree of nitrification by creating near-optimum conditions. Numerous types of biofilters are used, from simple gravel beds to sophisticated fluidized bed reactors in which numerous small particles of support medium are suspended by an upward flow of untreated water. In all cases, a film of nitrifying bacteria is formed on the surface of the support medium.

After nitrification, the water is moved through a hydroponic system where the plants remove the nitrogen. Plants are integrated into the system in several different ways. The simplest method is to float the plants on the surface of the water. Plants also can be grown directly in the biofilter. Other more sophisticated methods use either drip hydroponics or nutrient flow technique (NFT). Once the nitrogen has been removed, the water is cycled back into the fish tank.

Generally, the word "aquaculture" brings to mind ponds in warm climates or the salmon pens of Norway and the Pacific Northwest. Unless one is "in the know," the state of Massachusetts doesn't spring to mind. Nevertheless, this area is home to two integrated, recirculating, hydroponic/aquaculture operations. The location of these businesses is due, in part, to Hampshire College in Amherst where the founders of both companies initially explored their interests in this and other emerging appropriate technologies.

Josh Goldman (AquaFuture, Inc. in Montague) and John Reid (Bioshelters, Inc. in Amherst) both studied aquaculture/hydroponics during their time at Hampshire College.

AquaFuture, Inc.

The initial impression is one of cleanliness, organization and a significant investment in equipment. Currently housed in a solar greenhouse, a row of circular tanks occupy one side, with a single large tank running the length of the house on the other. Rows of hydroponic trays filled with basil are suspended over the tanks on racks.

Located outside the city of Greenfield in northwestern Massachusetts, AquaFuture raises tilapia and striped bass. According to Josh Goldman, AquaFuture is the first company to raise striped bass in a recirculating system. "Striped bass is a native to the East Coast, so there is less consumer education required for market acceptance."

In Massachusetts where winter temperatures can dip below zero for weeks or months, keeping 45,000 gallons of water at 75 to 86 degrees (24-30 C) can be a major expense. Goldman's company solved this problem by locating their operation in an industrial park and purchasing waste heat from a neighboring manufacturing plant. During the spring, summer and fall, solar energy provides much of the heat in their current location.

Unlike the systems discussed above, AquaFuture uses hydroponics to treat only the waste water generated through sludge removal. Fish culture can produce much more nitrogen than the plants can effectively remove, unless one had unlimited greenhouse space and miles of hydroponic trays. The low nutrient concentration and the large volume of water from the fish tanks make it difficult to use hydroponics to treat all the water. In contrast, the sludge waste water has a much higher nutrient concentration and there's much less of it, greatly reducing the size of the hydroponic system needed. In this operation, as in most integrated systems, the main product is fish; hydroponic plant produc-

169

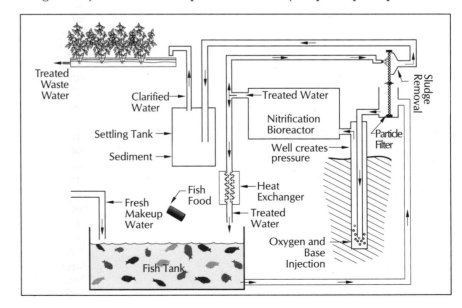

tion is part of the water treatment system.

Ten circular tanks, each holding about 2,000 gallons of water are used for striped bass culture. The single large tank used for tilapia holds about 25,000 gallons. Water flows from the fish tanks through a custom filtration system which removes the solids.

After filtration, the main volume of water is supersaturated under pressure with oxygen and a base is added to favor nitrification before it moves on to the biofilter. The water then passes into a sophisticated fluidized bed reactor where a continuous flow of water suspends filter particles that are coated with bacteria. The resulting nitrate is about 2,000 times less toxic to the fish than is ammonia. Nitrate levels are controlled through dilution — the water lost during sludge removal is replaced with fresh water. About 3,000 to 4,000 gallons of water (7 to 8 percent of the total water volume) is exchanged daily.

The water/sludge mix is pumped into a settling tank and water from this tank is pumped into the hydroponic trays. A standard NFT system is used with the plants supported in rockwool cubes. The water leaving the hydroponic system is clear and low in dissolved nutrients so that it can be discharged without further treatment.

Although they have grown a variety of salad greens, AquaFuture's main plant crop currently is basil. At harvest, the entire plant is sold — rockwool and roots included — as fresh produce. AquaFuture harvests and ships about 1,400 basil plants per week which provides about 25 percent of their income.

The striped bass begin their lives in Arkansas where they are raised in ponds. Arriving in Massachusetts as fingerlings, they grow rapidly to about 1.5 to 2 pounds in 10 months. AquaFuture produces their own tilapia fingerlings from brood stock that they maintain. Tilapia require about a year to grow to market size — about 1.25 pounds. At their present production level, about 300 pounds of striped bass and 100 pounds of tilapia are produced each week.

Bioshelters, Inc.

Bioshelters' unique approach is closely modeled on the relationships found in natural ecosystems. Immediately inside the door of the double walled poly greenhouse is a small area overflowing with a variety of plants. These plants act as a refuge and reservoir for lacewings, aphid lions, ladybugs and other biocontrol agents used to control aphids and whiteflies explained John Reid, director of Bioshelters, Inc.

In business since 1986, Bioshelters raises tilapia and basil, both of which currently have a strong market. The sale of basil provides about 25 to 30 percent of Bioshelters' revenue.

Two large circular tanks occupy one end of the solar greenhouse, separated from a series of smaller rectangular tanks at the opposite end by the water-filtering equipment. There is about 26,000 gallons of water in the system. Water from the tanks passes through a mesh filter which removes the large particles and then flows into a settling tank. After passing through a net-supported biofilter where nitrification occurs, about 25 percent of the process water flows through the hydroponic system before going back into the fish tanks. The hydroponic system initially appears to be a standard NFT system; however, upon closer examination, the volume of water passing through the trays is much higher than in a normal NFT system.

"The nitrogen concentration is about 30 ppm which is really low for

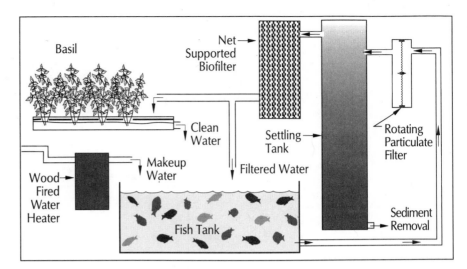

plants, so we compensate by using a high flow rate through the system. We started out trying different types of emitters, but right now we're not using any at all, and we're getting great plant growth" Reid said. The water goes directly from the hydroponic trays back into the fish tanks. Essentially, it's a closed system although a small amount of water is lost through evaporation and during sludge removal.

After experimenting with tomatoes, Reid switched to basil because of the shorter crop time and better market. "We just didn't make enough off the tomatoes" he said. "And harvesting basil is much easier."

Bioshelters produces all their basil from seed, using rockwool cubes. The entire plant is marketed, roots and all, direct to restaurants and produce wholesalers. It takes four to six weeks in the summer and up to eight weeks in the winter to produce a basil crop. Their production currently varies from 840 plants per week in the winter to 1,440 plants per week in the summer.

The amount of nitrogen released by the fish could grow more plants, but plant production is limited by the solar greenhouse size. Indeed, the entire greenhouse is filled with a "second floor" of hydroponic trays containing basil plants, suspended on a metal framework.

During the spring, summer and fall, all the light and the heat is provided by the sun. Thirty percent of the heat in the winter is solar and supplemental heat is provided by a wood/propane heater designed by Reid. High-pressure sodium lights are used in the winter to provide supplemental light and chelated iron is added periodically to the water. In the hottest part of the summer, large vents in the greenhouse are opened and evaporative cooling is sufficient to maintain temperatures.

Fish production is about 700 to 800 pounds per week. The production efficiency is good — about 1.2 to 1.4 pounds of feed is needed to produce one pound of fish. Bioshelters processes their fish in a neighboring facility and sells mostly to fish brokers or wholesalers. Supermarkets and restaurants are only a small part of their market, but are a segment that Reid hopes to expand in the coming years.

Hobby Systems

The commercial systems discussed above are on the cutting edge of large-scale integrated hydroponic/aquaculture techniques. Many of the same principles can work on a small scale for the home hobbyist. Doug

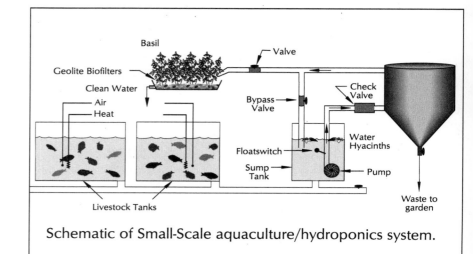

Schematic of Small-Scale aquaculture/hydroponics system.

Ernst is an aquaculturist who has worked on integrated tilapia/hydroponic production in the Caribbean and is currently working on innovative salmon hatchery management and design at Oregon State University. He has put together a system for tilapia culture in his small greenhouse in the central Willamette Valley of Oregon.

His system uses features of the solar-algae pond, although it is a recirculating, integrated system. The fish are raised in three tanks — two 150-gallon livestock watering tanks for brood fish and growout and one 100-gallon tank for rearing fry to fingerlings. Each fish tank has its own heater and aeration stone.

The drains of all three tanks are connected to a sump that also acts as a settling tank. Suspended in the sump tank is a pump that lifts the water into a centrifugal clarifier. Water hyacinths grow on the surface of the sump tank and begin the process of water treatment.

These floating plants reproduce with runners — like strawberries — and have a large root mass that hangs into the water. The water hyacinths grow so fast in the summer that "you can almost see them grow," according to Ernst.

"They make great primary filters. The roots trap a lot of suspended solids and they remove some nutrients from the water. The excess nutrients are available for hydroponics. And when they overgrow the surface of the sump tank, I just pull 'em out, rinse off the roots, and toss them in the fish tank. The fish love them, but I grow more than I can put in the fish tanks. The rest go to the compost pile. Hyacinths are a great source of greens and vitamins for the fish. Easy, clean, convenient." Fish are also fed a floating pelletized meal (dog food) that is about 25 percent protein.

The water in the centrifugal clarifier is constantly swirling around which causes the suspended solids to settle to the bottom. About a gallon of dilute sludge is removed every few days which is taken directly to the garden and applied as fertilizer. Water flows from the clarifier by gravity to geolite biofilters which are located over each tank. Coarse gravel or similar materials can also be used to construct the filter bed.

Each biofilter is about 2 to 3 square feet in area, and filled with the growing medium about 4 to 6 inches deep. The filter is gently sloped toward a drain on one end. Plants are grown directly in the biofilters.

Each biofilter is an independent unit that is easily removed for cleaning.

After several months, the biofilter/hydroponic media can become clogged with trapped solids, bacterial growth and plant roots. "By this time, the herbs or greens are ready for harvest and the whole filter, plants and all, can be taken outside for cleaning," says Ernst. "The geolite can be easily cleaned by placing it in a wire basket and spraying it with a hose. A layer of nitrifying bacteria remains on the surface of the media, so they begin oxidizing ammonia immediately when they are placed back in the system — there's no conditioning time."

Water flows from the biofilters back into the fish tanks. The pump operates periodically for about 6 hours each day, alternately flooding the biofilters and allowing them to drain. This flood-and-drain method of loading the filters assures adequate aeration throughout the filter for the nitrifying bacteria and the plants' roots.

Ernst has grown a number of different plant crops in his system and has found that greens — basil, lettuce, spinach — seem to work the best. These crops have a short turn-around time and thrive in the warm, humid conditions over the tanks. The crops of fish and greens are grown from early spring through late fall.

"Equally important, in a non-material way, are the aesthetics and educational value of a micro-ecosystem and knowing the history of the fish and greens I consume."

"From November through February, it becomes an issue of how much money you want to spend to heat the water. I've decided that it just isn't reasonable for me to produce during this time. I scale back during the winter, then grow crops of fish and greens in the spring and fall when production from outdoor gardens is limited. In the winter, I let the water temperatures go down to about 64 degrees (18 C) which is just warm enough to keep the fish healthy. I feed them just enough to maintain their weight. With less feed input, less filtration is needed. I also cover the tanks with a 'tent' of plastic to further conserve heat. In addition, the plastic reduces condensation in the rest of the greenhouse which can really be a problem when it gets cold outside."

Ernst hasn't kept strict production figures because his system is continuing to evolve. But, he figures that during the spring and fall he spends about $10 per month on electricity for pumping and heating. His last crop of basil produced for three months (he harvested by cutting) and his fish crop was about 40 half-pound fish. "It was one hellava a fish fry" he said, beaming with satisfaction.

First published in Volume 2, Number 4, page 28.

173

Hydroponic Food Production Indoors

by Lawrence L. Brooke

Not everyone who would like to grow their own food crops has the luxury of a greenhouse or garden. Some have nothing more than a spare room or a sunny windowsill. Through hydroponics, rapid growth and higher yields are possible in confined areas, making the home garden a possibility for just about everyone.

Using modern equipment and techniques, it is now possible to fulfill all plant needs, light, nutrition, oxygen, atmosphere and warmth. A table-top planter can add an extra dimension to any room. An extra bedroom or converted basement, attic or garage can become your family farm, generating fresh vegetables, herbs, fruits and ornamental plants year round.

The 'Bedroom' Garden

Before you dismiss indoor growing as too troublesome or too expensive, consider the following "bedroom" garden that not only provides its owner with plenty of fresh produce, but does so on a "break-even" or better basis.

The indoor garden that has provided us with the following data is located in Berkeley, California. The climate is mild — outdoor temperatures rarely drop below freezing or climb above 85 degrees (29 C). Water quality is exceptionally good, in the range of 30 to 50 parts per million (ppm) of total dissolved solids (TDS) with a pH of about 7.5.

The growing area was adapted from an unused bedroom, mostly by clearing the floors and lining the walls with a reflective material to maximize the effectiveness of the artificial lights. Lighting is provided by

COMMON PROBLEMS

Looking at this and other indoor garden operations, a few basic principles emerge that are worth repeating:

- Growth rate and yield are directly related to available light. With artificial lights, it is essential that the light be placed as close to the plants as possible without burning them. A good reflector for each lamp and a mechanism for moving the lamp over the crop are effective for improving light distribution. Modern high intensity discharge (HID) lamps are the most efficient for converting electricity into the light that high metabolism plants need during vigorous growth.
- For generating seedlings or cuttings, use a more gentle form of light to avoid stress or burning. Full-spectrum fluorescent lights are ideal for this purpose. Many types of tropical plants including orchids, African violets and typical indoor potted plants prefer gentle light for their entire lives.
- One of the most overlooked factors for successful indoor cultivation is atmospheric control. Plants require good cross ventilation to enable gas exchange. Remember, foliage absorbs carbon dioxide and roots absorb oxygen. If you plan to enrich the atmosphere with carbon dioxide, keep in mind that the roots will suffer if you don't provide fresh air to the root zone. Carbon dioxide poisoning of the nutrient solution is often indicated by a drop in nutrient pH

as carbonic acid is formed. In addition, carbon dioxide in concentrated form does pose some risk to human and animal life.
- Atmospheric and nutrient temperatures are also important to healthy plants. Select crops that will do well in the environment you intend to provide for them — spring or fall crops for cool areas and summer crops for warm areas. In general, cool weather crops can tolerate lower light levels. Nutrient temperature is easier to ignore, but is just as important. Warmer is not necessarily better. Cool nutrient can hold much more dissolved oxygen than warm nutrient, but a cold nutrient can slow plant growth. The ideal temperature is about 65 degrees.
- One of the most common problems encountered with home gardens is water quality. Very soft water — rainwater, or water purified by distillation, deionization, or the use of a reverse osmosis filter — generally provide the best growth rates, crop health and yields. Very hard water, high in calcium, magnesium carbonate, sulfates, sulfides and other dissolved minerals, can cause problems. Nutrients can "lock up," resulting in poor growth and increased susceptibility to diseases and insects. For most growers with poor quality water, the answer is to collect rainwater if possible, or use a reverse osmosis filter. — *Lawrence L. Brooke*

two metal halide lights, one 1000-watt and one 400-watt.

The grower's intention from the beginning was to minimize out-of-pocket operating expenses. One way to do that without sacrificing the size and productivity of the garden is to grow a cash crop. Because it is easy to grow and market, one of the best cash crops for the small grower is sweet basil.

A 5- by 8-foot area consisting of a single hydroponic unit (the AeroFlo system, General Hydroponics) with 104 plant sites was planted with one to two plants per site. The first harvest, about three pounds, was taken about six weeks after seeding. Harvests were taken weekly and average about four or five pounds each.

As of mid-April, 1992, the crop had been producing for four months. From past experience, harvests can be maintained for about a year, with proper care. The nutrient is mixed with a TDS of about 800 ppm, and pH is kept in the 5.0 to 6.5 range. Minor infestations of aphids and spider mites have been controlled with ladybugs and predatory mites.

The excess basil is sold to local restaurants for about $5 per pound, not enough to retire on, but more than enough to cover the $60 monthly light bills. Two more chambers on the same reservoir as the basil are planted with watercress, a total of 16 plant sites. Yield averages about 3/4 of a pound per week.

Other crops were grown in individual top-feed units (Aquafarm, General Hydroponics). Two of the units produced more than 15 pounds of Japanese eggplant during a five-month period, yielding excellent firm fleshed, shiny black fruits. Cilantro yielded about 1/4 pound per week. "Red Salad Bowl" lettuce grew faster than the grower could eat it, yielding more than 1/2 pound each week.

Pickling cucumbers grew up 5-foot stakes, down the other side and on to the floor. These required hand pollination and produced a cucumber every two days per unit for three months. Cantaloupe (Chantilly) grew much like the cucumbers, up the stake, down on to the floor, and across the room. Yield was about one melon per week, a total of 15. The first melons fell from the vines before they were fully ripe. Providing support for the heavy fruits allowed them to ripen on the vine. The quality was excellent, extremely sweet and firm.

Of course it is not necessary to stick with the tried and true food crops in your indoor garden. Since you control the environment, it is possible to experiment with unusual varieties and species. Our garden features a "Chinese Gooseberry," a relative of the Kiwi, provided as a cutting from the California Rare Fruit Society and rooted in an Ein-Gedi aero-hydroponic unit. The first fruit, somewhat tomato-like and great in salads, appeared in about two months.

Tomatoes, on the other hand, were a real disappointment. Sweet 100s grew wildly, but did not produce well. If a determinate variety is chosen and tended with care, yields might be improved.

We are in the early stages of an explosion in the growth of hydroponic technology worldwide for both commercial and home food production. Traditional farming was the horse and buggy; modern conventional farming is the automobile, fast but polluting; and hydroponics is the spacecraft of agricultural technology. Indeed, only hydroponics is used on NASA's space vehicles.

You, the home hobbyist, can enjoy the fruits of your investment and labor, even if you don't have a square foot of soil to call your own, using modern hydroponic technology and controlled environment techniques.

Supplement your diet, teach your children about plants and their relationship to other living beings on our small planet, and maintain your own relationship with nature by cultivating plants hydroponically.

First published in Volume 3, Number 4, page 18

An Interview with William Texier

The following interview with William Texier, owner of White Owl Water Farm, was conducted in early October, 1991. Since then, White Owl has landed a contract with one of the best known restaurants in the San Francisco Bay Area, a testament to the high quality of the crops produced. The facility consists of a 21- by 72-foot steel framed structure (Poly-vent) with a double poly cover and six multi-tube oxygen-intensive water culture units (AeroFlo-384 by General Hydroponics) for a total of 2,300 plant sites.

The Growing EDGE: Why did you choose a water culture system for your operation?

William Texier: First of all, no other system can deliver as much oxygen to the roots. Secondly and just as important, this type of system is ecologically sound since there is practically no growing medium to buy and dispose of, water use is minimal and once the system is installed, there are practically no recurring costs. We reuse the pots and gravel through many crops.

The hydroponic system and the greenhouse were selected together as a concept of a natural hydroponic system integrated into its environment. The sides of the greenhouse open with an automated thermostatic control, exposing the crop to generous cross-ventilation and allowing open access between the crop and the external environment. For the plants to be able to resist disease and insect infestation, a system was required that provided maximum growth and crop health. It is well established that the best protection for a crop is superb health and vigorous growth. It will always be the weakest plants that are attacked; strong, healthy plants will have natural resistance.

GE: What are the most important factors for success?

WT: The first requirement is to have good quality water available. Our well water tests at about 160 parts per million (ppm) of total dissolved solids (measured with a Hanna Dist-1 meter). Generally, water up to 250 ppm is acceptable. Above 250 ppm it may be necessary to use a reverse osmosis filter. Once a good quality water supply is established, it is essential to use a nutrient solution specifically designed for water culture.

GE: Describe the types of nutrient mixes you use.

WT: We run very mild nutrient solutions. This is one of the great advantages of water culture. We start a fresh batch of nutrient (Flora Nutrients by General Hydroponics) at about 600 ppm. With regular water top-off, plus nutrient added every two to three days, we allow the nutrient strength to drift up to 950 ppm over a period of four weeks. Complete system drainage and nutrient replacement is done at the end of a four-week cycle. We keep the solution pH in the range of 5.5 to 6.0. As a general rule, the plants feed a lot more during the vegetative growth stage than during the reproductive phase.

GE: What types of crops have you worked with?

WT: We tested a variety of crops for their value. We started with a "salad mix" consisting of loose head lettuces, endives, radicchio, arugula, escarole and such. These crops grow easily and fast, but are extremely labor intensive for both planting and harvesting. We tested snow peas, but even with very tight spacing between plants — we had 384 plants in 200 square feet — and enormous pods, this crop would only be viable during the off season when high prices prevail.

Primarily, we now grow colored sweet peppers, red and yellow, with good success. We had the first peppers on the market in our area, ahead by one month. We have been sustaining a constant yield of about 150 pounds per week from four 200-square-foot systems. The fruit development is constant and should continue through the winter.

We've also started a crop of sweet basil which shows promise with the approach of the off season. We harvested our first crop 20 days after transplant into the system. We also maintain a corner of the green-house for testing new crops.

GE: Could you be more specific about your yields?

WT: To give you a few examples, we have consistently harvested in excess of 20 pound per week of salad mixes from a single 200-square-foot system. With snow peas the harvest came about 30 days after transplanting. The yield was 145 pounds from a 200-square-foot system over a period of 30 days. We learned after we gave up on snow peas that if we had selected a variety specifically developed for greenhouse cultivation, our yields would have been practically double that. We are now experimenting with sweet basil and are expecting yields of at least 25 pounds per week from each system.

GE: What are your primary operating costs?

WT: By far, the electricity for running the pumps is the major expense. The cost to run each of the six systems is about $55 per month (at 15 cents per kilowatt-hour). The systems are set on timers to run all day and off at night, except for a one-hour on period in the middle of the night to recharge the nutrient with oxygen. Fertilizer is also an expense, but since we run a mild nutrient solution and change the nutrient infrequently, the cost is minor.

GE: How do you sell your crop and how much money do you think you can make with this type of system?

WT: We are blessed with an enormous market. The San Francisco Bay Area is known to be a gourmet paradise and Sonoma County, where we are located, is noted for the finest wines and outstanding restaurants. This environment is very conducive to an operation like ours since a strong market is close at hand.

The quality of our produce has enabled us to be introduced into the best kitchens around. Farmers markets can help you get the word around about the character and quality of your produce and they can be interesting secondary markets despite the fact that the clientele will often favor a bargain over superior quality.

Restaurants make the best clients since they purchase in volume and on the basis of quality over price and the regular contracts can be helpful in planning your crop. The ability to provide off-season produce can greatly enhance your competitive edge.

The amount of money you can make operating a facility like ours would vary greatly according to location. You *can* make money with water culture on a small scale, practically anywhere and without too large an investment. The possible markets and applications are far greater than you may first suspect.

GE: What problems have you had with insects and diseases?

WT: A clean environment is the first step to avoiding diseases. If a virus develops, it is best to eliminate the crop and sterilize the system with bleach. Insects pose far less of a problem — we look at them as part of the natural environment that the plants need.

We have found a large variety of living creatures including frogs, butterflies, bees, wasps, spiders, ladybugs and a controlled population of aphids and spider mites. Our plants have never suffered any significant damage from insects. We believe that it is because of the natural equilibrium that has developed in the greenhouse. We don't use any form of pest control, except for the introduction of a few ladybugs. We don't even use the mildest natural soap for fear of interfering with the natural equilibrium.

GE: What are the most labor intensive procedures in operating your facility?

WT: We start our seeds in a mixture of peat moss, perlite and vermiculite. We grow them in flats for a month or so, depending on the crop. Then we transplant into 3-inch net pots filled with clay pebbles for support. Depending on the crop, they can be planted one to six plants per cup. This is one of the most tedious procedures. Stringing up a crop of peppers or beans also takes a lot of time and patience, plus acrobatic skill. Harvesting can vary considerably according to the crop, from easy to unbearable. Harvesting the salad mixes was definitely tedious work.

The daily maintenance of the system is relatively fast and easy, generally consisting of nutrient top-up and unplugging an occasional nutrient injector. We are now able to operate the greenhouse between two people each working an average of two hours per day, skipping the occasional day.

GE: Is this type of hydroponic system appropriate for other uses and situations?

WT: It's not really a system, but a method. So it could be scaled from a small table-top planter, to a commercial facility covering acres. It is certainly simple enough for the home hobbyist and could easily be used to supplement a family's diet.

To use it as a commercial tool, you must have a market for your produce and be willing to make the investment in equipment. We do not yet have sufficient data on the cost and profit of other commercial hydroponic facilities to make a fair comparison.

GE: From your experience with White Owl Water-Farm, can you offer some general tips for other growers?

WT: Growing plants requires two skills: observation and communication. Looking closely and often at your plants will tell you more about their needs than any book can. A certain amount of time should be spent simply watching your plants. Your plants should not only grow, they should glow. Your job is to avoid problems, not cure them.

An advantage with water culture is the mild nutrient solution used. This prevents nutritional problems that can make life complicated for the grower. This gives you the time and energy to focus more closely on subtle changes in the condition of your crop. Tending plants means providing for the needs of another living organism and, for that while, forgetting your other worldly preoccupations.

There is an exchange of information between the grower and the crop. The grower can affect change in the crop through selection, pruning, nutrient manipulation and other environmental controls. They will communicate their needs through the color of their leaves, growth patterns and the speed of response to your stimulus. Remember, whatever you do to your plants, nutrient manipulation for example, it will be days before you can see the effect. Avoid excess! Your plants live in a time frame that is different from yours; you have to adapt yourself to that. Consider that the Bristle Cone Pine has a life expectancy of over 5,000 years, or that radishes can grow from seed to harvest in less than a month.

GE: What advantages and disadvantages does your hydroponic greenhouse offer over organic farming?

WT: Organic is God's way for plants to grow and it would be presumptuous to try to improve on nature, but there are other factors to consider. One is the explosion of human population; organic methods cannot keep up. In developed countries, organically grown produce has become an elitist item, available only to a limited segment of the population.

Over the years, organic growers have developed "gentle" means of pest control including soaps, copper sulfate and sulfur, pyrethrum insecticides and many other methods and materials. Our objective has been to establish a completely natural and self-sustaining environment, never disturbing the natural balance. We believe that by giving plants an edge by increasing their health, speed of growth and resistance to disease and insects, we can achieve a more natural environment with no need for these gentle methods of pest control. In Europe, where I grew up, we do not use the term organic. We say "biological." I think that this a more precise expression because it addresses the natural way in which plants feed. The bottom line is whether the plant depends for its nutrition on the biological breakdown of organic materials by bacteria and fungi, or upon the application of industrial chemical fertilizers.

In soil farming, the selection of "natural" vs. synthetic fertilizers has a significant impact on the environment and the crop. To be economically viable, commercial farmers are compelled to use large quantities of low-cost chemical fertilizers.

The dynamics of feeding a crop in a recirculating water culture system are significantly different from either of these soil methods.

We are compelled to use the highest grades of purified fertilizers in very low quantities since the roots live in a state of constant immersion. The application of fertilizer is calibrated according to the crops' actual consumption. And the environmental impact resulting from the disposal of exhausted nutrient is insignificant.

The most efficient drip irrigation systems still require many times more water per crop than recirculating water culture systems. This will have the greatest significance with the world's water supply becoming so rapidly depleted.

One reason that organically grown produce has received so much popular attention is the myth of superior product quality. This is only sometimes true. Everyone who has tried our produce has been convinced, sometimes to their great surprise, that our quality is at least equal to, if not better than, the best organically grown products.

GE: How does your operation differ from existing commercial facilities?

WT: First of all, we are very small. We are now ready to expand to 6,000 square feet of growing area, which would be the final stage of the project — three greenhouses with 22 200-square-foot water culture systems. This is still pretty small by international standards. But it should generate a substantial income and could be operated easily by the two of us.

Another important difference is our location. Hydroponics has flourished in colder climates. We are combining a powerful technology and a moderate climate with unbelievable results. Due in part to the climate, our yields greatly exceed those of the giant commercial hydroponic farms. Of course the materials, methods and equipment also have an effect.

We are not trying to cheat nature by growing crops that could not otherwise be grown here. We're working with nature to improve yields and quality. Frankly, I'm surprised that no one has experimented with this type of commercial operation before.

GE: What do you see as the future of food production and how does your operation fit into that future?

WT: When I first heard of hydroponic technology 20 years ago in Europe, I was very enthusiastic. I thought that mankind had come up with a technology that would alleviate world hunger and environmental stress. In fact, this technology has been used to generate profits for large corporations and has led to local pollution of ground water and the need to dispose of enormous amounts of used rockwool.

This state of affairs will change. Hydroponics can be the basis for a small family business that is ecologically sound. The units are light weight and could be integrated anywhere that there is water, sunshine and warmth. Instead of feeding the Third World with our surplus grain, which we pay for with corporate subsidies and damaged soils, we would be wiser to help those countries to achieve agricultural independence by applying hydroponic technology.

We are trying to promote that kind of hydroponics that can be integrated into nature, rather than trying to enclose the growing area and exclude nature. We believe that by developing this type of production facility we will help make it possible for small farmers in remote areas to create profitable businesses based on the needs of their own communities. The family farmer can be returned to business, the community's food supply can be improved and food can be generated where it is consumed, reducing transportation costs. This technology is in its infancy, but I think it will grow as a tool in the overall management of the planet and its resources.

First published in Volume 3, Number 2, page 28.

Chapter 8
Specialized Techniques

Thigmomorphogenesis — Plant Stress as a Cultivation Technique

by Kathleen Yeomans

Gardeners have been abusing their plants for centuries. Old-time stories tell of pegs and nails being pounded into tree trunks, while farmers were known to whip or shoot their trees to "inspire" them to grow well. At one time it was not unusual to see an orchard of trees with stones hanging from their branches. When stimulated in this manner, fruit trees were expected to bring forth heavier crops. Modern day growers may scoff, but the odd fact is that these folk remedies to increase plant production and control growth may actually have been scientifically sound.

Whipping and shooting, of course, are just rather energetic methods of thinning. Extra blossoms and fruit are knocked off, so the size and quality of the remaining fruit are improved. Shaking has a similar effect and, in addition, helps maintain plant health by dislodging insect pests. Driving nails into tree bark can improve fruiting by redirecting sap flow and hormone distribution. This same effect is obtained by "girdling," a technique used even today by conventional orchardists to minimize new shoot growth and concentrate plant energy on fruit and blossom production. Other forms of "plant abuse" may also have beneficial effects on plant growth and yield.

Why Beat Your Plants?

A 6-foot plant simply doesn't fit on the average windowsill. Indoor and greenhouse gardeners are constantly faced with the challenge of growing plants within space limitations. Under these circumstances any technique that helps control plant size is worth a try.

Commercial growers are also concerned with plant size. Not only because of container size or growing area limitations, but because uniformly sized plants are easier to maintain. Feeding and watering chores are more efficient and many tasks can be mechanized when plants are all of the same size. Furthermore, experience has proven that short, sturdy seedlings survive transport and transplantation better than tall, spindly seedlings.

Attractive shape, bloom size and bloom season are other reasons for growth control. In the past, hormone sprays and chemical growth retardants were used to obtain the desired results. Because of recent environmental and health concerns, many of these chemicals have been prohibited for agricultural use. Many growers, faced with these restrictions, have started using variations of the old-time practices to produce stocky, productive seedlings and marketable plants.

Type-A Plants

Many people perform best when under stress; the same can be said for some plants. Studies show that physical stress, such as wind, drought and adverse light conditions can make plants stronger.

American Horticulturist, (July, 1990) reports that studies done at Michigan State University demonstrate that plant height can be controlled simply with touch. Easter lilies that were "stroked" daily grew inches shorter than lilies that were not. One enterprising New Zealand grower has attached plastic fingers to a boom-watering system that "tickles" his plants each time they are watered.

Plant responses to mechanical stress, such as vibration, shaking or handling have been studied since the early 1800s. The term "thigmomorphogenisis"("thigmo" is Greek for "touch") was coined by M.J. Jaffe to describe this phenomenon. His experiments in 1973 showed that gentle rubbing reduced the growth of several plant species. He and others involved in similar experiments speculated that it was a plant growth hormone that caused this response.

Stress can make plants more tolerant of other stresses. According to Scientists at the United States Department of Agriculture Research

PRUNING

Pruning is a familiar application of plant stress used to control growth. Most hedging plants respond by growing bushier and thicker. The more one prunes, the better the hedge.

Fruit production can be boosted by cutting the terminal buds from branches, forcing the growth hormones to the side shoots, resulting in more fruit-bearing branches. Selective thinning of buds and blossoms also produces bigger, better fruits.

In addition to improved yields, pruning can produce other benefits, both aesthetic and functional, for the home gardener:

Pleaching is a method of tying the young side branches of neighboring trees together to form a tunnel. Many large estate gardens are famous for their long pleached drives and this technique was once a common treatment for street trees. Some towns have been able to preserve these pleached canopies in low-traffic areas.

Espalier is a technique that limits a plant, often a fruit tree, to a few main branches that are trained horizontally along wires or against a wall. Fruit produced on espaliered trees is frequently bigger and of better quality than that produced on trees growing more naturally.

Cordon is similar to espalier. A single stem is trained to grow vertically or at an angle, often along a garden wall or fence. Most pruning is done during the summer to avoid stimulating new shoots. This is a real space-saver. Many cordoned plants can fit into the growing area of a few uninhibited trees.

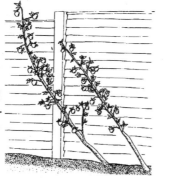

Topiary is a radical use of pruning to shape plants into ornamental figures, such as animals, people or geometric designs. These shapes have absolutely no resemblance to the natural growth pattern of the plant and frequent clipping is necessary to maintain the desired form. One would think that any plant subjected to this traumatic shearing would suffer, but some vigorous specimens have been maintained for generations.
— *Kathleen Yeomans*

184

Station in Beltsville, Maryland, Coleus plants that were subjected to inadequate lighting were better able to withstand cold temperatures than plants that were either untreated or grown under higher levels of light. In addition, enforced drought conditions also seemed to endow plants with increased chill tolerance. Another study showed drought-stressed plants were able to withstand heavy sulfur dioxide pollution.

How it Works

Jaffe was right. Plant hormones do have a great deal to do with the strength-building mechanisms of plants, and hormone distribution is affected by nearly all environmental conditions. When hormone levels are altered by light intensity, gravity, mechanical stress or temperature, the bloom season, fruit quality, size and shape of a plant are also changed.

Auxins, natural plant growth hormones, are produced in the growing tips of plants and distributed back to the roots. If an auxin-producing tip is removed, either by accidental breakage or deliberate pruning, the auxins will migrate to side shoots and form a shorter, bushier plant. Auxins are also affected by physical stress and respond to vibration or touch by slowing plant growth. This works so well that temporary dormancy has been produced in Liquidamber trees by merely shaking them.

Ethylene is a plant hormone that controls fruit ripening and sap flow. Ethylene activity causes trees to lean away from prevailing winds. This response to wind stress strengthens the plant to withstand further damage. Young trees that are blown about by the wind grow stronger and sturdier than trees that have grown with supporting stakes.

Another way a plant responds to stress is to close its leaf stomata. When stomata, the "breathing pores" of the leaf, are closed, transpiration and photosynthesis decrease and plant growth is slowed, resulting in shorter, sturdier plants.

No Pain, No Gain

It appears that some plants can benefit from "weight lifting." Hydroponically grown Belgian endive, often loose-leafed and floppy, is being improved by using pressure to produce tight, broad chicons like those obtained from soil planted roots. Researchers at the University of Massachusetts placed weighted boards over chicory roots to reproduce soil-grown conditions. They were rewarded with well-shaped chicons that had few loose or unusable outer leaves.

Another study showed that wind-ravaged banana plants with torn leaves have an advantage over plants that have been protected from wind damage. In bright sunlight, the whole leaves get hotter and temperatures can rise to near lethal limits. In these conditions, the plant protects itself by slowing photosynthesis and shutting down its fruit bearing functions. The plants with wind-torn leaves don't suffer from these high temperatures and therefore produce normally.

Other researchers have noticed that root-bound fig trees often bear more fruit than those that grow unrestricted. These examples show that stress can actually contribute to plant hardiness and productivity.

Environmental Stress

Keeping plants on the dry side will certainly slow growth, but at the risk of sacrificing plant health. However, some growers have had good

BONSAI — STRESS AS ART

The ultimate use of plant stress is in the practice of bonsai, where growth control has become an art form.

Wind-bent trees and shrubs were first collected from the wild and planted carefully in containers. Later, as it became harder to find worthy subjects in nature, seedlings and cuttings were used and the much-admired gnarled forms and twisted branches were artfully aged and weathered by wires, weights and pruning knife.

The Roots

The roots are the first part of a bonsai plant to be subjected to stress. A container many times smaller than would be considered adequate is chosen.

The plant is kept within bounds by periodic root pruning. At least annually, and sometimes more often, plants are removed from their containers, the soil carefully brushed away, and the roots are cut back by one-third. Rather than killing the plant, this encourages the growth of root hairs which can efficiently take up water and nutrients.

As if this weren't enough, roots are often exposed for artistic purposes. When the plant is removed for routine root pruning, some of the roots are left above the soil level by spreading them over a moistened rock and packing wet sphagnum or peat moss around them. After the roots are acclimated, the moist barrier is removed and the roots are left to grow.

Shaping

Since bonsai plants are protected from the stresses of nature, their interesting shapes are formed by man-made stresses. They are planted at a slant and trunks are bent with copper wire to achieve a wind-blown look. Weights may be hung on the branches to change the normal direction of growth. Other times upright branches are tied down to the pot to give the plant a drooping look. Wooden sticks and props are used for the opposite affect, when branches need to be raised.

Pruning

Bonsai plants are constantly pruned. Often, almost all the leaves are pinched off at a near-mature stage just to encourage the growth of tiny replacement leaves. Pine needles are frequently cut in half to keep them in proportion to the rest of the dwarfed plant. Snipping branches and rubbing away unwanted shoots is a grooming procedure sometimes performed daily to keep a bonsai plant under control.

Feeding and Watering

Bonsai plants are kept a little hungry and a little dry so that they don't grow too fast. The soil in which bonsai grow best is extremely fast draining, so that it may be necessary to water these plants more than once a day. Very dilute fertilizer is used at regular intervals to prevent a sudden growth spurt. Some bonsai trees are only 1 1/2 inches tall at maturity!

Flowers and Fruits

A bonsai tree in flower, or bearing fruit, is a stunning sight. The buds and blossoms may have been removed many times over to attain perfect blossoms or fruit; only a few are left on each shoot. Fertilizing stops and the tree is not fed again until after the blossoms drop so it can direct all its energies to blooming. Bonsai plants are living proof that judiciously applied stress "builds character." — *Kathleen Yeomans* results with unconventional watering practices. As reported in *American Vegetable Grower* (April, 1990), George Todd of Apollo Beach Florida, keeps his tomato seedlings short by watering them in the middle of the night. It seems that this night-time watering allows the plant to use up all of its water allocation before "bedtime" and puts it in a slight, but not significantly detrimental, "stress-condition."

Commercial growers often limit phosphorus when feeding plants in order to keep them short and stunted. Plants with a purple tinge, showing phosphorus hunger, are a common sight where this technique is used.

This type of "diet" can be maintained until close to sale or transplant time, but plants must be watched carefully, permanent damage can result from long-term phosphorus depletion. Now and then it's a good idea to add a small amount of phosphorus to the fertilizer to keep plants from starving to death.

Plants grown under intense light are shorter and sturdier than plants grown under low light conditions. To increase light intensity in greenhouses or indoors, use artificial lights or glass, which allows in more ultraviolet light than plastic.

Slow growth brought on by cool temperatures keeps plants short and stocky. Of course, in a very chilly environment, plants won't grow at all. Be aware that a temperature of 41 degrees (5 C) or less will completely halt the growth of most plants. Tropical and other heat-loving plants, especially tomatoes, peppers and begonias, don't tolerate low temperatures well and may never recover from this sort of treatment.

What's the DIF?

DIF refers to the difference between day and night temperatures and is an important growth control factor. Plants grown in conditions with warmer daytime temperatures (positive DIF) are taller than plants grown with equal day and night temperatures (zero DIF) or those grown in warmer night conditions (negative DIF).

Because germination benefits from constant temperature, DIF techniques should only be used after the first set of true leaves has developed. Vegetable seedlings are especially responsive to this type of conditioning and transplants can easily be kept short and sturdy by growing them in negative DIF environments.

DIF is most effective when night periods are longest. William Carlson, a horticulture professor at Michigan State University, suggests in *American Vegetable Grower* maintaining a day temperature of 62 degrees (17 C) and a night temperature of 68 degrees (20 C) for best results.

Exercise

Shaking, tickling and vibrating may be the growth control technique of the future. Hormones stimulated by these mechanical shocks produce short, sturdy and healthy seedlings. Automation will be the key to commercial success.

We probably won't see plantsmen taking a whip or a gun to their plants, but it may become routine to see certain forms of physical stress applied to manipulate plant size, bloom season and fruiting qualities. So try giving your plants a gentle thrashing to keep them within bounds and "inspire" them to grow better.

First published in Volume 2, Number 4, page 22

Drip Irrigation — The Basics

by Tom Bressan

Because it is so adaptable, drip irrigation is successfully used in a wide variety of climates and for a wide variety of plants and soil types. Systems range in size from a few plants to a few hundred acres and cover open fields, steep slopes, back yards and roof tops. Drip irrigation has allowed the cultivation of slopes thought to be unusable and land that has been left idle.

Most drip irrigation installations have been for large, commercial operations. It is an ideal method for watering fruit and nut orchards and vineyards, as well as other crops including strawberries, cotton and jojoba. The newest and fastest growing use of drip irrigation, however, is by homeowners for watering containers, gardens and landscaping.

Advantages

With drip irrigation, almost all of the water used is accessible to the roots of the plants. Weed patches, walkways and areas between rows and plants remain dry. Wind does not carry water away and water lost to evaporation is negligible. The net result is substantial water savings which, with our increasingly limited supply of water, can only become more important in the future.

In addition to saving water, drip irrigation can also save time. Watering time is reduced to almost nothing — just turning on and off a valve or hose bib. And, with automatic controls, that isn't even necessary.

The deep, localized waterings made possible by drip irrigation deliver water directly to the root zone of the plant. This, along with the regularity of watering, prevents the shock that plants suffer with other methods. The difference in the health and growth of plants is obvious. The concept behind drip irrigation was inspired by a leaky faucet that provided lush growth of nearby weeds.

Drip irrigation systems are simple to design and easy to install. And it doesn't take long for the benefits to outweigh the initial expenditure of time and money. You don't have to be an engineer or irrigation contractor to drip irrigate or even automate your gardens and landscaping.

Hardware

The "head" is the connection between the source of water and the drip irrigation system. For most small systems it occurs at the hose bib. It usually includes a filter, a pressure regulator and an adapter to connect to the polyethylene tubing of the drip system. It can also include an automatic valve, a vacuum breaker or back flow preventer and a fertilizer injector (see illustration on page 194 for the proper installation order).

Of these components, two are essential to all drip systems: the filter which prevents small particles from clogging emitters; and the pressure regulator which reduces the pressure in the system to 20 or 30 pounds per inch (psi) and ensures the proper functioning of the tubing, fittings and emitters.

From the head, water travels through tubing to the plant, where the emitter is attached. These lines are called mains (supply lines) and laterals (where the emitters are attached). They are usually 1/2-inch in diameter, although 3/8 inch lines are sometimes used when the flow is very low. Polyethylene tubing is preferred for several reasons. It is resistant to the damaging effects of the sun's ultraviolet rays. It is flexible and easy to work. It has "memory," so that it seals around holes when emitters are inserted and holds the tee and elbow fittings so that no glue or clamps are needed.

The emitter is the most important part of any drip irrigation system. It ensures that each plant receives the desired amount of water. The emitter you choose should be designed to deliver water at the rate you intend. It should resist clogging and it should compensate for variations in water pressure, especially if your system requires long lateral lines or if your lines must run up or down hills. Better quality emitters might increase a system's cost by 10 percent, but they are worth it. The most common types of emitters are:

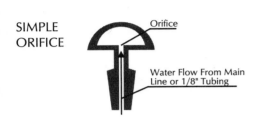

SIMPLE ORIFICE

Orifice

Water Flow From Main Line or 1/8" Tubing

Simple Orifice — This type of emitter is the least expensive and, as one might expect, the least effective. It limits the discharge by means of a small hole.

Laminar Flow — This type of emitter uses a larger opening than the simple orifice emitter. In so doing, it partially eliminates the problem of clogging. The discharge is limited by forcing the water to travel through a long spiral or a maze-like complex of interconnected chambers before it reaches the orifice.

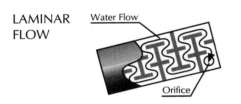

LAMINAR FLOW

Water Flow

Orifice

Vortex — This type of emitter has a larger orifice and is partially pressure compensating. Water enters a circular chamber inside the emitter at an angle causing a circular flow. This motion diffuses the pressure around the outside wall creating an area of reduced pressure at the center where the orifice is located.

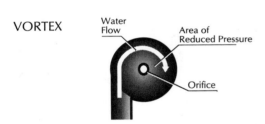

VORTEX

Water Flow

Area of Reduced Pressure

Orifice

Diaphragm — These emitters are pressure compensating and flush automatically at the beginning and end of each watering cycle. The diaphragm opens under low pressure conditions and restricts the flow as pressure increases, balancing the rate of drip under a wide range of pressures.

Watering is easy with drip irrigation but automatic controllers make it even easier. Most controllers are plugged in to a AC outlet and are set to water for however long and often watering is needed. A control wire runs from the valve or valves to be operated. The solenoid valve, which runs on a low-voltage DC current, opens and closes as directed. When shopping for a controller, make sure it can handle the complexity and duration of your watering schedule.

Less expensive battery operated controllers are now available. These controllers can be installed between the hose bib and the system and programmed to turn the water on and off at certain times.

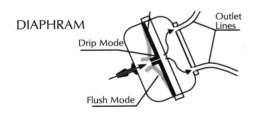

DIAPHRAM

Outlet Lines

Drip Mode

Flush Mode

Applications

The flexibility of drip irrigation allows the removal of individual emitters from the system by replacing them with a "goof" plug, or the addition of new emitters and lines with little worry about the design of the system.

A common landscaping problem is that plants with different water requirements are often planted together. A partial solution is to place multiple or higher output emitters at the plants needing more water. Lines can be buried or mulched to hide them from view. A 2-inch depth will hide the tubing and still show a wet spot on the surface for inspection. If a line is accidentally cut, it can easily be repaired with a connector. (It is best to keep a few on hand just in case.)

Vegetables prosper when adequate water is provided, but overhead watering tend to encourage rust, mildew, blossom damage and disease. Closely spaced emitters can be used to thoroughly wet an area of soil without wetting plant leaves. A 1/2-gph emitter will generally suffice for an area 16 inches in diameter. In coarse soils 1-gph emitters should be used for more lateral coverage. If plants are more widely spaced and deeper rooted, such as tomatoes or squash, a single emitter can be placed at the base of each plant.

For row crops, a lateral with emitters placed every 16 inches will give complete watering down the row. Crops such as carrots, onions and radishes can be planted two or more deep on either side of the lateral. With plants such as corn, strawberries and peppers, one row on each side of the lateral is preferred. Tomatoes and bush squash require one lateral per row.

With intensive gardening methods, set up the system on a grid with laterals 16 inches apart and emitters every 16 inches on the laterals. With a 4-foot wide bed, three laterals will give complete coverage for the entire bed. One advantage is that the system does not have to be changed as the plantings are changed.

Trees and Shrubs

Drip irrigation is widely accepted for use in commercial orchards. It allows for a slow, deep watering. Better growth is achieved with less water and without the problems associated with flood or sprinkler irrigation.

Young trees can be started with one emitter at the base and additional emitters added as the tree grows. If you have young trees, it is important to design a system that will grow with them.

The number and placement of emitters depend on the size of the tree, the amount of rainfall and the structure of the soil. If you have large trees, less than 16 inches of annual rainfall and a sandy soil, you'll need more emitters. (See the chart on the next page for estimating the number and placement of emitters.)

There are four common ways to set up emitters around trees:
- Run a lateral down a row of trees with emitters placed on the lateral.
- Run two laterals along the row of trees 3 feet out from either side.
- "Tee off" individual laterals with a loop around each tree.
- Use a multi-outlet emitter at the base of the tree, opening more outlets as the tree grows.

Container Gardens

Container gardens present special watering problems for the home grower. Sprinklers are inappropriate because of the spacing and placement of plants. Until now, the only option has been hand watering which, if done properly, can make the grower a virtual slave during the dry season. An automated drip system can not only improve the health of container plants, but can free the grower from this daily chore.

The setup is simple. In most cases 1/2- or 3/8-inch line is run below or behind the plants with transfer barbs connecting it to smaller tubing going up to the plant with an emitter placed on the end. A 1/4-inch transfer barb should be used for any line with 10 or more plants on it.

SELECTION, NUMBER AND SPACING OF EMITTERS

Plant Type	Flow Rate (gallons/hour)	Number of Emitters	Placement
Low Shrubs (2-3')	1.0	1	At Plant
Shrubs and Trees:			
3-5'	1.0	2	6-12" Either Side
5-10'	2.0	2-3	2' From Tree
10-20'	2.0	3-4	3' Apart
20'+	2.0	6+	4' Apart
Potted Plants	0.5-1.0	1	At Plant
Flower Beds	1.0	1	At Plant
Ground Covers	1.0	1	At Plant
Vegetables:			
Closely Spaced	0.5-1.0	1	Every 16"
Widely Spaced	1.0-2.0	1/plant	At Plant

Use 1/4-inch tees and lines to individual plants. (Most emitters use 1/4-inch transfer barbs, but some use 1/8-inch. Know which you have before you buy your parts.) The maximum flow rate for 1/8-inch line is 3 to 5 gph on any one transfer barb, while 1/4-inch line can at least double that.

For different sized containers, use 1/2, 1 or 2 gph emitters. Use multiple emitters for extra large containers. Number 5 insulated staples are excellent for attaching the small tubing to decks and planters.

Planning and Design

For most people, knowledge about the effects of friction and elevation on pressure are unnecessary for designing your own drip system. If it uses less than 250 gallons per hour, your laterals are less than 200 feet in length, you use pressure compensating emitters and you have a 25 or 30 psi pressure regulator, no technical design considerations are needed.

Most home systems use less water than the hose bib is capable of delivering and can be run as a single unit. If, however, your system needs more water than the hose bib can deliver at one time. it can be divided into as many subsystems as needed. To determine hose bib capacity, run the water at full force into a measured bucket and time how long it takes to fill. If, for example, a 5-gallon bucket takes 30 seconds to fill (10 gallons per minute), then your capacity is 600 gallons per hour. To maintain a margin of safety, design your system so that it doesn't use more than 75 percent of the bib's capacity.

To aid in the planning and design, all systems should be sketched out on paper first. The sketch should include all buildings, walkways, fences and other obstructions, as well as shrubs, trees, containers, and vegetable and flower beds. Use graph paper and a long tape measure to make your drawings to scale. Scale drawings allow you to easily calculate the length of tubing and the number of other parts needed. The drawings need not be elaborate, but they should be clear and accurate.

Since you should design your drip system starting at the plants and moving back toward the water source, your first task is to determine how many emitters to use and where they should be placed. The two most important considerations on this point are the type of soil and the root structures of the plants.

Soil structure is important in the design and use of drip irrigation as it will directly affect the number and placement of emitters. In sandy soil, where the spaces between the grains are relatively large, gravitational forces affect water movement more than capillary action. In finer soils such as clay, capillary action is much stronger and water will move laterally before penetrating very deeply. An emitter in sandy soil may water an area 16 inches in diameter, the same emitter in clay soil may water an area 24 inches in diameter.

A field test can be useful in making your decisions. This can be done by setting up a plant or section of your garden and observing the effect of the slow dripping of water on the soil. Be sure to dig down into the soil, away from the obvious wet spot on the surface, to see the true area covered. After you have determined the number, output and placement of emitters, put them on your sketch. You can put in laterals where emitters need to be placed, noting the length of tubing, connectors needed and total flow of the system.

Once you know the total flow, you can easily select the appropriate sized filter, pressure regulator and tubing. Generally, for systems of 180 gph or less, an in-line filter, hose thread pressure regulator and female hose tread to compression fitting are used. (This set up and that for larger systems are illustrated on page 194.)

There are pressure variations in all systems. Two factors affect pressure: elevation and friction. Elevation can either add to the pressure if the tubing is running downhill, or reduce the pressure if the tubing is running uphill. With friction, pressure is always lost as water travels through the tubing. Friction is greater at higher flow rates and in smaller diameter tubing.

If the highest point in your system is not more than 20 vertical feet above the valve, the difference in pressure is acceptable. Tubing needs to be sized properly to keep pressure loss due to friction in the acceptable range. Half-inch tubing should be used for all mains and laterals with a flow of up to 320 gph, and 3/8-inch tubing for mains and laterals of 120 gph or less. Not all suppliers carry 3/8-inch tubing. If not, substitute with 1/2-inch.

The above calculations assume that pressure compensating emitters are used. These emitters allow for a wider range of acceptable pressure differences. This will simplify design and allows the use of smaller tubing since emitter output varies little under a wide range of pressures. If you use non-compensating emitters, more care is needed in the design to keep pressure and flow within acceptable limits. The maximum flow figures given above should be reduced by at least one-third.

Remember, you can't make the correct purchasing decisions or finish your installation without knowing what parts you need. The scale drawing will help furnish you with that information. Ask your dealer, if you have questions about products or your specific needs. But keep in mind that the dealer's advice is only as good as the information you give to him or her. Take your scale drawing with you when you shop to clear up any questions that might arise.

Assembly   Installing drip irrigation is surprisingly easy, but here are a few tips to make the process go even smoother:

- Care should be taken to keep dirt out of the tubing during assembly.
- Allowing the tubing to sit in the sun will make it easier to handle and assemble. If it's cold, dipping the end of the tubing in hot water will make it easier to connect fittings.
- Install the system from the water source and work out to the laterals.
- When threaded connections are made, wrap the treads with Teflon tape, available from your dealer or plumbing supplier, before connecting.
- Do not tighten plastic fittings with a wrench. If Teflon tape is used, hand tightening will be enough.
- When installing pipe under a sidewalk or other obstruction, let water do the digging for you. Attach a garden hose to s stiff piece of pipe. With the water turned on high, work the pipe under the obstruction.
- Many parts for the head assembly have an arrow on them. Install so that the arrow is pointing in the direction of the water flow.
- If you want to use your hose bib for other purposes, connect a Siamese or Y-valve. This turns the hose bib into two outlets, each with its own shut-off valve.
- Be aware of differences in thread types. Forcing a hose thread onto a fitting with pipe threads can strip threads and cause leaks. If you are in doubt as to the type of thread on any component, consult your dealer before installing.

Head Assembly

For simplicity, we will describe two types of systems: a simple backyard system, and a larger system with more options included (see illustration on page 194. There are many possibilities between these two, but with the information given here you can pick and choose what is applicable to your situation. Simple home systems should include at least three items:
- An in-line screen filter attached to the hose bib.
- A hose thread preset pressure regulator placed after the filter.
- A female hose thread to compression fitting that will connect the pressure regulator sized to fit the system tubing.

   In some areas you will be required to use a vacuum breaker to prevent siphoning of the system water back into the water system. If you wish or are required to use a vacuum breaker, it should be placed between the hose bib and the screen filter.

Complex systems also begin with a vacuum breaker. Some automatic valves, which are connected to a controller unit to turn the system on and off automatically, have a built-in vacuum breaker. The valve usually has female pipe threads on both sides, so you will need a pipe thread nipple to connect to most fertilizer injectors (optional).

   A Y-filter can be connected directly to the automatic valve or injector (if used). the pressure regulator is installed last so that the pressure to the systems is at the desired level. Most pressure regulators for this size of system have female pipe threads on both sides, allowing connection to the Y-filter without an adapter. The tubing is then connected to the head by a male pipe thread to compression adapter. Occasionally, connections are made between two female, two male, or pipe and hose thread fittings; there are adapters to solve these problems.

Lines and Emitters

One of the advantages of using "poly" tubing is that its fittings require no glue or clamps. With both compression and barbed fittings, the

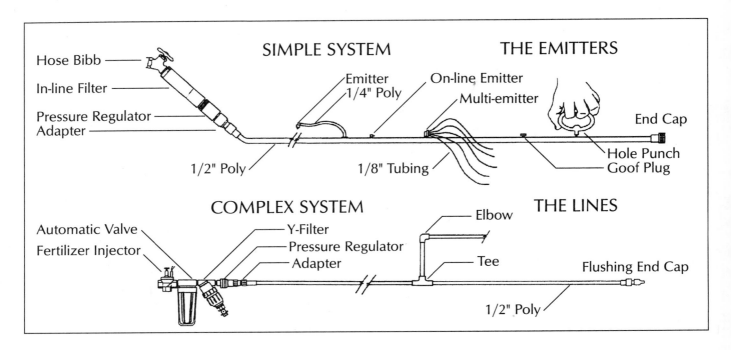

SIMPLE SYSTEM

- Hose Bibb
- In-line Filter
- Pressure Regulator Adapter
- 1/2" Poly
- Emitter 1/4" Poly
- 1/8" Tubing
- On-line Emitter
- Multi-emitter

THE EMITTERS

- End Cap
- Hole Punch
- Goof Plug

COMPLEX SYSTEM

- Automatic Valve
- Fertilizer Injector
- Y-Filter
- Pressure Regulator
- Adapter
- 1/2" Poly

THE LINES

- Elbow
- Tee
- Flushing End Cap

WATERING GUIDE

Plant Type	Time (hours)	Interval (days)
Low Shrubs (2-3')	2	3
Shrubs and Trees:		
3-5'	3	4
5-10'	4	5
10-20'	5	6
20'+	6	7
Potted Plants:		
1-gallon	1/6	1
5-gallon	1/3	1
25-gallon	1 1/4	2
Flower Beds	1	2
Ground Covers	1	2
Vegetables:		
Closely Spaced	1	2
Widely Spaced	1 1/2	2

tubing is pushed into place and its elasticity, or "memory" hold it secure. To avoid complications the system illustrated uses compression fittings only.

Lateral lines are connected to the main lines with a "tee" fitting which splits the flow of water. The last of the laterals or sharp turns can be made with "elbow" fittings. At the end of the last line, install an end cap that can be removed for flushing.

As the lines are laid out, the tubing might have to be secured until it takes shape. This can be done by piling soil on top of the lines or by using stakes designed for that purpose. Leave a little slack in the lines to allow for expansion and contraction due to changes in temperature. This will help prevent the emitters from moving out of place.

Once the lines are in place and before the emitters are installed, flush the system with water. To install emitters, punch a hole in the tubing with a hole punch (available from your dealer), and slip the barbed end of the emitter into the hole. For best results hold the punch at a right angle to the tubing and press firmly. If a hole is punched in the wrong place, relax. It can be capped with a "goof plug."

There are three basic way in which emitters are installed. The most common method is to place the emitter directly on the line. This way, you only have to punch the hole and slip in the emitter. For plants that are not near enough to the main or lateral to be served by an on-line emitter, install a transfer barb into the line, run 1/4- or 1/8-inch tubing (depending on the size of the fitting on the emitter) to the plant, and push the emitter into the end of the tubing. An alternate method is to attach the tubing directly to an on-line emitter and run it to the plant.

Operation

The object of drip irrigation is to bring the moisture in the root zone up to a satisfactory level and, by repeated waterings, to maintain that level. Too much water all at once can cut off oxygen to the roots and leach nutrients deep into the soil.

There are many factors the affect watering: soil type, root depth, temperature, humidity and the plant's stage of growth. The chart on page 194 lists times and intervals for watering different plants. Observe plant and soil conditions, consult local authorities and adjust watering time and intervals to maximize water use. In systems with mixed plantings compromises have to be made. Part of the difficulty can be avoided by placing more emitters or emitters of higher output on more demanding plants. But some compromises will have to be made in the watering schedule. It is better to error in favor of shallow rooted plants that are less able to withstand dry conditions.

Maintenance

Regular maintenance should be carried out on all drip irrigation systems. It includes occasional inspection of the emitter flow rates, flushing of lines, and cleaning filters. The design of a system using filtration and quality emitters will make this an easy job. Visual inspection of lines and emitters can be done while gardening.

If a problem with water delivery develops, do the standard maintenance procedures first. If the problem is with a single emitter, replace it. If it is system wide, look for a break in the line. With buried line, a break will sometimes appear as a damp spot on the surface. If you can't find anything wrong, it may be a problem with your basic design, or with the quality of your tap water. In either case, consult your dealer.

First published in Volume 2, Number 4, page 44.

Allelopathy — Bio-Weapon of the Future

by Kathleen Yeomans

Allelopathy — it sounds like something you get if you don't eat your carrots. Scientific research has shown that plant roots exude chemical compounds, some of which are active and can migrate through the soil to affect nearby plants. In addition, aromatic compounds given off by plant leaves can attract or repel insects. Sulfides and phenolic acids present in some plants have antibiotic and antiseptic properties that can kill certain fungi and bacteria.

These chemical interactions between plants have been recognized for centuries. Allelochemics refers to the study of these interactions. Allelopathic compounds are produced by most plants and this effect is the basis for the traditional practice of "companion planting." Modern crop rotation and the use of "green manures" also employ allelopathic strategies.

Although they didn't have a name for it then, allelopathic effects were reported as early as 300 B.C. Theopratus noted that chick pea (Cicer arietinum) does not "reinvigorate the ground" as other legumes do, but rather "exhausts" it. Pliny (1 A.D.) reported the adverse effects on soil and crops from such plants as barley, fenugreek, bitter vetch and walnut. In 1633, Culpepper wrote of the antipathy between various herbs, such as basil and rue, and also claimed the grape and cabbage plants won't grow near each other. Is this true? Do plants really interfere with each other in this way?

In 1948, T.M. McCalla and F.L. Duley found that wheat straw mulch reduced corn germination by half. Further work by these same two researchers concluded that these effects were produced by toxins released by plant material and by fungi that are stimulated by its close proximity.

Although these early studies concentrated on the adverse effects of allelopathy, later work proved that the interrelationships between plant chemicals could be used advantageously.

Effects on Growth

Keeping your garden weed free does more than just improve its appearance. Seeds of many common weeds release allelopathic chemicals that inhibit the germination of some vegetable seeds. Pepper, tomato, lettuce and cucumbers are especially sensitive. Residues of crops and weeds can also have allelopathic effects; nutsedge, quackgrass and foxtail have been shown to reduce growth in corn, soybeans and alfalfa by up to 50 percent.

Weeds aren't the only allelopathic culprits. Fresh residues of broccoli, barley, beets and rye severely inhibited or killed lettuce plants. Chemicals released by the decomposition of these plants are toxic to certain other plants.

I observed this effect in my own garden this year after planting tomatoes in a bed where I sheet-composted kitchen waste. Anxious to get an early start, I planted the tomato seedlings before the kitchen scraps, including broccoli, cabbage and cauliflower, were completely composted. The seedlings just sat there. Their color was poor and they grew very slowly. Tomatoes planted in another bed on the same day had fruits long before those plants even blossomed.

Detoxification takes place eventually, brought about by complete break down of the plant residues and the activity of microorganism which help deactivate the chemicals. Sheet composting and the use of green manures are good techniques for enriching the soil, but be sure to allow plenty of time for the plant residues to decompose before planting your main crop.

Rice farmers commonly plow under left over stubble in order to add organic material to the soil. However, the second crop is often smaller than the first. When studies were made, the fields in which the stubble was left proved to have higher concentrations of toxins that inhibit the growth of rice. Furthermore, these toxins seemed to inhibit nitrogen fixation, forcing farmers to use great quantities of chemical fertilizers to maintain productive yields.

Rice farmers who are aware of these facts can save money and increase production by rotating crops. In southern Taiwan, soybeans or other legumes are planted in rotation with the rice. The rice stubble is removed or burned and the yields of both crops have increased..

Soviet scientists have been studying allelopathy for years. They have found that some varieties of legumes are detrimental and others are beneficial. Roots of the pea (*Pisum arvense*) and hairy vetch (*Vivia villosa*) exude substances that aid in photosynthesis and the absorption of phosphorus in barley and oats. They also stimulate the uptake of nitrogen, potassium and calcium in these cereals. This type of beneficial allelopathic effect has encouraged the Soviets to work on developing new varieties of legumes specifically for use in mixed culture with corn and other food crops.

196

Effects on Plant Disease

Some plant diseases are caused by the direct action of plant residues. Lupine roots have been found to secrete ethyl alcohol in concentrations high enough to attract zoospores of the disease-causing fungus *Phytophthora cinnamomi*. Other plant illnesses are caused by nutritional deficiencies brought about by allelopathic influences in the soil. Allelopathic chemicals can make phosphorous and nitrogen unavailable to some crop plants.

Allelopathic chemicals can act in a number of ways to weaken and, therefore, make a plant more susceptible to infection. But on the other hand, the disease fighting properties of some plant-produced antibiotics are well known.

Plants in the onion family, especially garlic, have disease fighting properties that can be reproduced in the laboratory. Garlic (*Allium sativum*) has long been considered a useful medicinal, as well as culinary, herb. Several sulfur compounds are found in garlic oil, including one called *allicin*. Allicin is the compound that gives garlic its characteristic odor. It's also a potent antibiotic, effective against certain *staphylococci* and *E. coli*. Garlic paste was used in wartime to treat wounds when other antibiotics were not available. It has been found to be active against some plant bacteria and fungi.

African and French marigold (*Tagetes erecta* and *T. patula*) are resistant to root-knot nematodes and can apparently pass this resistance to other plants. Fewer nematodes infested fields that had grown *Tagetes* as a cover crop. Nematodes are also sensitive to phenyl acids given off by the roots of mustard plants.

Some of the disease controlling effects of allelopathy are derived from the activity of microorganisms in the soil. Beneficial microorganisms aid photosynthesis and nutrition, while the pathogenic microorganisms disrupt plant growth and cause disease. Populations of these microorganisms can be stimulated or depressed by plant root exudates, another way in which allelopathy affects plant health.

Zonation

Is successful competition the reason for the distribution patterns of plants, or does allelopathy play some role?

The "fairy ring" is a good example of plant distribution. This phenomenon of plants growing in a circle with a relatively plant-free center is a common growth pattern for certain fungi. Sunflowers are also seen to grow in this pattern and experiments have shown that it is a chemical released by the sunflowers themselves that is responsible. When soil from the inner circle is replaced with soil from outside the circle, sunflower growth in the center is normal.

Some plants simply refuse to grow next to certain other plants. Very few plants will grow under the black walnut tree, or even in soil where a walnut tree has grown in the past. Sunflowers, artemesia, certain salvias and pines are some of the plants that appear to strongly inhibit other plants.

In 1964, California scientists noted that few herbaceous plants would grow within 2 feet of certain native shrubs. Bare patches occurred around *Salvia leucophylla* and *Artemisia californica*. Studies proved that soil, moisture and predation were not the causes of this zonation. The evidence suggested that chemical inhibitors might be responsible for the zones, a theory that was latter proven to be true. Six terpenes were extracted from the leaves of these plants and found to be toxic to cucumbers and other plants. These types of volatile oils are present in many other plants.

So What?

While they may find the research interesting, most home gardeners are probably unaware of the potential of allelopathy beyond simple companion planting. It can be used to prevent weeds, repel insects and stimulate growth in cultivated plants.

Plants that inhibit germination and growth can be used for weed control. Carefully chosen crops, planted in rotation, can take advantage of the allelopathic effect. In a recent article in *Horticulture* magazine, Lewis Cook reported that witchgrass (*Agropyron repens*) can be totally eliminated by a planting of buckwheat. Cook sowed buckwheat in the spring, tilled it under six weeks later and then sowed it again. Winter rye was sown in the fall and tilled under the following spring. Although it was a time consuming process, Cook was rewarded with a richer soil that was free of witchgrass.

Rye suppressed certain weeds when used in rotation with vegetable crops. Its high nitrogen content adds nutrients to the soil as the residue breaks down. Other crops that work well in rotation are alfalfa, buckwheat and cereal grains. It is reported that purslane and crabgrass have been reduced by as much as 94 percent when grain sorghum residue is added to the soil. Sunflowers are also a good weed deterrent, if used with care. Remember, sunflowers will inhibit the growth of some desirable plants as well.

Some vegetable varieties can also be added to the allelochemical arsenal. Cucumbers effectively control barnyard grass and red pigweed. Care should be taken, though, some plants are autoallelopathic; asparagus, peach trees and alfalfa produce compounds that are toxic to replantings of their own kind.

Some plants are not only resistant to insect and disease attack, they can pass this resistance through the soil to other plants. C.Y. Li and his assistant found that many phenolic compounds in the roots of various plants, and especially red alder (*Alnus rubra*) inhibited the growth of a root rot fungus (*Poria weirii*). This antagonistic activity can be used in the biological control of plant diseases.

In California and Mexico, some interesting results have been obtained by solarizing soil after digging in chopped cruciferous plants (cabbage, broccoli, cauliflower, kale, radish, mustard). After 15 days under a clear plastic cover, previously infected soil was found to be free of fusarium wilt. Researchers noted that although a later cabbage crop grew exceptionally well, tomatoes grew poorly. That result may be due to allelopathic chemicals that are released by the partially decomposed cruciferous plants.

Farmers in Mexico have been using this "plant medicine" for ages. They traditionally allow a certain weed (*Bidens pilosa*) to grow with their corn. Cultivation consists of cutting the weed back every month or so. Francisco J. Rosado-May and his colleagues from the University of California at Santa Cruz found that the weed's roots secrete compounds that destroy fungi and nematodes that typically attack corn plants. If kept trimmed, the weeds appear to control these pests without robbing the soil of essential nutrients. Experiments in the United States with another corn field weed, *Brassica kaber*, yielded similar results.

Some plants produce compounds that stimulate the growth of other plants. Yugoslavian studies in 1974 showed the corn cockle (*Agrostemma githago*) promoted the growth of wheat. Residues from corn and giant foxtail appeared to benefit soybean production.

It's common for some farmers to interplant crops in order to increase total crop yields. The combination of corn, pumpkins and beans is a traditional crop mixture that is especially successful.

Beans and peas have long been used by farmers to replace soil nitrogen. These plants release nitrogen as they grow, so they can be interplanted with other crops to increase available nutrients. One study at Iowa State University showed that corn crops were boosted by more than 10 percent when interplanted with soybeans.

As synthetic pesticides go the way of man-made fertilizers, allelopathic control of nematodes and other pests will be vital to farmers and gardeners. Plant chemicals are already being used in commercial pesticides and the search for these substances continues. Meanwhile, more emphasis is being placed on natural methods of plant pest and disease control. Allelopathy, in conjunction with prevention and selective breeding is a vital bio-weapon of the future.

First published in Volume 2, Number 2, page 33

ALLIES AND ENEMIES

Plants for weed control:

Alfalfa	Sunflower
Flax	Chick pea
Barley	Sorghum
Coffee arabica	Sudan grass
Buckwheat	Rye

Plants for insect control:
Marigold *Tagetes*
Bird Bush *Crotolaria agatiflora* (nematode)
Asparagus (nematode, especially with tomatoes)
Fetid Marigold *Dyssodia papsosa*
Nicotiana
Anabasis aphylla
Chrysanthemum cinerariaefolium
Ryania speciosa
Echinacea angustifolia

Plants for disease control:
Bird Bush *Crotolaria agatiflora*
Marigold *Tagetes*
Mustard
Garlic
Corn cockle *Agrosemma githiago*
Bouncing Bet *Saponaria ocymoides*
Chamomile *Matricaria recutita*
Echinacea angustifolia

Plants to feed the soil:

Pea *Pisum arvense*	Hairy Vetch *Vivia villosa*
Soybeans	Sudan grass
Clover	Alfalfa
Corn cockle	

Enemies:
These plants have strong allelopathic exudates and can adversely affect the growth of many plants. Plants most often affected are listed in parenthesis:
Rye (Wheat)
Thistles (Oats)
Spurge *Euphorbia* (Flax)
Pincushion Flower *Scabiosa* (Flax)
Sunflower (Flea Bane *Erigeron, Rudebeckia*)
Mexican Bush Sage *Salvia leucophylla* (many annuals)
California Sagebrush *Artemesia californica* (many other plants)
Wheat straw (Cotton)
Yellow nutshedge (Alfalfa)
Quackgrass (Corn)
Giant foxtail (Alfalfa, Corn, Soybeans)
Asclepias syriaca (many plants)
Crucifers, members of the mustard family (Lettuce, Tomatoes)

199

Index

Sources

CANADA

Brite-Lite/Qué-Pousse
2215 Walkley
Montreal, Quebec
Canada H4B 2J9
514-489-3806, 514-489-3805 FAX

Everything for the indoor grower: Hydrofarm, Sun Circle, Green Air, Grodan, lighting, CO_2, Eco, organic fertilizers, environment controls, plant care books, hydroculture. Ebb-and-flow table and optimum liquid nutrient. State-of-the-art equipment. Canada's top supplier since 1969. Free catalogue (Canada). Mail-order or in store.

Frank's Magic Crops Inc.
480 Guelph Line
Burlington, Ontario
Canada L7R 3M1
800-668-0980 Canada wide
905-333-3282, 905-639-9190 FAX

Forty-two years of experience in hydroponics, NFT and soilless systems for the hobbyist and commercial grower. Consulting services available. Canadian distributor for Australian Clonex, Hydrofarm Gardening Products, Wilder Agriculture Products. Custom lighting systems, fiberglass parabolics and horizontal air cooled reflectors. Fiberglass flood and drain trays and Green Air Products. Custom nutrient solutions: Optigrow and Optibloom. Dutch Hydrocorn Aggregates. Soilless and organic growing supplies. Free catalogue and mail order service.

Homegrown Halide & Hydroponics, Inc.
2717 Weston Road, Weston
Ontario, Canada M9M 2R4
416-745-5007
800-463-6476 Canada only

Established 1985. Eight locations throughout Ontario. Expert advice. Retail and commercial. Canada and USA. Homegrown brand lighting systems, ebb and flow, aeroponics, NFT and drip. Advanced custom nutrients. Full line of latest technology for controlled environment growing. Large stock. Free catalogue.

UNITED STATES — ARIZONA

Aqua Culture, Inc.
700 West 1st Street
Tempe, AZ 85281
800-633-2137, 602-966-6429

We manufacture an extensive line of quality hydroponic equipment and supplies including the Solar Shuttle, Brightstar horizontal lighting systems, Freedom Garden and Garden of Ease hydroponic systems, CO_2 regulators and Aquagrow hydroponic nutrients. **Introducing the all new Star Trak.** Wholesale and retail. Call for free catalog or a distributor near you.

CALIFORNIA

American Hydroponics
824 L Street #3
Arcata, CA 95521
800-458-6543 Nationwide
707-822-5777 in California

Manufacturer and distributor of growing equipment you can count on: Sun Circle™, Baby Bloomer™, Vegi-Table™, and small commercial ebb-flow systems. We stock an extensive line of nutrients, lamps and hydroponic accessories for hobby and small commercial growers. Call or write for free information, catalog or the dealer nearest you.

Diamond Lights
628 Lindaro Street
San Rafael, CA 94901
800-331-3994
415-453-8311

World's largest manufacturer of gardening lights for hobby and commercial growing. In business since 1980. Over 60 garden centers, nurseries and grow shops carry our lights and supplies. Atmospheric controls, fans, blowers, Earth Juice, General Hydroponics products. Call for a location near you or for direct mail order.

General Hydroponics Co.
15 Koch Service Road Unit J
Corte Madera, CA 94925
800-37-HYDRO, 415-924-3390
415-924-3392 FAX

Our aero-hydroponic system, the "RainForest," is manufactured under exclusive license by Ein-Gedi Israel. It is the most advanced propagation system in the world and is used at the University of California and Utah State University for research in plant propagation. We also offer the "Advanced Nutrient System" and the "AquaFarm System." Contact us for more information.

Grobots International, Inc.
PO Box 549
Garberville, CA 95440
707-431-1882 in California
800-547-6268 Nationwide

Harvest year round — conserve water! Grobot System I- The Hydrobot: An automated plant growing system. Features revolutionary computer controlled Light-Deprivation-System. Use the sun's free power, force flower or fruit plants anytime! Choose your growing and watering method; solar power pack for remote use. No mess feeding organic plant food teas.

Pure Food Company
3385 El Camino Real
Santa Clara, CA 95051
408-247-5410, 408-247-5424 FAX

Step into the future and grow your own soil and pesticide-free fruits, vegetables, flowers and herbs. Suppliers of growth and lighting systems for pure produce to both beginner and professional growers. Distributors of high-tech hydroponic units developed in Silicon Valley, including exclusive dealership of the AQUADUCTS hydroponic system.

ILLINOIS

Chicago Indoor Garden Supply
297 N. Barrington Rd.
Streamwood, IL 60107
708-885-8282

For the home gardener and home brewer, we have what you need: lights, hydroponics, organics, and the largest selection of Grodan Rockwool available in the U.S. Our selection of home brewing supplies is without equal. Beer! If you can't taste it, why bother?

Worms Way, Inc.
3151 South Highway 446
Bloomington, IN 47401
800-274-9676 Retail & Wholesale

No one has a product selection like Worm's Way! Stores with large grow rooms in Indiana, Florida, Massachusetts, and Missouri to meet all gardening needs. Authorized national distributor for General Hydroponics, Eco, Olivia's and others with hundreds of products in stock. Call or write for our free full-color catalog!

MICHIGAN

Brew & Grow of Michigan
33523 W. Eight Mile Road #F-5
Livonia, MI 48152
313-442-7939

For the home gardener and home brewer, we have the largest selection of indoor gardening supplies, organics, and home brewing supplies in Michigan. We carry Hydrofarm, Diamond, General and American Hydroponics, and the full line of Grodan rockwool. Call for free catalog.

Superior Growers Supply, Inc.
4870 Dawn Ave., East Lansing, MI 48823
800-227-0027
Superior Growers Supply, Inc.
29217 Seven Mile Rd., Livonia, MI 48152
800-227-0027

SGS is your connection with state-of-the-art Dutch growing technology. Manufacturers of the EUROPONIC ROCKWOOL SYSTEM & NUTRIENTS. We are the largest and oldest high-tech garden center in the Midwest. A full line of products to help the indoor/greenhouse gardener. Call toll-free or write for a free copy of our latest catalog.

MINNESOTA

Brew & Grow of Minnesota
8179 University Avenue N.E.
Fridley, MN 55432
612-780-8191

For the home gardener and home brewer, we have what you need: lights, hydroponics, organics, and the largest selection of Grodan Rockwool available in the U.S. Our selection of home brewing supplies is without equal. Beer! If you can't taste it, why bother?

NEW YORK

East Coast Hydroponics
439 Castleton Avenue
Staten Island, NY 10301
718-727-9300
718-727-9313 FAX

Located in New York City. Home of the "MAXIMUM" horizontal light. The most fully-stocked indoor grow shop on the East Coast. We only stock the best halides, sodiums, hydroponics, bat guano, soil and soilless mixes, grow bags, CO_2 systems, pumps, timers, tools, fans, rockwool distributor and much more! Home brewing supplies. Visit our retail store or call for price quotes (no catalog).

OREGON

American Agriculture/Halide of Oregon
9220 S.E. Stark
Portland, OR 97216
800-433-6805
503-256-2400

Eleven years in business. Portland's most complete indoor/outdoor horticulture supplier. Your hydroponic specialist. Manufacturers of indoor climate controllers, digital event timers and infrared monitor controllers. Customer satisfaction is our #1 goal. Call or write for information. Working hydroponic systems on display.

Beautiful Plants Brand
PO Box 383
West Linn, OR 97068

Manufacturers of **Bioactive nutrients** for hydroponic and soil growing. A living nutrient formula capable of exceeding all known standards of hydroponic plant yields and health. Also manufacturing: the highest quality fish emulsion, seaweed amendments, rockwool conditioner, micronutrient supplements for use with chemical fertilizers and Bioactive supplements used in conjunction with chemical fertilizers.

The Genesis Formula
PO Box 1318
Gresham OR 97030
503-663-2000

Green Air Products equipment and supplies are available in nearly every hydroponic store throughout the United States, Canada and beyond. The Genesis Formula, as with all Green Air Products, has and will continue to reflect the finest of today's technology. Our chemists and horticultural staff have spent years in the lab and greenhouse coordinating their efforts to formulate the most complete feeding program available today. The Genesis Formula is innovative in its design and composition, providing the most versatile nutrient package on the market. The four-part system allows flexibility to belnd nutrients to meet the nutritional requirements of any crop in any stage of growth.

Green Air Products
PO Box 1318, Gresham, OR 97030
503-663-2000

Manufacturers of professional quality indoor growing equipment for laboratory-like control of your micro climate. Ask your dealer to see our full line of atmospheric controllers, timers, CO_2 generators, CO_2 bottle emitters, air cooled lighting, and The Genesis Formula plant nutrient.

Light Manufacturing Co.
1634 S.E. Brooklyn, Portland, OR 97202
800-669-5483, 503-231-1582

Makers of Living System™ Hydroponics. Retail distributors of high intensity discharge lights, light moving devices, custom nutrients and other horticultural products. Free phone consultation.

TENNESSEE

New Earth Indoor/Outdoor Garden Center
139 Northcreek Boulevard
Goodlettsville, TN 37072
800-982-GROW (4769), 615-859-5330

Great service and the BEST prices on lighting, hydroponic equipment and all indoor garden supplies. Visit our thriving grow/show room or call for a FREE 43 page catalog. FREE shipping on orders over $300 for *Growing EDGE* readers. Your gardening success is always our top priority! Hydroponic experts since 1987.

VERMONT

Green Thumb Gardening, Inc.
PO Box 235/Park Street
Underhill, VT 05489
800-56-HYDRO Vermont only
802-899-4323

Northern New England's number-one stop for professional quality indoor/outdoor gardening equipment. Specializing in hydroponics, H.I.D. lighting equipment, and specialty organics. Authorized dealer for Hydrofarm, Light Rail III, Diamond Lights, American Hydroponics, Green Air Products, Higher Yield, Wilder Agriculture and many more. Come Grow with us. USER-FRIENDLY, WATER-WISE, ECOLOGICALLY SAFE.

WASHINGTON

Discount Garden Supply, Inc.
14109 E. Sprague #5, Spokane, WA 99216
800-444-4378, 509-924-8333

Ten successful years in business. Large enough to handle all your indoor growing needs, yet small enough to help with your individual needs. Our business is growing indoors.

Eco Enterprises, 1240 NE 175th St.
Suite B, Seattle, WA 98155
800-426-6937

Twenty-one years in business. EcoGrow and EcoBloom plant nutrients. Hydroponics, indoor growing systems, hydroponics equipment, pumps, timers, etc. Free catalog.

Green Gardens
12748 NE Bel-Red Road
Bellevue, WA 98005
206-454-5731

Greenhouse and indoor garden supplies. Halide and sodium light systems, replacement parts, bulbs, horizontal reflectors, light movers, fans, timers, pumps, multilight timed breaker panels, growing media, fertilizers, CO_2, hydroponic equipment and supplies. Open weekdays 10 to 6, Sat 12 to 5. Mail orders shipped same day.

WISCONSIN

Brew & Grow of Wisconsin
19555 W. Bluemound Rd. #36
Waukesha, WI 53186
414-789-0555

For the home gardener and home brewer, we have what you need: lights, hydroponics, organics, and the largest selection of Grodan Rockwool available in the U.S. Our selection of home brewing supplies is without equal. Beer! If you can't taste it, why bother?

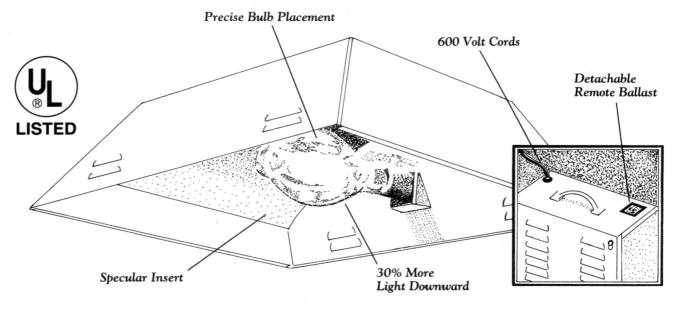

Precise Bulb Placement

600 Volt Cords

Detachable Remote Ballast

UL LISTED

Specular Insert

30% More Light Downward

THE WORLD'S MOST SUPERIOR GROW LIGHT JUST GOT BETTER

The new Diamond LumenArc™ II design truly is the new standard for the indoor gardener. Features include a replaceable white reflector insert and a re-engineered, completely enclosed socket assembly. UL listed systems include a unique detachable remote ballast with 600 volt rated cords for your safety. The optional Specular insert is a "mirror-like" piece of aluminum that provides an average of 30 percent increase in downward light over that of normal white paint reflectors. This new hood is by far the finest advancement to date in the indoor gardening industry.

DIAMOND
INNOVATIVE GARDENING TECHNIQUES SINCE 1980

---

628 Lindaro Street, San Rafael, CA 94901-3936, (800) 331-3994 or call the distributor nearest you.

American Agriculture™

INDOOR CLIMATE CONTROLLER

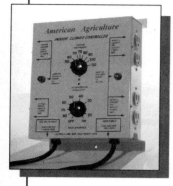
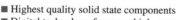

- Highest quality hydraulic thermostat
- Quality dehumidifying humidistat
- Large knobs designed to fit adult hands
- Large professional housing (10 x 8 x 4") with easy to read instructions on the face with 8 power outlets
- Outlet provided for CO_2 equipment
- CO_2 equipment turns *off* at night and when temperature or humidity turns exhaust fans *on*
- Superior design of air vents for truly professional air sensing
- 24 hour temperature and humidity control
- Compare to equipment costing much, much more
- No interfacing relay needed!

DIGITAL EVENT TIMER

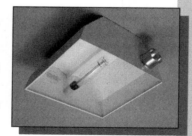

- Highest quality solid state components
- Digital technology for super high accuracy
- Simply flip a switch for exact timing
(No more searching for settings as with the old style equipment)
- Heavy duty grounded power cord
- Instructions on the face of the timer make it easy to use and understand
- Powder coated white enamel paint reflects light and heat while resisting moisture
- A high accuracy repeat cycle timer for *both* long and short durations!

THERMOSTAT

- Thirteen amp. professional quality cooling thermostat with U.L. listing
- Hydraulically actuated exposed coil for reliable air sensing
- Heavy duty power cord with built in power outlet for convenient exhaust fan plug in

LOW HEAT LAMP REFLECTOR

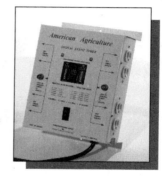

- Eliminates heat build up in your growing area from hot bulbs
- May be used with or without fans
- For your convenience it may be purchased with or without glass, ducting adapters, or socket
- New superior design eliminates hot spots and gives an even light pattern
- Aluminum construction is half the weight of other brands (won't damage light movers and tracks because of excess weight)

CO_2 MONITOR CONTROLLER

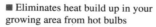

- Revolutionary infrared design with digital readout
- Superior one box design eliminates confusing wires
- No fault and simple instructions are silkscreened right on the front for super easy use
- Exacting control of CO_2 for laboratory results!

Manufacturer ♥ Distributor ♥ Wholesaler ♥ Retailer

American Agriculture 9220 S.E. Stark, Portland, OR 97216 ☎ Voice Phone: 1-800-433-6805 & 1-503-256-2400 Ⓕ Fax Phone: 1-503-256-2402

AQUACULTURE INC

PICK YOUR GARDEN!

GARDEN OF EASE - NUTRIENT FLOW TECHNIQUE

Ideal for small to medium plants such as lettuce, herbs, flowers and even small tomatoes.

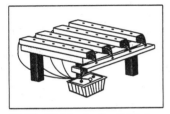

GE 24 - Mini Garden 2' x 3', 24 plants 3 gal. reservoir, stand included.

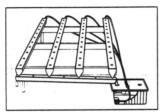

GE 51 - Floor unit 4' x 6', 51 plants 3 gal. reservoir, 4 trays.

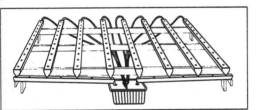

GE 102 - Floor unit 8' x 6', 102 plants 9 gal. reservoir, 8 trays.

GE 45 - Wall unit 5' x 6' x 1', 45 plants, 3 gal. reservoir, 4 trays, mountings included.

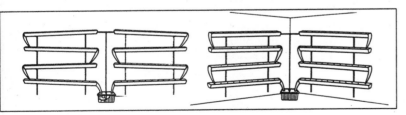

GE 200 - Floor unit 12' x 6', 200 plants , 15 gal. reservoir, 16 trays.

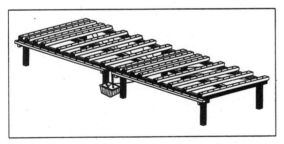

GE 90 - Wall units 5' x 6' x 1', 90 plants, 9 gal. reservoir, 8 trays, mountings included. Can be placed flush or mounted on corner walls.

FREEDOM GARDENS - FLOOD AND DRAIN SYSTEM

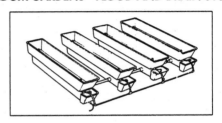

Top growing tray is filled with Garden Gro-Rock. Bottom tray is a 10 gal. reservoir. Expandable to six trays. Maximum space between each tray of 4'. Each tray is 1' x 6' x 1'.
FG 1 - One tray **FG 4** - Four trays **FG 6** - Six trays

OTHER EQUIPMENT AND SUPPLIES

- Original Solar Shuttle™ • CO2 Regulators • Pumps
- Complete line of Horizontal HID Light Systems
- pH Pens and DiST Pens • pH Reducer and pH Up
- Calibration Solution - tests BOTH pH and DiST pens with one solution • Blower Fans
- Hygrometers • Barometers • Thermometers
- Grodan™ Rockwool • Aquagrow™ Plant Nutrients
- Plus many other items!

HOME PRO - NUTRIENT FLOW TECHNIQUE

1000 Tomatoes in Two Months!! Designed for vining plants such as tomatoes, beans, peas, and cucumbers, uses rockwool cubes in a flexible sleeve.

HP 16 - 2 Sleeves, 4' x 10', 16 plants, 15 gal. reservoir.

(602) 966-6429   **AQUACULTURE INC**   (800) 633-2137

700 W. 1st Street Tempe, Arizona 85281

Call for your free catalog or dealer nearest you. Visa and Mastercard accepted. Sorry, no COD's. Dealer inquiries welcome!

THE ECOGROW FAMILY OF SCIENTIFIC PLANT NUTRIENTS

21st CENTURY GROWING POWER

IS HERE TODAY, AS NEAR AS YOUR PHONE!

The research labs of Eco Enterprises in Seattle, Washington have expanded their product line to include convenient, easy to use liquid formulas. Ecogrow "L" and Ecobloom "L" are two-part formulas providing all the growing power of our conventional water-soluble powered nutrients. Highly concentrated, 1 teaspoon of each part per gallon makes a high-potency solution for soil or soilless growing. Economical and Ecological, these pH adjusted formulas are "CLIMATE FORMULATED" for finest plant growth with or without soil. Available in bottles or in bulk.

In dry powder or new liquids, Eco nutrients contain every major and trace element necessary for the finest plant growth.

FORMULA	N-P-K	RECOMMENDED USES—SELECTION GUIDE
Ecogrow	10-8-14	Temperate zone plants, houseplants, gardens, hydroponics or in soil.
Ecogrow "S"	15-7-12	Sub-tropical plants and flowers, good light, with or without soil.
Ecogrow "M"	20-6-12	Tropical formula for lush growth in good lighting conditions.
Ecobloom	3-35-10	Low N, high P promotes flowers, fruit while slowing growth rate.
Ecogrow "R" **Ecobloom "R"**	14-6-17 6-25-17	Formulated for rockwool growing to counteract its alkaline nature, proven ideal for hydroponics or soil. (Two part formula)
Ecogrow "L" **Ecobloom "L"**	4-2-4 2-4-3	Superior, highly concentrated 2 part liquid formula for soil, hydroponics, houseplants, gardens and greenhouses. Ideal for aeroponic and drip systems.

Call or write today and receive a free Eco hydroponic Catalog and Guidebook!

 **ECO ENTERPRISES**
1-800-426-6937

1240 NE 175th St. Suite B, Seattle, WA 98155   FAX (206) 363-9983

THE CHOICE FOR AMERICAN GROWERS...

Is the Nutrient Preferred by Dutch, Canadian and Australian Grower

FloraGro™ • FloraMicro™ • FloraBloom™

General Hydroponics "Advanced Nutrient System", Research Grade Technology in an Easy to Use Form.

Imagine a plant nutrient so advanced that hydroponic growers worldwide choose to import it from America. This is the nutrient used to grow vegetables served by the finest gourmet restaurants. "Flora" nutrients were developed by Dr. Cal Herrmann, senior scientist with the University of California Water Technology Center and water specialist for NASA. The formulas are based on research done in Holland. We have furthered the Dutch achievements by providing three highly concentrated components that can be mixed in various strengths and ratios to create precise mixes for specific applications. "Flora" nutrients are extremel concentrated – you get more value for your investment. "Flora" nutrients contain unique 'pH buffers'. You won't have to check o adjust your pH as often as with other plant nutrients. If you're investing your time and money in hydroponics, use the bes nutrients, use "Flora" nutrients.

GH **GENERAL HYDROPONICS**

For your nearest distributor:
Call 415/924-3390 or FAX 415/924-3392
General Hydroponics
15 Koch Road, Unit J, Corte Madera, California 94925, U.S.A.

Simply The Most Advanced Gardening Products

Ten years and Still Growing!

EUROPONIC
ROCKWOOL SYSTEM

For 10 Years SGS has remained a leader in the field of indoor growing by manufacturing innovative hydroponic systems and lighting systems of the **highest quality** and functionality. Our shops, located in East Lansing, Michigan and the Greater Detroit Area offer the **largest selection** of hydroponic gardening equipment in the midwest. Others make this claim but don't come close. To see for yourself, stop in or call for our **free 1993 catalog**. We carry all the leading products, both those that we manufacture and products of other leaders in the industry.

- Nutrients • Clonex • Organic Fertilizers • Rockwool
- High Tech Garden Equipment • Flower and Vegetable Seeds

Everything you need to get started growing indoors!
ALSO- SGS carries a complete line of HOME BREWING SUPPLIES!
Home Produce, Home Brew...always the most satisfying.

Superior
Growers
Supply, Inc.

East Lansing, MI - 4870 Dawn Ave. 48823 (517) 332-2663
Livonia, MI - 29217 Seven Mile Rd. 48152 (313) 473-0450
CALL TOLL FREE - (800) 227-0027
Visa - Mastercard -American Express and C.O.D..'s welcome

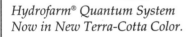

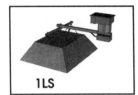

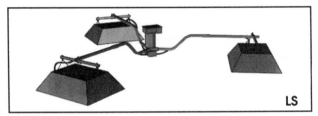

The
GENESIS
Formula

If your dealer doesn't have it... You need a new dealer!

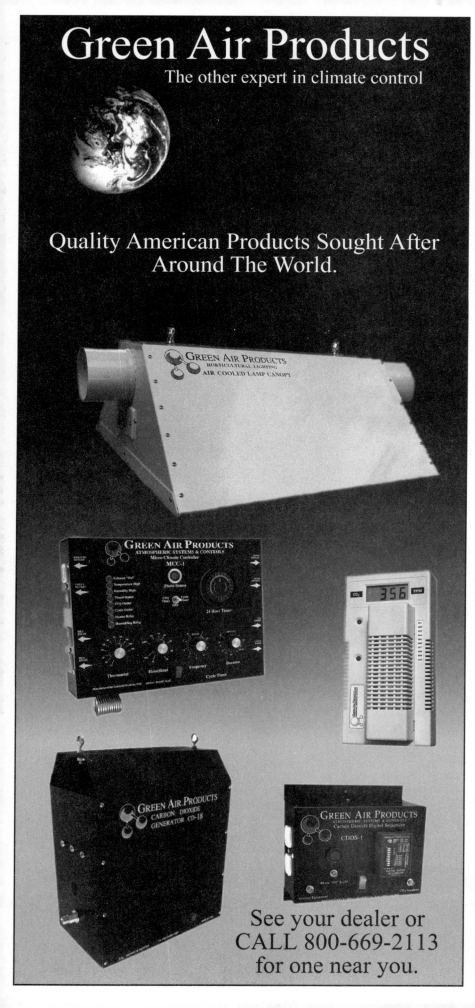

GROW FOOD WHERE IT HAS NEVER GROWN BEFORE!

AQUADUCTS™ are produced in our own extrusion dies and are cost-effective in any size installation. Ducts come in 2.5', 5', 10' and 20' lengths.

AQUADUCTS are uniquely modular. Join modules to increase output.

AQUADUCTS are manufactured from high- grade PVC with special ultra-violet inhibitors to avoid sunlight degradation.

AQUADUCTS have a "V" shaped cavity. This makes the roots grow in a "V" shape. Roots are suspended in air with the tip of the root receiving nutrient, while the top receives oxygen. This causes massive absorption of nutrients into the root structure. Plants grow faster and stronger and are more resilient to pests allowing growers to have pesticide-free produce. Food is clean, tastes better and is more nutritious as it now has a full compliment of trace minerals. Plants can be picked with their root structure intact. This gives an extremely long shelf life.

AQUADUCTS have two heating or cooling cavities beneath the "V" for optimum root zone temperature control. This allows heating or cooling of the plant.

AQUADUCTS' closed system *does not allow any algae growth to develop!*

AQUADUCTS use no sand or gravel substrate at the root structure thereby eliminating cleaning problems and changing PH levels.

REMOVABLE TOPS can be variable spaced for giant tomatoes to be planted at 24" intervals while lettuce can be planted at 6" intervals. The covers also allow access for cleaning ease.

MAINTENANCE IS INFREQUENT With *no evaporation loss,* Aquaducts use the absolute minimum amount of water. Every drop of water goes to the plant. Aquaducts use small rock wool cubes or neoprene inserts for cuttings. There is no material that can change PH levels. Aquaducts' low water usage and infrequent need for PH changes means systems need less supervision.

DEALER INQUIRIES WELCOME. FREE CATALOGUE.

PURE FOOD
HYDROPONICS

3385 EL CAMINO REAL
SANTA CLARA, CA 95051

(408) 247-5410   FAX (408) 247-5424

From Australia
Hydroponics video, book and magazine!

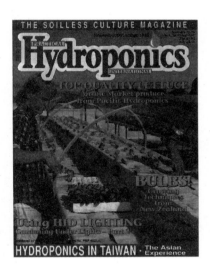

Practical Hydroponics is Australia's only dedicated hydroponics magazine. Designed for both the commercial and hobby grower, PH brings its readers up to date with the latest news, ideas and growing techniques being employed in Australia and around the world.

Each bimonthly issue includes reviews and reports on the latest products, as well as in-depth feature articles on a range of hydroponic enterprises.

Now everyone can discover how easy and exciting it is to grow plants hydroponically. "Hydroponic Gardening" is a simple step-by-step video designed for beginners of all ages. It teaches you the basics of hydroponic cultivation – nutrients, pH control, growing media, easy hydroponic systems, lighting, transplanting, and cloning.

Hydroponics for the home gardener is an economical and simple way to turn your backyard (no matter how big or small) or balcony into productive vegetable and flower gardens.

Hydroponic Gardening teaches the basics of hydroponics – how to grow hydroponic plants from seed, and to feed them with naturally balanced nutrients. This book is ideal for all hydroponic growers.

These products are made in Australia and distributed in the U.S. and Canada by New Moon Publishing

For further pricing and ordering information, contact:

NEW MOON PUBLISHING

New Moon Publishing
P.O. Box 1027, Corvallis, OR 97339
503-757-8477   FAX 503-757-0028
1-800-888-6785 (U.S. only)

Subscription and Back Issue Order Form
(Please check each back issue requested)

Indoor & Outdoor Gardening for Today's High-Tech Grower

☐ **VOL. 1 #1**
Hydroponics: The Growing
   Technology for the '90s
Organic Hydroponics
Hard Rock Gardening: Rockwool
Mycorrhizal Associations
The Basics of HID Lighting
Nutrient Management Techniques
Winter Grown Tomatoes
Environmental Dynamics: Part I
Oyster Mushrooms at Home

☐ **VOL. 1 #2**
Basil Production for the Small Grower
Propagation in Rockwool
Biological Pest Control
The Fine Art of Micropropagation
Hydroponic Nutrient Solutions
Phytofarms of America
Toxics in the Garden
Environmental Dynamics: Part II
Wine-Red Stropharia

☐ **VOL. 1 #3**
Bananas: Grown in Oregon
In-Store Hydroponics in Houston
Pest Management for Hydroponics
Bioponics: Part I
Hydroponics for the Home Hobbyist
Quebec's Hydroponic Tomatoes
Shiitake Mushrooms

☐ **VOL. 1 #4**
Build Your Own Hydroponic System!
Plant Selection for Hydroponics
Water Should Taste Good to Plants!
Basil Production: An Update
Mid-South Greenhouse
Look Out Holland, Here Comes B.C.!
Grow Your Own Mushrooms Indoors
Softwood Cloning for Beginners

☐ **VOL. 2 #1**
Aero-Hydroponics
A Computer in Your Garden
Hydroponic or Organic?
Deep Water NFT
The Earth as Greenhouse
The Sip of Life: Cutting Survival
Optimizing High Pressure Sodiums
Growing Oyster Mushrooms Indoors

☐ **VOL. 2 #2**
Low-Tech, High-Performance Hydro
Allelopathy: Bio-Weapon of the Future
Bioponics: Part II
Recycling Nature's Gifts
Brooklyn Botanic Garden
NASA's Ames Research Center
SLUG: Garden for the Environment
(Very) Basic Hydroponics

☐ **VOL. 2 #3**
Rockwool: Cube and Slab Gardens
Foliar Feeding: Fast Food for Plants
Hydroponic Herbs at Home
Artificial Lighting in Horticulture
Bioponics: Part III
Desert Botanical Gardens

Assault on Eden!
Shiitake Growing Indoors
Computer Control Systems

☐ **VOL. 2 #4**
Plant Abuse as a Cultivation Technique
Integrated Hydro/Aquaculture Systems
Bioponics: Part IV
Drip Irrigation: The Basics
A 'Sound' Diet for Plants
New Efficiency for Home Lighting
Electric Water Vortexes

☐ **VOL. 3 #1**
The Origin of Botanical Species
New World Fruits
Hardy Kiwi for Every Climate
The Garden Hacker
Plant Plane Hydroponics
The Struggle for Sunlight
The Sununu Effect vs.
   the Greenhouse Effect

☐ **VOL. 3 #2**
Carbon Dioxide Enrichment
White Owl Waterfarm
Subirrigation Systems Indoors
Subirrigation on the Cheap
Nitrogen Fixing Plants
The Domesticated Citrus

☐ **VOL. 3 #3**
Growing Bananas Indoors
Hydroponics for the Rest of Us
The Garden Hacker: Part III
Planetary Healing with Biology
Nature's Pharmacy: Medicinal Plants
Clean Air Update
Water Wise Garden

☐ **VOL. 3 #4**
Bedroom Garden
Goldfish Production
Designing With Nature
Gardening at the South Pole
Small Scale Solutions
Cloning Techniques
The Garden Hacker: Part IV
The $50 Greenhouse

☐ **VOL. 4 #1**
Hydroponics — A Global Perspective
Iceland — Land of Fire, Ice & Flowers
Paradise Found — Indoor Palms
Pest Control for Greenhouse Growers
Seeding Diversity, Reaping a Future
Sekol's Gourmet Sprouting Co.
Understanding Plant Names

☐ **VOL. 4 #2**
Dynamic Sustainable Agriculture
Hot Drinks You Can Grow
Biological Alchemy and
   the Living Machine
A Moment of Hope by John Todd
Bioponics: Part V
Mutation Breeding: Part I
High-Tech Nursery
Gases in Nutrient Solutions

An Orchard of Lettuce Trees
Demystifying Plant Propagation
Hydroponic Solutions for Beginners

☐ **VOL. 4 #3**
Seedlings, Cuttings and Transplants
Seeds — Embryonic Plants
The Orchid Environment
A Down-to-Earth Space Garden
Mutation Breeding: Part II
Healing a Wounded Planet
The Fruit/Herb Dryer
More Oxygen for your NFT

☐ **VOL. 4 #4**
Hydro-Organics
Bioponic Greenhouse
A Microbial Culture Chemostat
Organic Nutrient Extractor
Urban Hot Spots
Rain Gutter Hydroponic System
Strategies for Survival

Site Selection for Beginners
Seedless Grapes
The Fabric of Plant Diversity

☐ **VOL. 5 #1**
Hydroponics in Schools
Leaf Analysis Techniques
Mist & Fog Propagation Systems
Oxygen Intensive Water Culture
Basic Backyard Breeding
Pesticides in Our Communities
Winterize Indoor Plants
Systems for Beginners

☐ **VOL. 5 #2**
Building a Better Tomato
Computerize Your Garden
Gardening on Ice
S&S Aquafarm — Hydro/aquaculture
Agriculture for the Millennium
The Wheelchair Garden
Backyard Marketing Strategies

Note: Supplies are limited to stock on hand at the time of order. Information given here on prices and availability was current as of January 1, 1994 and is subject to change. For up-to-date information on products available from New Moon Publishing, write to the address below or call 1-800-888-6785 (1-503-757-8477 outside the U.S.).

The Growing EDGE (prices include shipping and handling):
☐ Back issues (Single issues are $6.50 in the U.S. and Canada, $10 overseas. Four or more are $5 each in the U.S. and Canada, $7.50 overseas.) .... $_____
☐ 1 year subscription (4 issues, U.S. only) $17.95
☐ 2 year subscription (8 issues, U.S. only) $34.00
☐ First Class 1 year subscription (U.S. and Canada) $24.95
   Sent First Class mail in a protective envelope
☐ Overseas subscription (1 year, 4 issues) $45.00
   Sent Air Mail in a protective envelope
                    Total Cost (U.S. funds only) $_____

SEND TO:

Name _____

Address _____

City _____ State/Province _____

Country _____ Zip or Postal Code _____

I have enclosed payment: Personal check, money order (U.S. funds. Personal checks will delay delivery), or bill my charge card: VISA, MASTERCARD, DISCOVER OR AMERICAN EXPRESS.
No. _____ _____ _____ _____ Exp. Date: _____ /_____

Telephone number (charge card orders): _____

Cardholder Name _____

Signature _____

Charge card orders 1-800-888-6785 (U.S. only)
Please send order and payment to:
New Moon Publishing, P.O. Box 1027, Dept. BGE, Corvallis, OR 97339
(503) 757-8477   FAX (503) 757-0028